# Managing the Dream

## Other Titles by Warren Bennis

Beyond Leadership (co-author)
Beyond Bureaucracy
Co-Leaders (co-author)
Douglas McGregor on Management (co-author)
Leaders: Strategies for Taking Charge (co-author)
Leaders on Leadership (editor)
Learning to Lead (co-author)
Managing People Is Like Herding Cats
Old Dogs, New Tricks
On Becoming a Leader
Organizing Genius (co-author)
Reinventing Leadership (co-author)
The Temporary Society (co-author)
The 21st Century Organization (co-author)
The Unreality Industry (co-author)
Why Leaders Can't Lead

# Managing the Dream

## Reflections on Leadership and Change

## Warren Bennis

*Foreword by Tom Peters*

BASIC
BOOKS

Member of the Perseus Books Group
New York

Special thanks to Rob Asghar for his assistance in organizing and editing this volume.

Many of the designations used by manufacturers and sellers to distinguish their products are claimed as trademarks. Where those designations appear in this book and Basic Books was aware of a trademark claim, the designations have been printed in initial capital letters.

Copyright © 2000 by Warren Bennis, Inc. Foreword Copyright © 1993 by Tom Peters
Previously published by Perseus Publishing
Published by Basic Books, A Member of the Perseus Books Group

A CIP record for this book is available from Library of Congress

ISBN 0–7382-0332-7

Find us on the World Wide Web at http://www.basicbooks.com

Books published by Basic Books are available at special discounts for bulk purchases in the U.S. by corporations, institutions, and other organizations. For more information, please contact the Special Markets Department at the Perseus Books Group at 11 Cambridge Center, Cambridge, MA 02142, or call (617) 252-5298 or (800) 255-1514 or e-mail special.markets@perseusbooks.com.

Text design by the Clarinda Company

# Permission Acknowledgments

# Contents

# Foreword

Curiosity invariably gets the best of Warren Bennis. Lots of us are better off as a result. These pages are a wonderful tribute to a perpetually curious seventy-five-year-old, who is as puzzled and thoughtful now as at age six or seven.

Bennis is a pioneer, and prescient. His work at MIT in the 1960s on group behavior foreshadowed—and helped bring about—today's headlong plunge into less hierarchical, more democratic and adaptive institutions, private and public. He's always burned his intellectual candle at both ends. While conducting meticulous research into the minutiae of social interaction, Warren was also risking self and soul as a leader of some of the first T-groups at the National Training Labs in Bethel, Maine. These intimate inner explorations, though, didn't stop him from engaging in the most oceanic prophecies. In a landmark 1964 *Harvard Business Review* article (see chapter 10), he and colleague Philip Slater astonishingly claimed that "democracy is inevitable." Only those of us who lived through McCarthyism and Khrushchev's shoe pounding at the United Nations can appreciate how outrageous such an idea sounded at the time. (The *Harvard Business Review* did Slater and Bennis the favor of reprinting the article in 1990; few of us have the opportunity of being able to say publicly, "I told you so.")

On the heels of that bold proclamation, just two years later, in 1966, came "The Coming Death of Bureaucracy" (chapter 9), in which Bennis insisted—bizarre, again, in the context of the times—that the centuries-old command-and-control, pyramidal organizational structures were doomed and that "adaptive, rapidly changing temporary systems" would be required to do tomorrow's work in the face of a society and economy beset by "chronic change." If only IBM, in whose *Think* magazine the article first appeared, had listened!

Warren's curiosity got the best of him again in 1967, when he began a decade of practicing what he had so long preached, first as provost at SUNY Buffalo and then as president of the University of Cincinnati. But to say he merely practiced what he preached is a gross understatement, for it turned out that leading in practice was a whole different kettle of fish from leading through influence via the printed page. The experience—containing at least as many potholes as peaks—tore Warren apart and doubtless contributed to his massive heart attack at age fifty-three.

With a stupendous career behind him, his place in the annals of social science ensured, scars up one side and down the other, inside and out, why bother with more? That damnable curiosity won out again, that's why. Bennis now turned his full attention and energy to figuring out where he'd been, and a series of methodically researched, landmark works on leadership ensued—with this, a personal reflection, the latest and in many senses the best.

Why best? Leadership, Bennis concluded while at the University of Cincinnati, is ultimately about the relationship between the leader-as-individual and the organization. In these pages he undertakes the sort of self-exploration and reflection that must be part and parcel of *any* successful leader's journey and makeup.

I love this book. It reflects humanity, openness, courage, and rigorous thinking in equal measures—and is a marvelous example (just the latest, in Warren's case) that good social science can be as scintillating and literate as it can rigorous.

I love this book, selfishly, because it confirms me in my perpetual confusion. On the one hand, Bennis has been constant in his concern with change, democracy, and bureaucracy for more than three decades. And yet he is as inconstant and fresh—and as timely and challenging—now as he was when I, as a neophyte MBA student in 1970, first came across his work ("The Coming Death of Bureaucracy" was one of our first assigned readings at Stanford).

Bennis admits to having been mesmerized by his early mentors—Captain Bessinger, the high school dropout who was his company commander in 1944, when, at age nineteen, Bennis became the youngest infantry commander in the European theater of operations, and Doug McGregor, the social science giant whose thinking spurred much of Bennis's later work. I too am mesmerized by my mentors, and Warren is one of the most important. A reporter once asked me what I wanted my epitaph to be. After declaring in no uncertain terms that I wasn't in any rush, I said, "He was curious to the end." Upon reading and reflecting on these pages, which came my way after that conversation, I know that I was, in a way, merely mouthing the words that are the signature of Warren Bennis's extraordinary career and life. Neither Bennis nor I is ready for epitaphs. But for those of you who wish to be inspired by the idea—and practice—of the curious life, richly spent, you'll do no better than to thoughtfully consider what follows.

*Tom Peters*

# Preface

"In dreams begin responsibilities," William Butler Yeats wrote. Nowhere is this demonstrated more vividly than in the lives of effective leaders. All humans possess an overpowering desire to understand and predict the future; but a leader takes real responsibility for molding it by embracing and "managing" a tangible dream for the future. In essence, a leader *incarnates* a dream for that future.

The future is for me a portmanteau word, one that embraces a number of notions. First, it involves an exercise in imagination which allows us to compete with and try to outwit events that lie ahead. Second, the attempt to control what is to come is a social invention that legitimizes the process of forward planning. There is no other way I know of to resist the "tyranny of blind forces" than by looking circumstances in the face (as we experience them in the present) and extrapolating how they may unfold; nor is there any other sure way to detect a compromise of goals or values.

Carl Sandburg observed that "nothing happens unless first a dream." Indeed, a dream is a roadmap to a rendezvous with destiny—a set of imaginative hypotheses groping toward whatever vivid utopias lie at the heart of our consciousness.

Martin Luther King's famous utopian line, "We shall overcome" is only a partial quote. He actually said, "We shall overcome *someday*." The dream through which he directed his followers' energies anticipated not an immediate outcome but a long and arduous struggle toward victory.

This focus on the notion of a dream may be irrelevant to some, especially to persons who may believe that lofty dreams are the domains of the Martin Luther Kings and that bottom lines are the domain of the rest of us. Couldn't such a person safely toss out the airy ideals, cut to the chase and focus on the study of the nuts and bolts of managing a business or institution well?

As my studies and my experiences have shown over the years, such a person may prove to be a successful manager for a certain length of time; but he or she would never in fact be a true leader of others. A dream can offer incomparable power to draw others alongside a leader, especially when they can find their own home within it. A dream need not be immense in scale, but it must be large enough to house a multitude. Indeed, a person will generally not leave a mark as a leader if he or she fails to manage a dream that makes room for other humans' essential need to belong, to contribute and to create. This book, then, is fundamentally about the relationship of the leader to his or her dream, and the relationship of his or her organization to that dream.

This collection of essays and stories represents a journey through various dreams of leadership over the past three and a half decades. I believe that, in an era in which the very pace of change is accelerating with each new day, there is a tremendous learning experience to be had from looking back at what was being written at earlier stages of the field of organizational dynamics. Some utterances and prophecies were remarkably accurate, while others were complicated by unanticipated societal and technological developments. Still, I hope they can be of real value in helping us make informed guesses about the kind of leadership and organizations we will need tomorrow.

For myself, I have been thinking about leadership almost as long as I have been thinking. My older brothers were my first teachers on this subject that would fascinate me for a lifetime. They were—and are—identical twins, alike in almost everything but their ability to lead. When we were growing up, one of my brothers was the archetypal natural leader, able to talk his teenage peers into doing things that parents never dreamed of, including ditching school for long periods of time. My other brother was the exact opposite, an innate follower without power, or even voice, within the group.

My brothers taught me the first two things I learned about leadership: that it is a function of character as well as behavior, and that leading is better than following. As a child I began scrutinizing leaders, starting with my more charming, more authoritative brother, to discover how they controlled and shaped their domains. I was hoping to learn their secrets: how to become a leader, and even more important, how leaders make things happen. Before I was out of my teens, I was studying leadership not in my living room or neighborhood but on the battlefields of Europe during World War II. Overnight I learned that a leader is not simply someone who experiences the personal exhilaration of being in charge; a leader is someone whose actions have the most profound consequences on other people's lives, for better or for worse, sometimes forever and ever.

This volume contains the essence of what I have learned about leadership and change. It contains some intensely personal essays, including an autobiographical sketch and an intellectual memoir. The latter piece sheds some light on how social science research a few decades ago altered the prism through which we view organizations and the means by which people can be motivated to make contributions that are enriching both to themselves personally and to their organizations.

Readers will discover how World War II, Antioch College, graduate school in Cambridge, Mass., and other events and institutions shaped my work. They will learn what my years as a university administrator practicing my theories in complex settings revealed to me about those theories themselves.

We are all children of our times, and my time—our time—has been one of the most remarkable in human history. In reading these essays, which I have woven together with some introductory comments that provide context, you will glimpse the beginnings of one revolution after another (the information explosion is only one), and you will see why I have come to believe that change is the only constant.

A close reading will reveal that each essay is a product of its times, and some of the early ones contain now-painful-to-behold references to the leader as "he" or "him." These were obviously written before the women's movement reminded us that language can oppress as well as liberate and that many of our best and brightest are women. You may also notice in these essays that I believe in repeating some of the most powerful anecdotes.

Over the years I have given corporate executives and other leaders counsel on how best to lead, sharing such insights as the necessity of leading as opposed to managing. But perhaps the most durable advice I can give leaders is to stay nimble. In this age of uncertainty, leaders must prepare for what has not yet been imagined. Leading today is like being a first-time parent—you have to do the right thing long before you fully understand the situation. Just one example: When I co-wrote "Is Democracy Inevitable?" in 1964, no one imagined how profoundly Japan would shape the philosophy and practice of management, either domestically or globally. And yet the corporations from that era that survived were those which were flexible enough to respond quickly to the paradigm shift spurred by Japan. Muhammad Ali was right: You have to flit like a butterfly and sting like a bee.

This book is part meditation, part how-to manual. I tend to share what I've learned in short bursts rather than extended analyses. Whenever possible I show rather than tell. Most of the substance in this book is contained in stories. In this I wonder whether my teachers were not the deathless authors of the New Testament, who routinely used parables to make their points. They realized people would learn more about selfless compassion from the story of the Good Samaritan than from any long-winded treatise on altruism. Indeed,

I think there is too much pseudoscientific jargon written about organizations. We need more good stories.

Most of the essays in this book deal with facilitating leadership and managing change. But the essays in Section Three focus on character and ethics, which I've found to be pivotal assets for leaders who are in the business of leaving a true legacy. Every organization tempts its leaders to become preoccupied with the priorities of the moment at the cost of overarching questions that determine the quality of all our lives, such questions as: Is this right? Is it good for our children? Is it good for the planet? The fact is that the best leaders in corporate and public life remember their societal obligations as well as their organizational ones.

Thirty-five years ago I was considered a futurist. Essentially, that meant I had the chutzpah to predict what might happen, instead of limiting my analysis to what had already happened. This book, however, ends not with new predictions for the future but rather a series of questions that I believe must be answered successfully by those leaders and students of leadership who have a stake in creating new dreams for that future. Even in these complex and vexing times, my great confidence is that we are up to the task.

*Warren Bennis*
*Santa Monica, 2000*

# Introduction |

## The Dreams—and Nightmares—of Leaders

It would be helpful to begin with some candid reflections on the gaping chasm that can exist between a leader's ideals and the realities that scorn them. At the time that I was launching a scholarly career in Boston more than four decades ago, many of my talented colleagues and I firmly held joint possession of a conviction that we could make history and that our collective work could transform the social architecture of human institutions.

We had considerable motivation. With the "shadow of Hitler's ghost" (a phrase from a seminal essay by Barbara Kellerman) still in plain view, and with the embers of the horrific Second World War still redolent, we sensed the need to reinvent social organizations in a way that would allow democracy to renew itself and immunize itself against fascism and tyranny. In that context, the study of effective leadership had the broadest implications imaginable.

More than a decade of intensely studying leadership gave way in 1967 to more than a decade of intensely practicing it. First, I left a comfortable and rewarding position on the faculty of MIT to serve as provost at the up-and-coming State University of New York at Buffalo for four years. Then in 1971, I left SUNY Buffalo to take the presidency of the University of Cincinnati. Chapter 18 of this book paints in great detail my experiences at those institutions; but my desire here at the outset is to offer some insights into what happened when this academician took his theories to the crucible to see first-hand how they would fare in the high temperatures of complex social organizations.

At the time, and in fact to this day, my colleagues at MIT thought this was the stupidest move I'd ever made. For myself, however, the motives for suspending a scholarly career at its moment of greatest velocity have become clearer to me with the passage of time.

One thing that has become clear is that *why* I chose to go into administration and *what I learned* were two quite separate things. Who ever knows all the "why's" of one's own motivation, but here are some of them:

Ever since my days at Antioch College, I wanted to follow in the footsteps of Antioch president Douglas McGregor, my mentor, as the head of a college or university. I won't argue that that's rational, but it was a powerful motivation.

I was tired of being a Montaigne in the bleachers. Montaigne once confessed, "If it were my due to be believed I wouldn't be so bold." It had been easy enough to be bold for someone in the bleachers, a detached analyst and objective observer, several terrain features away from the action. I wanted to be bold *in the arena,* to see if my written words could be embodied in the practitioners' world where deeds more than words counted. I recalled the words of Robert Graves's poem:

> Experts ranked in seried rows
> Fill the enormous plaza full;
> But only one is there who *knows*
> And he's the man who fights the bull.

It wasn't quite "fighting the bulls" that I had intended, but it turned out to be a marvelous 11-year validity check on my ideas.

Related to that, I suppose, is what every composer or playwright must desperately want, getting his or her work fully realized. How would a composer know how the music *sounds* unless he or she hears it; how would a playwright know how his or her words actually *play* without seeing and hearing it. How else could I truly know if my words had resonance or practical consequence for the world of management?

I also had ideas about higher education and I wanted an opportunity to see if I could push the higher education world in new directions.

A sense of purpose and an impulse to make a palpable difference in the lives of others were also powerful motivations. Our school motto at Westwood High (N.J.) was *Res non Verba,* Deeds not Words. Perhaps that helped lead some years later to an epiphany (and I don't use that word lightly) while visiting Michael Murphy in his San Francisco apartment in 1966 or so. The founder of Esalen and brilliant expositor of New Age philosophy was lamenting a recent story about Esalen in *Life* magazine. He was appalled by the story, featuring not Esalen's intellectually challenging ideas, but only the hot tubs and massages and the one nude group. (Hey, this *was* the 60s!) What made matters worse, Michael felt, and for good reason, was that the cover of that issue featured a different kind of nude group—dead, naked Biafran children, stacked grotesquely like cordwood, the result of a brutal tribal war. I was appalled by the juxtaposition of those two stories and wanted to get beyond disembodied analysis, beyond disengagement and detachment: *To do something!*

There were many other ineffables that even when I look back through the shining ether of time, I'm unclear about, and when I try to express them, they sound tritely jumbled. John Cage once said, "I have nothing more to say but I'm going to say it anyway." I shall resist the temptation.

*What* I learned during those 11 years was far more important than the preceding ruminations about why I embarked on that road. The dreams I cherished often snapped with the sensation of cold water splashing my face to bring me back to reality; other times I felt the dreams transfigured into outright nightmares. Regardless, here is a summary of what I learned:

**About power:** In my academic writings, I underplayed most forms of power while emphasizing the role of the leader as "facilitator," and stressed, to use Doug McGregor's famous metaphor, an "agricultural model" of seeding, nurturance and climate building. I utilized a domesticated version of power, emphasizing the process by which authorities attempt to achieve collective goals and to maintain legitimacy and compliance with their decisions, rather than the perspective of potential partisans, which involves diversity of interest groups attempting to influence the choices of authorities. Put differently, I realized that an organization was as much a political model (i.e. allocating scarce resources) as a human-relationship model.

**About change:** Similarly, my writings had implied a rather simple model of change, based on gentle nudges from the environment coupled with a truth-love strategy; that is, with sufficient trust and collaboration, along with knowledge, organizations would progress monotonically upwards and onwards along a democratic continuum. In short, the organization of the future I had envisaged would most certainly be, along with a Bach Chorale and Chartres Cathedral, the epitome of Western Civilization.

One other thing about change that I learned and that was in order to be an effective leader *qua* change agent, you had to adhere simultaneously to the symbols of tradition and stability and to the symbols of revision and change. I was seen by many constituents as emphasizing the latter and tone-deaf to the former. I think there is more than a little validity to that perception. As president of the University of Cincinnati, I could have done well to learn much more about the city and its proud traditions. Further, some of my interventions appeared to slight the sensibilities of longtime faculty members.

**About bureaucracy:** It was a lot more stubborn and obdurate than I had thought. Not a bad lesson for someone who was called the Buck Rogers of Organizational Change in a book review of one of my books.* Perhaps universities are more resistant than most. The old saw about universities being

---

*Changing Organizations,* McGraw-Hill, 1966.

harder to move than cemeteries has a ring of truth about it. The clogged cartography of stakeholders in a modern university is both breathtakingly confusing and filled with conflict. Much like internal stakeholders, interests vary and that brings up another old saw, that the way to success for a university president is to provide sex for students, a winning football team for alumni and a parking place for the faculty.

When I was president at Cincinnati I would hold "Open Hours" every Wednesday afternoon where anyone could come in and surface their problems, complaints, ideas, etc. It was an expedient move, I thought; so many people wanted a hearing that this was a way I could manage to squeeze everyone into a 2–5 p.m. time slot. At first, I would see students, faculty or administrators—or for that matter, anyone from the community—one-on-one. Then word got around and more and more people wanted an "audience with the president." Both to keep order and have a decent place to wait, I opened up the adjacent board room and stocked it with soft drinks and cookies. Finally, it got so jammed with petitioners that the board room was no longer adequate to contain all comers, at which point I invited everyone to sit in my office. Open hours began to resemble something like a 15th Century Persian court, supplicants of various kinds crowded into my office. Most of the problems were bureaucratic glitches and upsets.

Not wanting to make decisions that should be left to the appropriate department chair, dean or vice-president, I invited other university officers to attend. The university ombudsman was always present to take notes and follow up. The sessions often went into the evening hours and it was not unusual for me to leave the office after seeing the last person out at 8 or 9 at night. Often, people came in groups to lobby me; frequently "townees" would come to register their complaints about unruly students, or parents would come to express their unhappiness with their children's grades. Many of the sessions were also hilarious and, if they accomplished nothing else, they exposed to me the DNA of the university.

I noticed one woman in her 60s who came every week and sat quietly observant, knitting and looking on quite contentedly. One Wednesday I asked her if she had an issue she'd like to raise or a question she'd like to ask. "No," she replied, "I'm here because it's the best show in town."

After three years of presiding over open hours, I hadn't noticed any differences in the kabuki-like routine of the university's bureaucracy. I was hard-put to show that these sessions had any visible effect on bureaucratic inertia. I had hoped, naively, that I would set a model that other university administrators would emulate. Even more naively, I had the unrequited wish that somehow or another, these sessions, along with other administrative interventions would de-bureaucratize the campus and make it more responsive to faculty and students. Perhaps I should have kept at it longer, I'm not sure, but it was a painfully revealing—going back to my Antioch roots—"learning experience."

It wasn't fatalism which gripped me, only realism.

**About leadership (and me):** Those eleven years at Buffalo and Cincinnati were arduous, difficult and enormously important. *Doing it* is remarkably different than *writing about it*. Business professors are especially vulnerable to a dangerous chasm between the practice of management and the study of management. In most professions, take medicine, medical school professors are clinicians as well as teachers and researchers. Of course, there a few who only conduct research, usually those who hold dual Ph.D. and M.D. degrees. But for the most part, medical school teachers and researchers also practice; they not only chair departments, but also maintain a practice. Consulting, as many management professors do, is not the same as doing management. Faculty who teach direction and production at USC's top-ranked Cinema and TV School also direct and produce films; faculty teaching screen writing also write screen plays. I don't think it's possible to understand a profession, as compared to an academic discipline such as physics or English literature, without practicing it. There is a profound difference, it seems to me, between reading up on something and performing it, between observed truth and participative truth. Eleven years of actually "running something" provided an understanding of the thick texture of leadership, the triumphs and tragedies of it, the personal underworld that leaders experience. It's not for everyone, I know, but those years on the ground grounded me in an understanding of management that, speaking as an experiential freak, I couldn't have gotten any other way.

In many ways, I have to add quickly, it wasn't for me either. Not for the long run, anyway. The truth is that I wouldn't have missed it for the world and I wouldn't want to do it again. It's no false modesty to say that while I had a curious admixture of shortcomings and competencies as an academic leader, I knew in my heart that there were others who could do it as well or better. It simply wasn't my calling. There was a definite turning point, a glistening moment in time, when that realization crystallized.

I was delivering an evening lecture to the faculty and students of Harvard's School of Education, sometime in 1976. They invited me to speak on the topic of academic leadership and I spent an inordinate amount of time preparing for it. The auditorium was full and I thought I was at my best, enjoying myself enormously as I described wittily and ironically the existential groaning, the ups and downs, the backstage gossip of governing a large, urban university. As I think back to that evening I was part social anthropologist and part standup comic. The audience seemed to enjoy it as much as I did. And then came a question from the Dean of the School, Paul Ylvisaker, one of the most respected figures in all of higher education, a consultant to the Ford Foundation and man whose wisdom was sought after by everyone from the President of the United States to the President of Harvard. He was the uncontested elder statesman of higher education.

Now I thought that my experience responding to questions was sharpened to a fine point after so many years of teaching as well as spending a lot of time with the media who loved asking embarrassing and difficult questions. My singular conceit, shortly to end, was that there wasn't a question I couldn't respond to in a convincing (and winning) way. At the least, I thought I was beyond being stumped. Paul was sitting near the back of the room and the question came at me like a long, high lob, floating lazily over the audience and masking its astuteness in that self-effacing (and deceptive) mid-western drawl of his. It was short. "Warren," he asked, "do you *love* being President of the University of Cincinnati?" I don't know how many seconds passed before responding. The room was suddenly so quiet that I could hear my heart beating. Finally, I looked up at Paul and haltingly said, "I don't know." Actually, that was the moment I knew the answer but hadn't yet told myself.

The truth is that I didn't love it and didn't have the passion for it and that what I was doing wasn't my own voice. I wanted to *be* a university president. I didn't want to *do* university president. Now that was a huge lesson for me, because if there is one single thing I have found out about leaders is that, by and large if not every day, they seem to love what they're doing. C. Michael Armstrong, the exemplary CEO and Chairman of AT&T, told me recently that his favorite day of the week is Monday. I told him that he should have his license plate read, TGIM, Thank God, It's Monday.* It won't be Jack Welch's strategic genius that will be remembered as the signature of his almost 20 years of GE's leadership. It will be the way he has mobilized and energized hundreds of thousands of workers across many types of businesses into constructive activity that will mark his place in business history. And when I co-teach a course on leadership to undergraduates with USC's President, Steve Sample, I realize how much he loves what he's doing. I felt that fund raising was an unnatural act; this man loves it and loves dealing with the daily conflicts, the numbing daily

---

*Incidentally this is the title of a splendid book by Ken Cloke and Joan Goldsmith, Irwin Press, 1997.

interactions, in his car always on the phone, trying his best to keep his Sundays "free" but not always successfully, and the countless other responsibilities that goes with leading a major, research university. No one can be a great leader without that passion and love.

Ylvisaker's question made me aware that administration wasn't for me. I didn't have the passion and love for it. That epiphanic moment I had was later confirmed over the following twenty years researching the qualities of exemplary leaders. The simple fact is that all exemplary leaders have found their unique voice, their trademark. They know who they are and that what they do, no one else can quite do their way. The late Jerry Garcia, the great, gray presence of the Grateful Dead, said it better than I just did. He once observed, "You do not merely want to be considered just the best of the best. You want to be considered the only one who can do what you do."

To this day I don't know what Ylvisaker was picking up in my delivery or my body language that informed his question. It may have been my casual, detached delivery or something in my eyes. Perhaps he had read the W.H. Auden poem I recently came upon:

> You need not see what someone is doing
> To know if it is his vocation,
> You have only to watch his eyes:
> A cook mixing his sauce, a surgeon
> Making a primary incision,
> A clerk completing a bill of lading
> Wear the same expression,
> forgetting themselves in a function.

He must have known that I couldn't forget myself in that function. This was no disaster, however. I now know I wasn't destined to be to management what a Michael Jordan or Magic Johnson was to the hardwood. Perhaps I was more of a Phil Jackson or a Pat Riley—someone who had once sweated in the arena, but who ultimately made his greatest contribution as a student of the game and as a coach of others.

Indeed, many of our greatest coaches were marginal players, and many of our greatest players fail miserably as coaches. I found my calling as an adviser and coach to leaders in corporate, government and academic life. What helped me immeasurably in this role was my newfound ability to appreciate the exhausting complexity of the worlds which they inhabited.

In short, I found my place within the dream. It took some time to find, and it was not the place I had at times envisioned, but it was the one which was right for me and for many others.

# Part 1

*Negotiating the Dream:*
*Lessons in the Art of Leading*

# 1
## Managing the Dream

*The buzz has grown almost deafening over the past decade regarding the need for "global leadership," as if it were something distinct from effective management of the past. I'm increasingly convinced that good leadership has always looked the same regardless of time and place. When this essay was written in 1990, American industry was being overtaken by Japan on one side and the New Europe on the other. A decade later, it's clear that Japanese and German industry didn't enjoy any built-in advantages over that of the United States, which has again assumed world leadership at all levels. This helps confirm that the dominant players may change over time but the principles of good leadership don't, either at the global or local level.*

*True, the "global manager" has to find ways to understand and empathize with other cultures. But domestic organizations—especially in the era of mass mergers of widely disparate businesses—typically have multiple subcultures that can be just as mysterious as any lost tribe and that must also be mastered before the organization can work. However many area codes are involved, the effective leader understands this diversity and embraces it.*

$P$ick up any business magazine or newspaper and you'll find the same story: pessimism about America's capacity to compete successfully in the new, spirited global economy. *The Wall Street Journal* laments, "The sudden emergence of America as the world's largest debtor, Japan as the globe's richest creditor, and the Soviet Union as its most ardent preacher of pacifism seems, to many Americans, to have turned the world upside down, raising doubts about whether America can or should lead." The *Washington Post* kicks in with "Kiss Number One Goodbye, Folks." A headline in the *International Herald Tribune* warns, "America, Europe Is Coming."

If there is reason to despair and join the handwringing and headshaking of doomsayers, it's because traditional American managers were brought up in a different time, when all they had to do was build the greatest mousetraps, and the world beat a path to their doors. "Leadership in a traditional U.S. company," says R.B. Horton, CEO of BP America, "consisted of creating a management able to cope with competitors who all played with basically the same deck of economic cards." And it was an American game. The competition was fierce but knowable. If you played your cards right, you could win.

But the game has changed and strange new rules have appeared. The deck has been shuffled and jokers have been added. Never before has American business faced so many challenges, and never before have there been so many choices about how to face those challenges. Uncertainties and complexities abound. The only thing truly predictable is unpredictability. The new chic is chaos chic. As Yogi Berra put it, "The future ain't what it used to be."

Constant change disturbs some managers—it always has, and it always will. Machiavelli said, "Change has no constituency." Well, it better have one—and soon. Forget about regaining global leadership. With only a single, short decade remaining before the 21st century, we must look now at what it's going to take simply to remain a player in the game. We can do that because the 21st century is with us now. Cultures don't turn sharply with the pages of the calendar—they evolve. By paying attention to what is changing today, we know what we must do better tomorrow.

## Leaders, Not Managers

Given the nature and constancy of change and the transnational challenges facing American business leadership, the key to making the right choices will come from understanding and embodying the leadership qualities necessary to succeed in a mercurial global economy. To survive in the 21st century, we're going to need a new generation of leaders— leaders, not managers.

The distinction is an important one. Leaders conquer the context—the volatile, turbulent, ambiguous surroundings that sometimes seem to conspire against us and will surely suffocate us if we let them—while managers surrender to it. There are other differences, as well, and they are crucial:

- The manager administers; the leader innovates.
- The manager is a copy; the leader is an original.
- The manager maintains; the leader develops.
- The manager focuses on systems and structure; the leader focuses on people.
- The manager relies on control; the leader inspires trust.
- The manager has a short-range view; the leader has a long-range perspective.
- The manager asks how and when; the leader asks what and why.
- The manager has his eye on the bottom line; the leader has his eye on the horizon.
- The manager accepts the status quo; the leader challanges it.
- The manager is the classic good soldier; the leader is his own person.
- The manager does things right; the leader does the right thing.

Field Marshal Sir William Slim led the 14th British Army from 1943 to 1945 in the reconquest of Burma from the Japanese—one of the epic campaigns of World War II. He recognized the distinction between leaders and managers when he said: "Managers are necessary; leaders are essential. . . . Leadership is of the spirit, compounded of personality and vision. . . . Management is of the mind, more a matter of accurate calculation, statistics, methods, timetables and routine."

I've spent the last 10 years talking with leaders, including Jim Burke at Johnson & Johnson, John Scully at Apple, television producer Norman Lear, and close to 100 other men and women, some famous and some not. In the course of my research, I've learned something about the current crop of leaders and something about the kind of leadership that will be necessary to forge the future. While leaders come in every size, shape and disposition—short, tall, neat, sloppy, young, old, male and female—every leader I talked with shared at least one characteristic: a concern with a guiding purpose, an overarching vision. They were more than goal-directed. As Karl Wallenda said, "Walking the tightwire is living; everything else is waiting."

Leaders have a clear idea of what they want to do—personally and professionally—and the strength to persist in the face of setbacks, even failures. They know where they are going and why. Senator Howard Baker said of President Reagan, whom he served as Chief of Staff, "He knew who he was, what he believed in and where he wanted to go."

## Managing the Dream

Many leaders find a metaphor that embodies and implements their vision. For Charles Darwin, the fecund metaphor was a branching tree of evolution on which he could trace the rise and fate of various species. William James viewed mental processes as a stream or river. John Locke focused on the falconer, whose release of a bird symbolized his "own emerging view of the creative process"—that is, the quest for human knowledge.

I think of it this way: *Leaders manage the dream.* All leaders have the capacity to create a compelling vision, one that takes people to a new place, and the ability to translate that vision into reality. Peter Drucker said that the first task of the leader is to define the mission. Max De Pree, former CEO of Herman Miller Inc., the Zeeland, Mississippi, office furniture maker, put it another way in *Leadership Is an Art:* "The first responsibility of a leader is to define reality. The last is to say thank you. In between, the leader is a servant." Managing the dream can be broken down into five parts. The first part is communicating the vision. Jung said: "A dream that is not understood remains a mere occurrence. Understood, it becomes a living experience."

Jim Burke spends 40 percent of his time communicating the Johnson & Johnson credo. More than 800 managers have attended J&J challenge meetings, where they go through the credo line by line to see what changes need to be made. Over the years some of those changes have been fundamental. But like the U.S. Constitution, the credo itself endures.

The other basic parts of managing the dream are recruiting meticulously, rewarding, retraining and reorganizing. Jan Carlzon, CEO of Scandinavian Air System (SAS), is a leader who embraces all five parts.

Carlzon's vision was to make SAS one of the five or six remaining international carriers by the year 1995. (He thinks that only five or six will be left by that time, and I think he's probably right.) To accomplish this, he developed two goals. The first was to make SAS 1 percent better in 100 different ways than its competitors. The second was to create a market niche.

Carlzon chose the business traveler—rather than college students, travel agent deals or any of a host of other possibilities—because he believed that this would be the most profitable niche. In order to attract business travelers, Carlzon had to make sure that every interaction they had with every SAS employee was rewarding. He had to endow every interaction with purpose, relevance, courtesy and caring. He estimated that there were 63,000 of these interactions each day between SAS employees and current or potential customers. He called these interactions "moments of truth."

Carlzon developed a marvelous cartoon book, *The Little Red Book,* to communicate the new SAS vision to employees. And he set up a corporate college in Copenhagen to train them. Just as important, he has "debureaucratized" the whole organization. The organization chart no longer looks like a pyramid; it looks like a set of circles, a galaxy. In fact, Carlzon's book, which is called *Moments of Truth* in English, is titled *Destroying the Pyramids* in its original Swedish.

One of those circles, one organizational segment, is the Copenhagen–New York route. All the pilots, the navigators, the engineers, the flight attendants, the baggage handlers, the reservations agents—everybody who has anything to do with the Copenhagen–New York route—are involved in a self-managed, autonomous work group with a gain-sharing plan so that they all participate in whatever profits that particular route brings in. There's also a Copenhagen-Frankfurt organizational segment, and so on. The whole corporation is structured in terms of these small, egalitarian groups.

General Electric CEO Jack Welch said: "Yesterday's idea of the boss, who became the boss because he or she knew one more fact than the person working for them, is yesterday's manager. Tomorrow's person leads through a vision, a shared set of values, a shared objective." The single defining quality of leaders is the capacity to create and realize a vision. Yeats said, "In dreams begins responsibility." Vision is a waking dream. For leaders, the responsibility is to transform the vision into reality. By doing so, they transform their dominion, whether an airline, a motion picture, the computer industry or America itself.

Thoreau put it this way: "If one advances confidently in the direction of his dreams, and endeavors to live the life he has imagined, he will meet with a success in common hours. . . . If you have built castles in the air, your work need not be lost. It is where they should be. Now put the foundation under them."

## The New Global Alliances

Jan Carlzon also illustrates one element that I believe will distinguish the vision of 21st-century leaders from the current model. His is a global vision; he is fully aware of the need for transnational networking and alliances.

Carlzon is not alone. A recent United Research Co./ Harris survey of 150 CEOs of *Forbes 500* companies found that they saw the greatest opportunity and challenge for the future in the global market. In the same vein, senior-level managers polled in a Carnegie-Mellon University survey of business school alumni named competing effectively on a global basis as the most difficult management issue for the next decade.

Global interdependence is one of six pivotal forces working on the world today. (The others are technology, mergers and acquisitions, deregulation and reregulation, demographics and values, and the environment. Leadership is necessary for coping with each of these forces, but those are subjects for another time.) One of the first things the astute businessperson checks daily now is the yen-dollar ratio. Fifty percent of the property in downtown Los Angeles is owned by the Japanese.

Foreign investment in America—in real estate, finance and business—continues to escalate. But the changes aren't simply on our shores. In 1992, when Europe becomes a true Common Market, it will contain 330 million consumers, compared with 240 million in this country.

American leaders who want to be a part of that new market are planning now. Michael Eisner of Disney has sent Robert Fitzpatrick to France to head up the new EuroDisney project. CalFed, which already has a bank in England, is preparing for the future with plans for banks in Brussels, Barcelona, Paris and Vienna. In Spain, AT&T has spent $220 million for a semiconductor plant, and General Electric has budgeted $1.7 billion for a plastics facility. Ford, Nissan, Sony and Matsushita have opened factories in or near Barcelona in the last two years.

In most cases, however, buying into Europe is prohibitively expensive. The shrewd leaders of the future are recognizing the wisdom of creating alliances with other organizations whose fates are correlated with their own. The Norwegian counterpart of Federal Express—which has

3,500 employees, one of the largest companies in Norway—is setting up a partnership with Federal Express. First Boston has linked up with Credit Suisse, forming FBCS. GE has recently set up a number of joint ventures with GE of Great Britain, meshing four product divisions. Despite the names, the companies hadn't been related. GE had considered buying its British namesake, but ultimately chose alliance rather than acquisition.

Buying in is not the choice of the Europeans themselves: Glaxco, a British pharmaceutical firm, made a deal with Hoffman-LaRoche for the distribution of Zantac, a stomach tranquilizer, and knocked SmithKline Beecham's Tagamet out of the game. Kabi Virtum, a Swedish pharmaceutical company, is looking for a partner in Japan to build a joint laboratory, in exchange for which the Japanese would get help in licensing drugs in Sweden.

And as for Jan Carlzon, when he tried and failed to buy Sabena, a rival airline, he established an alliance instead. SAS also works with an Argentine airline and with Eastern Airlines, sharing gates and connecting routes.

The global strategy is firmly rooted in Carlzon's vision for SAS. All leaders' guiding visions provide clearly marked road maps for their organizations; every member can see which direction the corporation is going. The communication of the vision generates excitement about the trip. The plans for the journey create order out of chaos, instill confidence and trust, and offer criteria for success. The group knows when it has arrived.

The critical factor for success in global joint ventures is a shared vision between the two companies. If you're not sure of your company's vision, how can you tell what the advantages of an alliance would be? You must be certain you have the right map before embarking on the journey. If you think your company's vision lacks definition, here are some questions that may help give it color and dimension:

- What is unique about us?
- What values are true priorities for the next year?

- What would make me professionally commit my mind and heart to this vision over the next five to 10 years?
- What does the world really need that our company can and should provide?
- What do I want our company to accomplish so that I will be committed, aligned and proud of my association with the institution?

Ask yourself those questions today. Your answers will be the fire that heats the forge of your company's future.

# 2

# *The Four Competencies of Leadership*

*Much of what I've learned in decades of studying leadership was first distilled in this essay from 1984. The standard criteria for choosing top-level managers are technical competence, people skills, conceptual skills, judgment, and character. And yet effective leadership is overwhelmingly the function of only one of these— character. (Part three of this book examines this criterion in far greater detail.) If you ask subordinates what they want in a leader, they usually list three things: direction or vision, trustworthiness, and optimism. Like effective parents, lovers, teachers, and therapists, good leaders make people hopeful.*

For nearly five years I have been researching a book on leadership. During this period, I have traveled around the country spending time with 90 of the most effective, successful leaders in the nation; 60 from corporations and 30 from the public sector.

My goal was to find these leaders' common traits, a task that has required much more probing than I expected. For a while, I sensed much more diversity than commonality among them. The group comprises both left-brain and right-brain thinkers; some who dress for success and some who don't; well-spoken, articulate leaders and laconic, inarticulate ones; some John Wayne types and some who are definitely the opposite. Interestingly, the group includes only a few stereotypically charismatic leaders.

Despite the diversity, which is profound and must not be underestimated, I identified certain areas of competence shared by all 90. Before presenting those findings, though, it is important to place this study in context, to review the mood and events in the United States just before and during the research.

## Decline and Malaise

When I left the University of Cincinnati late in 1977, our country was experiencing what President Carter called "despair" or "malaise." From 1960 to 1980, our institutions' credibility had eroded steadily. In an article about that period entitled "Where Have All the Leaders Gone?" I described how difficult the times were for leaders, including university presidents like myself.

I argued that, because of the complexity of the times, leaders felt impotent. The assassinations of several national leaders, the Vietnam war, the Watergate scandal, the Iranian hostage crisis and other events led to a loss of trust in our institutions and leadership.

I came across a quotation in a letter Abigail Adams wrote to Thomas Jefferson in 1790: "These are the hard times in which a genius would wish to live." If, as she believed, great necessities summon great leaders, I wanted to get to know the leaders brought forth by the current malaise. In a time when bumper stickers appeared reading "Impeach Someone," I resolved to seek out leaders who were effective under these adverse conditions.

At the same time that America suffered from this leadership gap, it was suffering from a productivity gap. Consider these trends:

• In the 1960s, the average GNP growth was 4.1 percent; in the 1970s, it was 2.9 percent; in 1982, it was negative.

• The U.S. standard of living, the world's highest in 1972, now ranks fifth.

• In 1960, when the economies of Europe and Japan had been rebuilt, the U.S. accounted for 25 percent of the industrial nations' manufacturing exports and supplied 98 percent of its domestic markets. Now, the U.S. has less than a

20 percent share of the world market, and that share is declining.

- In 1960, U.S. automobiles had a 96 percent market share; today we have about 71 percent. The same holds true for consumer electronics; in 1960 it was 94.4 percent, in 1980 only 49 percent. And that was before Sony introduced the Walkman!

In addition to leadership and productivity gaps, a subtler "commitment gap" existed, that is, a reluctance to commit to one's work or employer.

The Public Agenda's recent survey of working Americans shows the following statistics. Less than one out of four jobholders (23 percent) says he or she currently works at full potential. Nearly half say they do not put much effort into their jobs above what is required. The overwhelming majority, 75 percent, say they could be significantly more effective on their job than they are now. And nearly 6 in 10 working Americans believe that "most people do not work as hard as they used to."

A number of observers have pointed out the considerable gap between the number of hours people are paid to work and the numbers of hours they spend on productive labor. Evidence developed recently by the University of Michigan indicates the gap may be widening. They found the difference between paid hours and actual working hours grew 10 percent between 1970 and 1980.

This increasing commitment gap leads to the central question: How can we empower the work force and reap the harvest of human effort?

If I have learned anything from my research, it is this: The factor that empowers the work force and ultimately determines which organizations succeed or fail is the leadership of those organizations. When strategies, processes or cultures change, the key to improvement remains leadership.

## The Sample: 90 Leaders

For my study, I wanted 90 effective leaders with proven track records. The final group contains 60 corporate executives, most, but not all, from Fortune 500 companies, and 30 from the public sector. My goal was to find people with leadership ability, in contrast to just "good managers"—true leaders who affect the culture, who are the social architects of their organizations and who create and maintain values.

Leaders are people who do the right thing; managers are people who do things right. Both roles are crucial, and they differ profoundly. I often observe people in top positions doing the wrong thing well.

Given my definition, one of the key problems facing American organizations (and probably those in much of the industrialized world) is that they are underled and overmanaged. They do not pay enough attention to doing the right thing, while they pay too much attention to doing things right. Part of the fault lies with our schools of management; we teach people how to be good technicians and good staff people, but we don't train people for leadership.

The group of 60 corporate leaders was not especially different from any profile of top leadership in America. The median age was 56. Most were white males, with six black men and six women in the group. The only surprising finding was that all the CEOs not only were married to their first spouse, but also seemed enthusiastic about the institution of marriage. Examples of the CEOS are Bill Kieschnick, chairman and CEO of Arco, and the late Ray Kroc of McDonald's restaurants.

Public-sector leaders included Harold Williams, who then chaired the SEC; Neil Armstrong, a genuine all-American hero who happened to be at the University of Cincinnati; three elected officials; two orchestra conductors; and two winning athletics coaches. I wanted conductors and coaches because I mistakenly believed they were the last leaders with complete control over their constituents.

After several years of observation and conversation, I have defined four competencies evident to some extent in every member of the group. They are:

- management of attention;
- management of meaning;

- management of trust;
- management of self.

*Management of Attention*

One of the traits most apparent in these leaders is their ability to draw others to them, because they have a vision, a dream, a set of intentions, an agenda, a frame of reference. They communicate an extraordinary focus of commitment, which attracts people to them. One of these leaders was described as making people want to join in with him; he enrolls them in his vision.

Leaders, then, manage attention through a compelling vision that brings others to a place they have not been before. I came to this understanding in a roundabout way, as this anecdote illustrates.

One of the people I most wanted to interview was one of the few I couldn't seem to reach. He refused to answer my letters or phone calls. I even tried getting in touch with the members of his board. He is Leon Fleischer, a well-known child prodigy who grew up to become a prominent pianist, conductor and musicologist.

When I called him originally to recruit him for the University of Cincinnati faculty, he declined and told me he was working with orthopedic specialists to regain the use of his right hand. He did visit the campus, and I was impressed with his commitment to staying in Baltimore, near the medical institution where he received therapy.

Fleischer was the only person who kept turning me down for an interview, and finally I gave up. A couple of summers later I was in Aspen, Colorado, while Fleischer was conducting the Aspen Music Festival. I tried to reach him again, even leaving a note on his dressing room door, but I got no answer.

One day in downtown Aspen, I saw two perspiring young cellists carrying their instruments and offered them a ride to the music tent. They hopped in the back of my jeep, and, as we rode, I questioned them about Fleischer.

"I'll tell you why he is so great," said one. "He doesn't waste our time."

Fleischer finally agreed not only to be interviewed but to let me watch him rehearse and conduct music classes. I linked the way I saw him work with that simple sentence, "He doesn't waste our time." Every moment Fleischer was before the orchestra, he knew exactly what sound he wanted. He didn't waste time because his intentions were always evident. What united him with the other musicians was their concern with intention and outcome.

When I reflected on my own experience, it struck me that when I was most effective, it was because I knew what I wanted. When I was ineffective, it was because I was unclear about it.

So, the first leadership competency is the management of attention through a set of intentions or a vision, not in a mystical or religious sense, but in the sense of outcome, goal or direction.

## Management of Meaning

To make dreams apparent to others, and to align people with them, leaders must communicate their vision. Communication and alignment work together.

Consider, for example, the contrasting styles of Presidents Reagan and Carter. Ronald Reagan is called "the great communicator"; one of his speech writers said Reagan can read the phone book and make it interesting. The reason is that Reagan uses metaphors with which people can identify.

In his first budget message, for example, Reagan described a trillion dollars by comparing it to piling up dollar bills beside the Empire State Building. Reagan, to use one of Alexander Haig's coinages, "tangibilitated" the idea. Leaders make ideas tangible and real to others, so they can support them. For no matter how marvelous the vision, the effective leader must use a metaphor, a word or a model to make that vision clear to others.

In contrast, President Carter was boring. Carter was one of our best informed presidents; he had more facts at his finger tips than almost any other president. But he never made the meaning come through the facts.

I interviewed an assistant secretary of commerce appointed by Carter, who told me that after four years in his administration, she still did not know what Jimmy Carter stood for. She said that working for him was like looking through the wrong side of a tapestry; the scene was blurry and indistinct.

The leader's goal is not mere explanation or clarification but the creation of meaning. My favorite baseball joke is exemplary: In the ninth inning of a key playoff game, with a 3 and 2 count on the batter, the umpire hesitates a split second in calling the pitch. The batter whirls around angrily and says, "Well, what was it?" The umpire barks back, "It ain't *nothing* until *I* call it!"

The more far-flung and complex the organization, the more critical is this ability. Effective leaders can communicate ideas through several organizational layers, across great distances, even through the jamming signals of special interest groups and opponents.

When I was a university president, a group of administrators and I would hatch what we knew was a great idea. Then we would do the right thing: delegate, delegate, delegate. But when the product or policy finally appeared, it scarcely resembled our original idea.

This process occurred so often that I gave it a name: the Pinocchio Effect. (I am sure Geppetto had no idea how Pinocchio would look when he finished carving him.) The Pinocchio Effect leaves us surprised. Because of inadequate communication, results rarely resemble our expectations.

We read and hear so much about information that we tend to overlook the importance of meaning. Actually, the more bombarded a society or organization, the more deluged with facts and images, the greater its thirst for meaning. Leaders integrate facts, concepts and anecdotes into meaning for the public.

Not all the leaders in my group are word masters. They get people to understand and support their goals in a variety of ways.

The ability to manage attention and meaning comes from the whole person. It is not enough to use the right buzz word or a cute technique, or to hire a public relations person to write speeches.

Consider, instead, Frank Dale, publisher of the Los Angeles afternoon newspaper, *The Herald Examiner*. Dale's charge was to cut into the market share of his morning competitor, *The L.A. Times*. When he first joined the newspaper a few years ago, he created a campaign with posters picturing the *Herald Examiner* behind and slightly above the *Times*. The whole campaign was based on this potent message of how the *Herald Examiner* would overtake the *Times*.

I interviewed Dale at his office, and when he sat down at his desk and fastened around him a safety belt like those on airplanes, I couldn't supress a smile. He did this to remind me and everybody else of the risks the newspaper entailed. His whole person contributed to the message.

No one is more cynical than a newspaper reporter. You can imagine the reactions that traveled the halls of the *Herald Examiner* building. At the same time, nobody forgot what Frank Dale was trying to communicate. And that is the management of meaning.

## Management of Trust

Trust is essential to all organizations. The main determinant of trust is reliability, what I call constancy. When I talked to the board members or staffs of these leaders, I heard certain phrases again and again: "She is all of a piece." "Whether you like it or not, you always know where he is coming from, what he stands for."

When John Paul II visited this country, he gave a press conference. One reporter asked how the Pope could account for allocating funds to build a swimming pool at the papal summer palace. He responded quickly: "I like to swim. Next question." He did not rationalize about medical reasons or claim he got the money from a special source.

A recent study showed people would much rather follow individuals they can count on, even when they disagree with their viewpoint, than people they agree with but who shift positions frequently. I cannot emphasize enough the significance of constancy and focus.

Margaret Thatcher's reelection in Great Britain is another excellent example. When she won office in 1979, observers predicted she quickly would revert to defunct Labor Party policies. She did not. In fact, not long ago a *London Times* article appeared headlined (parodying Christopher Fry's play) "The Lady's Not for Returning." She has not turned; she has been constant, focused and all of a piece.

## Management of Self

The fourth leadership competency is management of self, knowing one's skills and deploying them effectively. Management of self is critical; without it, leaders and managers can do more harm than good. Like incompetent doctors, incompetent managers can make life worse, make people sicker and less vital. (The term *iatrogenic,* by the way, refers to illness *caused* by doctors and hospitals.) Some managers give themselves heart attacks and nervous breakdowns; still worse, many are "carriers," causing their employees to be ill.

Leaders know themselves; they know their strengths and nurture them. They also have a faculty I think of as the Wallenda Factor, the ability to accept risk.

One CEO told me that if she had a knack for leadership, it was the capacity to make as many mistakes as she could as soon as possible, and thus get them out of the way. Another said that a mistake is simply "another way of doing things." These leaders learn from and use something that doesn't go well; it is not a failure but simply the next step.

When I asked Harold Williams, president of the Getty Foundation, to name the experience that most shaped him as a leader, he said it was being passed over for the presidency of Norton Simon. When it happened, he was furious and demanded reasons, most of which he considered idiotic. Finally, a friend told him that some of the reasons were valid and he should change. He did, and about a year and a half later became president.

Or consider coach Ray Meyer of DePaul University, whose team finally lost at home after winning 29 straight home games. I called him to ask how he felt. He said, "Great. Now we can start to concentrate on winning, not on *not* losing."

Consider Broadway producer Harold Prince, who calls a press conference the morning after his show opens, before reading the reviews, to announce his next play. Or Susan B. Anthony, who said, "Failure is impossible." Or Fletcher Byrum, who, after 22 years as president of Coopers, was asked about his hardest decision. He replied that he did not know what a hard decision was; that he never worried, that he accepted the possibility of being wrong. Byrum said that worry was an obstacle to clear thinking.

The Wallenda Factor is an approach to life; it goes beyond leadership and power in organizations. These leaders all have it.

## Empowerment: The Effects of Leadership

Leadership can be felt throughout an organization. It gives pace and energy to the work and empowers the work force. Empowerment is the collective effect of leadership. In organizations with effective leaders, empowerment is most evident in four themes:

• *People feel significant.* Everyone feels that he or she makes a difference to the success of the organization. The difference may be small—prompt delivery of potato chips to a mom-and-pop grocery store or developing a tiny but essential part for an airplane. But where they are empowered, people feel that what they do has meaning and significance.

• *Learning and competence matter.* Leaders value learning and mastery, and so do people who work for leaders. Leaders make it clear that there is no failure, only mistakes that give us feedback and tell us what to do next.

• *People are part of a community.* Where there is leadership, there is a team, a family, a unity. Even people who do not especially like each other feel the sense of community. When Neil Armstrong talks about the Apollo explorations, he describes how a team carried out an almost unimaginably complex set of interdependent tasks. Until there were women astronauts, the men referred to this feeling as "brotherhood." I suggest they rename it "family."

• *Work is exciting.* Where there are leaders, work is stimulating, challenging, fascinating and fun. An essential ingredient in organizational leadership is pulling rather than pushing people toward a goal. A "pull" style of influence attracts and energizes people to enroll in an exciting vision of the future. It motivates through identification, rather than through rewards and punishments. Leaders articulate and embody the ideals toward which the organization strives.

People cannot be expected to enroll in just any exciting vision. Some visions and concepts have more staying power and are rooted more deeply in our human needs than others. I believe the lack of two such concepts in modern organizational life is largely responsible for the alienation and lack of meaning so many experience in their work.

One of these is the concept of quality. Modern industrial society has been oriented to quantity, providing more goods and services for everyone. Quantity is measured in money; we are a money-oriented society. Quality often is not measured at all, but is appreciated intuitively. Our response to quality is a feeling. Feelings of quality are connected intimately with our experience of meaning, beauty and value in our lives.

Closely linked to the concept of quality is that of dedication, even love, of our work. This dedication is evoked by quality and is the force that energizes high-performing sys-tems. When we love our work, we need not be managed by hopes of reward or fears of punishment. We can create sys-tems that facilitate our work, rather than being preoccupied with checks and controls of people who want to beat or exploit the system.

And that is what the human resources profession should care most about.

# 3

# *On the Leading Edge of Change*

*In the 1990s I met with corporate and other leaders throughout Asia. I came away convinced that the key to competitive advantage will be a leader's ability to create an environment that generates intellectual capital. The day is past when an organization can thrive simply by implementing the ideas of a single leader. The effective leaders of the future will be those who are best able to facilitate and orchestrate ideas, whatever their source. This is a shortened version of the original essay.*

In his recent book *Adhocracy: The Power to Change,* Bob Waterman tells us that most of us are like the characters in Ibsen's play *Ghosts.* "We're controlled by ideas and norms that have outlived their usefulness, that are only ghosts but have as much influence on our behavior as they would if they were alive. The ideas of men like Henry Ford, Frederick Taylor, and Max Weber—these are the ghosts that haunt our halls of management."

Most of us grew up in organizations that were dominated by the thoughts and actions of the Fords, Taylors, and Webers, the fathers of the classic bureaucratic system. Bureaucracy was a splendid social invention in its time—the 19th century. In his deathless (and deadly) prose, the German sociologist, Max Weber, first brought to the world's attention that the bureaucratic, machine model was ideal for harnessing the manpower and resources of the Industrial Revolution. To this day, most organizations retain the macho, control-and-command mentality that is intrinsic to that increasingly threadbare mode. Indeed it is possible to capture the mindset created by that obsolete paradigm in three simple words—control, order, and predict.

## Recurring Themes

Over the past dozen years, interacting with and interviewing CEOs and leaders of all kinds, I am reminded of Tolstoy's remark that all happy families are alike. Several themes appeared again and again.

• *However much the CEOs differ in experience and personal style, they constitute a prism through which the fortunes of the modern world are refracted.* These leaders are emblematic of their time, forced to deal not only with the exigencies of their own organizations but also with a new social reality. Among the broader factors that underlie all their decisions: the accelerating rate and complexity of change, the emergence of new technologies, dramatic demographic shifts, and globalization. For me, all of these are reflected in a single incident. Several years ago I invited the Dalai Lama to participate in a gathering of leaders at the University of Southern California. The living embodiment of thousands of years of Tibetan spiritual wisdom graciously declined—by fax.

• *Each of these leaders has discovered that the very culture of his organization must change* because, as constituted, that culture is more devoted to perceiving itself than to meeting new challenges.

• *Each of these individuals is a leader, not a manager.* Jack Welch, Chairman and CEO of General Electric, has predicted (correctly, I believe) that: "The world of the '90s and beyond will not belong to *managers* or those who make the numbers dance, as we used to say, or those who are conversant with all the business and jargon we use to sound smart. The world will belong to passionate, driven *leaders*—people who not only have an enormous amount of energy but who can energize those whom they lead."

- *Each of these individuals understands that management is getting people to do what needs to be done. Leadership is getting people to want to do what needs to be done.* Managers push. Leaders pull. Managers command. Leaders communicate.
- *Without exception every CEO interviewed has become the Chief Transformation Officer of his organization.* As Robert Haas, Chairman and CEO of Levi Strauss & Co., observes, change isn't easy, even for those committed to it. "It's difficult to unlearn behaviors that made us successful in the past. Speaking rather than listening. Valuing people like yourself over people of another gender or from different cultures. Doing things on your own rather than collaborating. Making the decision yourself instead of asking different people for their perspectives. There's a whole range of behaviors that were highly functional in the old hierarchical organization that are dead wrong in the flatter, more responsive organization that we're seeking to become."

John Sculley, CEO of Apple, once told me: "The old hierarchical model is no longer appropriate. The new model is global in scale, an interdependent network. So the new leader faces new tests, such as how does he lead people who don't report to him—people in other companies, in Japan or Europe, even competitors. How do you lead in this idea-intensive, interdependent-network environment? It requires a wholly different set of skills, based on ideas, people skills, and values. Traditional leaders are having a hard time explaining what's going on in the world, because they're basing their explanations on their experience with the old paradigm."

Sculley also predicted that the World War II fighter pilot (the formative experience of several corporate heads, as well as President Bush) would no longer be our principal paradigm for leaders.

The organizations of the future will be networks, clusters, cross-functional teams, temporary systems, ad hoc task forces, lattices, modules, matrices—almost anything but pyramids. We don't even know yet what to call these new configurations, but we do know that the ones that succeed will be less hierarchical and have more linkages based on common goals rather than traditional reporting relationships. It is also likely that these successful organizations will embody Rosabeth Moss Kanter's "5 F's: fast, focused, flexible, friendly, and fun."

Recently, I spoke with Alvin Toffler, the all-time change maven whose paradigm-shifting book, *Future Shock,* was published in 1970. We were trying to name an organization that exists in today's environment that was immune to change and had been stable *and* prosperous. We couldn't think of one.

The CEOs I know best understand that contemporary organizations face increasing and unfamiliar sources of competition as a result of the globalization of markets, capital, labor, and information technology. To be successful, these organizations must have flexible structures that enable them to be highly responsive to customer requirements and adaptive to changes in the competitive environment. These new organizations must be leaner, have fewer layers, and be able to engage in transnational and nontraditional alliances and mergers. And they must understand a global array of business practices, customs, and cultures.

The question all these leaders are addressing, with apparent success, is: *How do you change relatively successful organizations, which, if they continue to act today the way they acted even five years ago, will undo themselves in the future?* (Remember that 47 percent of the companies that made up the Fortune 500 in 1980 were not on the list in 1990.)

## The ACE Paradigm

The CEOs are telling us that the new paradigm for success has three elements: Align, Create, and Empower, or ACE.

• *Align.* Today's leader needs to align resources, particularly human resources, creating a sense of shared objectives worthy of people's support and even dedication. Alignment has much to do with the spirit and a sense of being part of a team. Great organizations inevitably develop around a shared vision. Theodore Vail had a vision of universal telephone service that would take 50 years to bring about. Henry Ford envisioned common people, not just the wealthy, owning their own automobiles. Steven Jobs, Steven Wozniak, and their Apple cofounders saw the potential of the computer to empower people. A shared vision uplifts people's aspirations. Work becomes part of pursuing a larger purpose embodied in products and services.

• *Create.* Today's leader must create a culture where ideas come through unhampered by people who are fearful. Such leaders are committed to problem-finding, not just problem-solving. They embrace error, even failure, because they know it will teach them more than success. As Norman Lear once said to me, "Wherever I trip is where the treasure lies."

Effective leaders create adaptive, creative, learning organizations. Such organizations have the ability to identify problems, however troublesome, before they become crises. These organizations are able to rally the ideas and information necessary to solve their problems. They are not afraid to test possible solutions, perhaps by means of a pilot program. And, finally, learning organizations provide opportunities to reflect on and evaluate past actions and decisions.

• *Empower.* Empowerment involves the sense people have that they are at the center of things, rather than the periphery. In an effectively led organization, everyone feels he or she contributes to its success. Empowered individuals believe what they do has significance and meaning. Empowered people have both discretion and obligations. They live in a culture of respect where they can actually do things without getting permission first from some parent figure. Empowered organizations are characterized by trust and system-wide communication.

Whatever shape the future ultimately takes, the organizations that will succeed are those that take seriously—and sustain through action—the belief that their competitive advantage is based on the development and growth of the people in them. And the men and women who guide those organizations will be a different kind of leader than we've been used to. They will be maestros, not masters; coaches, not commanders.

Today the laurel will go to the leader who encourages healthy dissent and values those followers brave enough to say *no*. The successful leader will have not the loudest voice, but the readiest ear. His or her real genius may well lie not in personal achievements, but in unleashing other people's talent.

# 4

# Change: The New Metaphysics

*How change happens and how to make it happen.*

Change is the metaphysics of our age. Everything is in motion. Everything mechanical has evolved, become better, more efficient, more sophisticated. In this century, automobiles have advanced from the Model T to the BMW, Mercedes, and Rolls Royce. Meanwhile, everything organic—from ourselves to tomatoes—has devolved. We have gone from such giants as Teddy Roosevelt, D. W. Griffith, Eugene Debs, Frank Lloyd Wright, Thomas Edison and Albert Michelson to Yuppies. Like the new tomatoes, we lack flavor and juice and taste. Manufactured goods are far more impressive than the people who make them. We are less good, less efficient, and less sophisticated with each passing decade.

People in charge have imposed change rather than inspiring it. We have had far more bosses than leaders, and so, finally, everyone has decided to be his or her own boss. This has led to the primitive, litigious, adversarial society we now live in. As the newscaster in the movie *Network* said, "I'm mad as hell, and I'm not going to take it anymore."

What's going on is a middle-class revolution. The poor in America have neither the time nor the energy to revolt. They're just trying to survive in an increasingly hostile world. By the same token, the rich literally reside above the fray— in New York penthouses, Concordes, and sublime ignorance of the world below. The middle class aspires to that same sublime ignorance.

A successful dentist once told me that people become dentists to make a lot of money fast and then go into the restaurant business or real estate, where they will really make money. Young writers and painters are not content to practice their craft and perfect it. Now they want to see and be seen, wheel and deal, and they are as obsessed with the bottom line as are IBM executives. The deal for the publication of a book is far more significant than the book itself, and the cover of *People* magazine is more coveted than a good review in the *New York Times*. The only unions making any noise now are middle-class unions. Professors who once professed an interest in teaching are now far more interested in deals—for the book, the TV appearance, the consulting job, the conference in Paris—leaving teaching to assistants.

When everyone is his or her own boss, no one is in charge, and chaos takes over. Leaders are needed to restore order, by which I mean not obedience but progress. It is time for us to control events rather than be controlled by them.

## Avenues of Change

Change occurs in several ways.

- *Dissent and conflict.* We have tried dissent and conflict and have merely become combative. In corporations, change can be mandated by the powers that be. But this leads inevitably to the escalation of rancor. We are perpetually angry now, all walking around with chips on our shoulders.
- *Trust and truth.* Positive change requires trust, clarity and participation. Only people with virtue and vision can lead us out of this bog and back to the high ground, doing three things: (1) gaining our trust; (2) expressing their vision clearly so that we all not only understand but concur; and (3) persuading us to participate.
- *Cliques and cabals.* The cliques have the power, the money and the resources. The cabals, usually younger and always ambitious, have drive and energy. Unless the cliques can co-opt the cabals, revolution is inevitable. This avenue, too, is messy. It can lead to either a stalemate or an ultimate

victory for the cabals, if for no other reason than they have staying power.

- *External events.* Forces of society can impose themselves on the organization. For example, the auto industry was forced to change its ways and its products, both by government regulation and by foreign competition. In the same way, student activists forced many universities to rewrite their curricula and add black studies and women's studies programs. Academicians are still debating both the sense and the efficacy of such programs, as they have altered not only what students learn but how they learn it.
- *Culture or paradigm shift.* The most important avenue of change is culture or paradigm. In *The Structure of Scientific Revolution,* Thomas Kuhn notes that the paradigm in science is akin to a zeitgeist or climate of opinion that governs choices. He defines it as "the constellation of values and beliefs shared by the members of a scientific community that determines the choice, problems which are regarded as significant, and the approaches to be adopted in attempting to solve them." The people who have revolutionized science have always been those who have changed the paradigm.

## Innovators and Leaders

People who change not merely the content of a particular discipline but its practice and focus are not only innovators but leaders. Ralph Nader, who refocused the legal profession to address consumer problems, was such a person. Betty Friedan, in truthfully defining how women lived, inspired them to live in different ways.

It is not the articulation of a profession or organization's goals that creates new practices but rather the imagery that creates the understanding, the compelling moral necessity for the new way. The clarity of the metaphor and the energy and courage its maker brings to it are vital to its acceptance. For example, when Branch Rickey, general manager of the Brooklyn Dodgers, decided to bring black players into professional baseball, he chose Jackie Robinson, a paragon among players and among men.

How do we identify and develop such innovators? How do we spot new information in institutions, organizations and professions? Innovators, like all creative people, see things differently, think in fresh and original ways. They have useful contacts in other areas; they are seldom seen as good organization men or women and often viewed as mischievous troublemakers. The true leader not only is an innovator but makes every effort to locate and use other innovators in the organization. He or she creates a climate in which conventional wisdom can be challenged and one in which errors are embraced rather than shunned in favor of safe, low-risk goals.

In organizations, people have norms, values, shared beliefs and paradigms of what is right and what is wrong, what is legitimate and what is not, and how things are done. One gains status and power through agreement, concurrence, and conformity with these paradigms. Therefore, both dissent and innovation are discouraged. Every social system contains these forces for conservatism, for maintaining the status quo at any cost, but it must also contain means for movement, or it will eventually become paralyzed.

Basic changes take place slowly because those with power typically have no knowledge, and those with knowledge have no power. Anyone with real knowledge of history and the world as it is today could redesign society, develop a new paradigm in an afternoon, but turning theory into fact could take a lifetime.

Still, we have to try because too many of our organizations and citizens are locked into roles and practices that simply do not work. True leaders work to gain the trust of their constituents, communicate their vision lucidly, and thus involve everyone in the process of change. They then try to use the inevitable dissent and conflict creatively and positively, and out of all that, sometimes, a new paradigm emerges.

A Harris poll showed that over 90 percent of the people polled would change their lives dramatically if they could, and they ranked such intangibles as self-respect, affection and acceptance higher than status, money and power. They don't like the way they live now, but they don't know how to change. The poll is evidence of our need for real leaders and should serve as impetus and inspiration to potential leaders and innovators. If such people have the will to live up to their potential—and the rest of us have the gumption to follow them—we might finally find our way out of this bog we're in.

## Avoiding Disaster during Change

Constant as change has been and vital as it is now, it is still hard to effect, because the sociology of institutions is fundamentally antichange. Here, then, are 10 ways to avoid disaster during periods of change—any time, all the time—except in those organizations that are dying or dead.

**1.** *Recruit with scrupulous honesty.* Enthusiasm or plain need often inspires recruiters to transmogrify visible and real drawbacks and make them reappear as exhilarating challenges. Recruiting is, after all, a kind of courtship ritual. The suitor displays his or her assets and masks his or her defects. The recruit, flattered by the attention and the promises, does not examine the proposal thoughtfully. He or she looks forward to opportunities to be truly creative and imaginative and to support from the top.

Inadvertently, the recruiter has cooked up the classic recipe for revolution as suggested by Aaron Wildavsky: "Promise a lot; deliver a little. Teach people to believe they will be much better off, but let there be no dramatic improvement. Try a variety of small programs but marginal in impact and severely underfinanced. Avoid any attempted solution remotely comparable in size to the dimensions of the problem you're trying to solve."

**2.** *Guard against the crazies.* Innovation is seductive. It attracts interesting people. It also attracts people who will distort your ideas into something monstrous. You will then be identified with the monster and be forced to spend precious energy combating it. Change-oriented managers should be sure that the people they recruit are change agents but not agitators. It is difficult sometimes to tell the difference between the innovators and the crazies. Eccentricities and idiosyncrasies in change agents are often useful and valuable. Neurosis isn't.

**3.** *Build support among like-minded people,* whether or not you recruited them. Change-oriented administrators are particularly prone to act as though the organization came into being the day they arrived. This is a delusion, a fantasy of omnipotence. There are no clean slates in established organizations. A new CEO can't play Noah and build the world anew with a handpicked crew of his or her own. Rhetoric about new starts is frightening to those who sense that this new beginning is the end of their careers. There can be no change without history and continuity. A clean sweep, then, is often a waste of resources.

**4.** *Plan for change from a solid conceptual base.* Have a clear understanding of how to change as well as what to change. Planning changes is always easier than implementing them. If change is to be permanent, it must be gradual. Incremental reform can be successful by drawing on a rotating nucleus of people who continually read the data provided by the organization and the society in which it operates for clues that it's time to adapt. Without such critical nuclei, organizations cannot be assured of continued self-renewal. Such people must not be faddists but must be hypersensitive to ideas whose hour has come. They also know when ideas are antithetical to the organization's purposes and values and when they will strengthen the organization.

**5.** *Don't settle for rhetorical change.* Significant change cannot be decreed. Any organization has two structures: one on paper and another that consists of a complex set of intramural relationships. A good administrator understands the relationships and creates a good fit between them and any planned alterations. One who gets caught up in his or her own rhetoric almost inevitably neglects the demanding task of maintaining established constituencies and building new ones.

**6.** *Don't allow those who are opposed to change to appropriate basic issues.* Successful change agents make sure that respectable people are not afraid of what is to come and that the old guard isn't frightened at the prospect of change. The moment such people get scared is the moment they begin to fight dirty. They not only have some built-in clout, they have tradition on their side.

**7.** *Know the territory.* Learn everything there is to know about the organization and about its locale, which often means mastering the politics of local chauvinism, along with an intelligent public relations program. In Southern California, big developers are constantly being blindsided by neighborhood groups because they have not bothered to acquaint the groups with their plans. Neighborhood groups often triumph, forcing big changes or cancellations. They know their rights and they know the law, and the developers haven't made the effort to know them.

**8.** *Appreciate environmental factors.* No matter how laudable or profitable or imaginative, a change that increases discomfort in the organization is probably doomed. Adding a sophisticated new computer system is probably a good thing, but it can instantly be seen as a bad thing if it results in overcrowded offices.

**9.** *Avoid future shock.* When an executive becomes too involved in planning, he or she frequently forgets the past and neglects the present. As a result, before the plan goes into effect, employees are probably already opposed to it. They, after all, have to function in the here and now, and if their boss's eye is always on tomorrow, he or she is not giving them the attention and support they need.

**10.** *Remember that change is most successful when those who are affected are involved in the planning.* This is a platitude of planning theory, but it is as true as it is trite. Nothing makes people resist new ideas or approaches more adamantly than their belief that change is being imposed on them.

The problems connected with innovation and change are common to every modern bureaucracy. University, government and corporation all respond similarly to challenge and to crisis, with much the same explicit or implicit codes, punctilios and mystiques.

Means must be found to stimulate the pursuit of truth—that is, the true nature of the organization's problems—in an open and democratic way. This calls for classic means: an examined life, a spirit of inquiry and genuine experimentation, a life based on discovering new realities, taking risks, suffering occasional defeats, and not fearing the surprises of the future. The model for truly innovative organizations in an era of constant change is the scientific model. As scientists seek and discover truths, so organizations must seek and discover their own truths—carefully, thoroughly, honestly, imaginatively, and courageously.

# 5

# *Information Overload Anxiety (and how to overcome it)*

*I wrote the following tongue-in-cheek essay in 1979 to help friends and colleagues dismantle their "guilt shelf"—that spot, usually close to the bed, where memos, important mail, yellowing back issues of the New York Times and other unread documents accumulate.*

*More than two decades later, I find that the following pages' regimen for overcoming Information Overload Anxiety remains helpful and effective. I have added some observations at the end in acknowledgment of the obvious fact that the communications revolution has over the past decade doubled or even tripled the overload of previous years. But the same basic principle applies: Most of the material we insist on saving on our guilt shelf is of secondary or tertiary importance. As such, most of it goes in one eye and out the other. The challenge, then, is to put first things first when it comes to how we receive our information.*

Lance Shaw uses a timer. The timer technique is invaluable for *enforced skimming* of the many magazines he must read. He gives himself *no more than 15 minutes* on the timer for each periodical. When it rings, he tosses out the magazine and moves on.

—*EXECU-TIME*

As we all know, ours is a poly-saturated, paper-polluted society; one in which power resides in those who have the right information. Fortunes are made or lost, careers secured or shot, health enhanced or damaged by one factor —information. In our society information equals power.

Coterminous with the information=power equation is a dramatic increase in a national nervous disorder: Information Overload Anxiety (IOA). This disorder is characterized by an obsessive-compulsive tendency to read everything about everything from anemones to zyzomys.* This is a killer disease made more pernicious by our collective and willful neglect of it. IOA is simple to understand: When the amount of reading matter ingested exceeds the amount of energy available for digestion, the surplus accumulates and is converted by stress and overstimulation into the unhealthy state known as IOA.

The so-called cures of this disease are as pervasive as the information-pushers themselves. The Lance Shaw bell-timer method is only one of the many regimens available at your local newsstand. Another comes from Nobel Laureate Herbert Simon speaking in *People* magazine: "Reading daily newspapers is one of the least cost-efficient things you can do.... Read *The World Almanac* once a year. What's happening you'll hear by lunchtime anyway." Russell Baker copes with IOA by reading only the obituary page to make sure he hasn't died, and, after ascertaining that, goes out to celebrate. Cutting back to Simon's starvation diet, or trading cerebration for celebration are only a few of the wonder cures. Many IOA victims have tried others: keeping the abstract and digest pushers prosperous with subscriptions; sitting through speed reading courses; having an assistant predigest industry news and then picking his brains. Some have tried newspaper fasting by shifting to liquid Cronkite, and other sufferers have stopped their intake cold turkey.

None of this is necessary. Neither must you be sentenced to a death row of sentences. As a reformed IOA patient, I can recommend a formula for dealing with this disorder. It is the surest, safest way to attain your basic minimum information requirement. For those of you who genuinely *want* to change

---

*The surgeon general has determined that reading further may endanger your health.

and who feel that obituaries are unhealthy and the timer system mechanical, I present here the Fat-Free Daily Reading Diet guaranteed to satiate everyone from the freaky faster to the junk news junkie.

But first a word about the Fat-Free Daily Reading Diet (FFDRD). Who needs it? The ambulatory generalist, the well-educated, intellectually curious, overstimulated crisis expediter. In short, *you.* Second, many nutritious items beyond the ordinary nosher's price range, or inaccessible to those not adjacent to the kiosk on Harvard Square or the newsstand in the Citicorp Building, have been eliminated. Third, faddists need read no further. You will not again see mention of such exotica as *Cahiers du Cinéma, Blood, Iron Age, Running Times* or *Hungarian Art Nouveau.* These are to be put immediately into your Cuisinart and pulverized into fruit smoothies. I choose my products on the basis of their health-giving balance, practicality, consistency, and absence of bulk. Less is more, so to speak. This plan is based on experiential boredom, and has been laboratory tested by patients who once seemed hopelessly mired in decadent reading habits, but who are now reading normal healthy lives.

## Basic Maintenance Plan

FFDRD is the reading plan to follow the rest of your life. Once comfortable with it and sure of your new control, you may want to modify it to include in your daily diet the *Boston Globe.* But only as a substitute for a news magazine. And remember, only *every other* page of a daily is allowed—and first throw out the Metro and Entertainment sections.

Group I: Newspapers. One daily. But proceed slowly, and check first with your physician. Choose from the following: the *Wall Street Journal,* the *New York Times,* the *Washington Post,* or the *L.A. Times.* Absence of bulk clearly makes the *Wall Street Journal* the preferred choice, and none of the other three is delivered outside its region on the date of publication. Nor does the *WSJ* suffer any episodic regional virus, such as the *Post's* Potomac virus, leading to feverish stories about the identity of Jimmy Carter's tennis partner at 3:05 yesterday, or the *NYT*'s Big Apple syndrome, leading to information about where one can buy Albanian sausage on Second Avenue or on which Thursday you can dance the hora on Prince Street with your children.

The *WSJ*'s editorials are peppy, nutritious, and infused with vital life-giving substances. As a daily regimen you will find its reviews of cultural events hearty and fat-free.

Group II: News magazines. One to be selected from the following: *Newsweek, Time, U.S. News and World Report.* Diet must be limited to one. Ingesting two reveals serious addiction. Since the basic contents of *Newsweek* and *Time* do not vary significantly, reading both will throw your metabolism out of kilter. The *U.S. News* has slimmed down considerably and has at least one fat-free item each issue, but *Time*'s essays on Masters and Johnson, and the post-Vietnam American consciousness are superb supplements to a restricted diet. *Newsweek,* however, is less caloric. In five out of eight tests, *Newsweek* was found to contain fewer carbohydrates, and it regularly contains such tonics as Meg Greenfield and George Will.

My preference for both *Newsweek* and *WSJ* is also based on the belief that a healthy agent locates pain-in-hiding and identifies potential problems in the soft tissues of a listless society; it recognizes symptoms and points them out: racism *before* Dr. King's march, pollution *before* Rachel Carson, sexism *before* Betty Friedan, bureaucratization *before* William H. Whyte, Jr., consumer protection *before* Ralph Nader.

Group III: General Culture and Ideas. Few temptations here. Needed is one unsweetened, streamlined packet that reviews books, movies, dance, theater, music, TV, the plastic and performing arts, architecture, urban aesthetics, graphic design and the commercial arts. No such item exists in the U.S. In waiting rooms try *Vogue;* in England sample *The Listener;* on Sunday read the *Times.*

A warning about the Sunday *Times:* It has unquestionably brought more patients to terminal IOA than any other single diet component. It must be read only under doctor's supervision, and you must first remove bulk—information on street dances in Soho, all lingerie ads, travel pages, reports of recent polo deaths in Rhodesia. Leave in essential ingredients: discussions of architecture, drama reviews, essays on arts and culture. Again, be forewarned: Forty-year-old John C., a former patient, had cut his information overload to a tolerable level. At a neighbor's house he picked up a copy of the Sunday *Times* and read it voraciously. Next we heard he was into *Saturday Review, New York Review of Books,* and when last seen was munching a forbidden *Harper's* and stuffing heavy paper items underneath his sweater. Remember: Reading the Sunday *Times* is like eating one peanut.

Group IV: Reference Books. Do not be hooked by book clubs or by friends' seductive shelves of *Encyclopaedia Britannica.* The typical IOA patient may start off with a pocket dictionary, then cautiously proceed to the rather disappointing *London Times Atlas.* By then there's no stopping him. The two-volume *Who's Who,* the addictive *Oxford English* whatever, a dictionary of quotations, of phrase origins, of slang, of golf. From that it's on to almanacs: farmer's, gardener's, jogger's, swinger's, ball club owner's and—there you are, off the wagon again.

This diet includes only one reference book—a dictionary with intellectual heft and clarity; an untrendy dictionary, but one that doesn't shy away from "DNA" or "glitch"; a dictionary with *helpful* pictures, but no drawings of nailheads or cows; one with a first-rate etymology, and with type that can be read without an accompanying magnifying glass which makes you, no matter how hardy, feel like a geriatric case. The ideal dictionary also includes a section of the most commonly used German, French, and Spanish words, a basic manual of style, and some major dates in history. The dictionary that comes closest to meeting our minimum daily requirement is the *Random House Dictionary of the English Language*—unabridged. But unlike the new you, it is so overloaded with information you must not attempt to carry it about with you; instead, leave it in an accessible place with good light.

Reference supplements: To help you adjust without regressing to book clubs, libraries, and binges resulting in a three-year subscription to *Mother Jones* or *Popular Mechanics,* I refer you to the following extras containing no fat, but which may be read only by those who have their appetites under control.

*The National Directory of Addresses and Telephone Numbers,* a Bantam paperback, includes an index of 50,000 useful addresses and phone numbers: all U.S. companies with annual sales of $10 million and over, governmental agencies, foundations, educational institutions, museums, ballparks, symphony orchestras, public libraries, hotels, airlines, hospitals and all those organizations you've been wanting to write hate letters to all these years.

Free Items: The Morgan Guaranty Bank in New York offers a monthly report on the U.S. economy, and Metropolitan Life publishes a monthly *Statistical Bulletin* tracing important demographic trends and their consequences. Good, but not quite free, are *Manas,* an idiosyncratic charmer tending toward philosophy and history of ideas, and *Brain/Mind,* a model of less-is-more with a neat four-page format containing almost as much information as one issue of *Psychology Today.*

## The Basic Harold Laski Reading Diet

People vary in their reading metabolism. Some, like former president John F. Kennedy, have a high IOA threshold. It is rumored that he devoured everything in sight and still remained free from nagging symptoms. Harold Laski was famous for this too. He could digest an average book in minutes with only a bare expenditure of energy. For the lucky few who do not require a strict regimen, the following may be included as a supplement to the Basic Maintenance Program.

Group V: Management and Business. We live in a corporate society—the daily press's best-kept secret. If you can find the business section, you'll see it stuck somewhere between sports and classifieds. Business/management magazines, however, are burgeoning and old standbys with expensive facelifts like *Fortune* no longer resemble thick racing forms. Preferred by dieters: *Fortune, Barron's, Forbes* and *Business Week.* If restricted to these, the prudent patient should have no weighty problems. A favorite is *Business Week,* which is timely and easily digested. It tends to items you can take in from beginning to end on one page. Its longer features are superb fare: "Washington Outlook," "Social Issues," and "Book Reviews."

Group VI: Science and Technology. No noshing here. This group contains no junk additives. The "Comment" section in *Science,* for example, is a heavy meal-in-one—substantive, and comprehensive. If you're into "sieve areas in fossils" or "food-webs and niche space," *Science* just may be your main fare. *Scientific American* is well-known, but too often gives the specialist too little and the non-specialist too much. It leaves you either hungry or overstuffed. Its design, however, is mouth-watering, and its regular features offer thought for food.

*The New Scientist* comes from England and is staffed with perhaps the most able science-writers around. It is often intelligent and timely, so don't be put off by items like "the courtship patterns of the red-vented bulbul." It gives the slimmed-down layman an overview of everything from the economics of micro-processors to fossilized footprints.

If there were one all-purpose compound which included the most basically sound ingredients of all the science magazines, I would happily recommend it. And I hear by the grapevine that the publishers of *Science* will soon come out with something like that.

*So there you have it. The Fat-Free Daily Reading Diet. If you stick with it, you will enjoy the new trim-reading-you—the emaciated intellectual inside you just waiting to emerge. And if you fail? Well, there are weekly meetings of Readers Anony-*

*mous in every major city. Consult your National Directory—
and join me.*

• • •

## IOA Self-Evaluation Test

*Directions*

*Please try to answer all of the following questions. If you are uncertain, go on to the next question and come back to the one(s) you left incomplete. Before starting test, please take your pulse per 10-second interval. If your pulse-rate rises in responding to 15 or more of the questions, call your doctor immediately. If your pulse-rate increases in responding to 10 questions, do not continue. We do recommend, however, in such cases that you do make an appointment with your physician.*

*Start*

## DOES YOUR PULSE RISE WHEN YOU:

1. Don't know if the ZAP count of a microwave oven is more or less than four dental X-rays or a Sunday drive within a 150-mile radius of Harrisburg?
2. Wonder if you should invite a quark for cocktails next week, especially one of the "charmed" quarks?
3. Put on your carcinogenic, flameproof 'jammies or your non-carcinogenic 3 a.m. flashpoint "nighties?"
4. Debate insurance against crowbars falling from space platforms or emergent Loch Ness monsters?
5. Calculate your chances of myocardial infarction from family history, exercise habits, stress, cholesterol in your bile (alleviated by bran), lipids (reduced by yogurt), smoking, weight, or all of the above?
6. Read conflicting reports about the overall value of jogging?
7. Argue about whether we will have one more year of double-digit inflation and Fred Kahn? About whether we will have one more year of double-digit inflation and James Schlesinger?
8. Wonder if Black Holes and Pot Holes have nothing/something/everything in common?
9. Question whether the Supreme Court is threatening or protecting the rights guaranteed under the Fourth and First

Amendments? And are not completely certain what those rights are (or were)?

## *Please Take Your Pulse*

10. Can't be sure if dolphins are really getting admitted to Harvard Medical School?
11. Can't describe in 5,000 words or less President Carter's energy policy and whether or not it will make any difference (Carter's energy policy, that is)?
12. Can't describe in 3,000 words or less what SALT II is and whether or not it will make any difference?
13. Aren't certain whether Pres. Carter is getting stronger or weaker, softer or harder and whether or not it will make any difference?
14. Can't tell whether Pres. Carter shifted his hair style from left to right or right to left and whether or not it will make any difference?

## *Please Take Your Pulse*

15. Don't know how serious George Steinbrenner III is about re-hiring Billy Martin for the 1980 season? Or how serious Johnny Carson is about quitting NBC? Or how serious Jerry Brown is about Linda Ronstadt?
16. Cannot respond to a question asking you to identify the winners ('79) of the National Book Award and if they are worth buying (in hard cover)?
17. Can't for the life of you think of the *questions* to the following answers taken from the May 12, '79 *New York Times* quiz. The answers were: 1) Diet soda and hard liquor; 2) "Utatuba" (Hint: a large granite structure that once stood outside an East Side art gallery; 3) Bob Hope; 4) Does not; 5) Harold Clurman; 6) Philip Caldwell will succeed him.
18. Haven't heard of Sparky Anderson?
19. Are uncertain whether it's worth driving 500 miles out of your way to attend a performance of the Houston Opera? Are even more confused about 1,000 miles?
20. When you can identify without trouble the last names of the following: Lennie, Woody, Scotty, Maggy, Jimmy, Billy, Jerry,

Ronnie, Reggie, Archie and Deng (Xiaoping), but are bewildered when it comes to knowing the *first* names of the following famous personages: Jacuzzi, Franco, Sadat, Marcos, Masters, Johnson, Garp, Hayakawa, Khomeini (Hint: It is *not* Ayatollah), Brezhnev, Giscard d'Estaing, Somoza, Tito, Gilbert, Sullivan, and Hildegarde (not Neff).

21. Don't know what the following five men have in common: Alan Ladd, Jr., Henry Ford II, Johnny Paycheck, Michel Bergerac, and "Catfish" Hunter?

22. Can't match the names (left column) with the countries they represent:

| | |
|---|---|
| Yao Grunitsky | Togo |
| Ionatana Ionatana | Tuvalu |
| Ousman Ahmadou Sallah | Gambia |
| Aristides Royo | Panama |
| Abel Muzorewa | Rhodesia |
| Mamady Lamine Conde | Guinea |

### *Not Too Far to Finish, Please Take Pulse*

23. Have never heard of Denis Thatcher?

24. Don't know if what the following have in common are any of these: 1) Office or house furnishings; 2) Slang for cocaine; 3) A purloined list of the Dallas Cowboys' draft choices for the 1980 season; 4) Prime Minister Joe Clark's cabinet members; or 5) Baseball players. After reading the following names, please circle one: Speed, Reed, Dent, Harrah, Rice, Bonds, John, Nettles, Lamp, Bench, Rose, Lemon, North, Rivers, Fell, Valentine, Swisher, Spikes, Cage, Hood, Page, Office, Gross, Wise, Klutts, May, Abbott, Waits, Porter, and Ford.

• • •

*Please Take Pulse and Compute Your IOA Score*

# Postscript

In 1979 no person on the planet had conceived what might come along later to complicate our lives further. Thus, in the spirit of the original IOA Self-Evaluation Test, we might add a few newer and more pertinent questions.

DOES YOUR PULSE RISE WHEN YOU:
- Realize that, if you stay awake just thirty minutes longer, you can be one of the first persons to read the next day's *New York Times* on its web site?
- Skip going to a movie with your family rather than having to turn off your wireless phone?
- Sit down to decide whether it's time to buy the latest wireless web technology or hold out three months for another technology to replace it?
- Think back to the day you found out that you probably knew the names of more world leaders than George W. Bush did?
- Pause to consider the authenticity of the witty and provocative e-mails you receive regarding the Neiman-Marcus cookie recipe, harvested human kidneys, Christmas tree fireproofing techniques and other weighty matters?
- Have to choose between preparing for your important early-morning meeting, answering the fifteen e-mail messages you received overnight, or squeezing in a few online trades?
- Find that your e-mail browser doesn't have enough space to bookmark all of your favorite sites?
- Argue at a cocktail party that, if only we had more technology in our public schools, the system would improve dramatically?
- Recall that you actually believed the e-mail message forwarded all across cyberspace was a major commencement speech delivered by Kurt Vonnegut at MIT rather than merely a pithy essay written by a columnist at the *Chicago Tribune?*
- Skim through the Wall Street Journal while watching a high-speed chase on the local television newscast and waiting for your daughter to free up your home office's high-speed connection to the Internet?
- Have the opportunity to inform someone smugly that Kazakhstan was a part of the former Soviet Union and not a nuclear power bordering India?
- Have to send your staff yet another terse memo reminding them to keep CNN on all day in the employees' lounge?

PLEASE TAKE YOUR PULSE


For a half-century, we've been guessing wrong about the impact of the computer. Some early designers worried greatly about its Orwellian implications. A 1950 East Coast newspaper article on an early digital differential analyzer opened with the chilling question: "Will people become obsolete?" Others painted rosier scenarios, speculating that the computer would rid us of hard labor and mountains of paper and would inaugurate the world's first true leisure society. With our electronic friends doing our bidding without disobedience or fatigue, what would be left for the rest of us but to play golf?

Of course, most of the experts missed the mark. But there has been a tyrannical aspect of our life with computers, caused not by those who build or control them, but rather by the technology's inherent capacity to rapidly multiply and distribute information. The computer has hardly made humans' lives more manageable. If anything, our lives are more chaotic than ever. And any leaders who have tried to ignore the tsunami of technology have been swept away. By 1999, home computer ownership had almost doubled over the previous four years, as 50% of American households had at least one computer. Nearly 70% of college graduates have computers at home. One in four American households already had Internet access, with the figure growing every day. Internet access had increased by over 40% in the previous year alone.

What a breathtaking development for a society already exhausted by information overload! As I stated earlier, however, the basic principle of making time for essential information allows us to pull ourselves out of the slough of extraneous information. But the level of discipline required to do this in a paper-filled society must be even higher in an electronic one. May your e-mail in-box be compact and your browser bookmarks be lean.

# 6

# *Cope with Speed and Complexity (Raplexity)*

*Leadership usually requires skill in the art of introducing change to a static organization and its constituencies. Yet the great truth of our times is that our environment is never static; we move quickly along the rapids, needing to adjust quickly and constantly to rocks and branches ahead. Our plans for change, then, have to factor in the dizzying uncertainty of what lies before us. The following short essay offers some ideas for how this can be accomplished at the individual and organizational level.*

I think that the problems facing executives, whether they be in large or small organizations, are related to the speed at which issues hit them, and the complexity of those issues. I use the word *raplexity* to signify rapidity and complexity.

Information and communication technology will change not just the degree but also the kind of leadership that we're going to need. Because, as we democratize the workplace and as we develop the kinds of technologies and digital interactivity that we are now seeing, our communication is going to become more, should I say, rampant. We will be able to talk simultaneously to a lot more people than we ever thought possible. And we are going to have a lot more information at our fingertips. This will democratize the workplace even more.

This means that leaders are going to have to be very comfortable with advanced technology and the changes that it's going to bring. Many of them aren't. I have a board in my leadership institute, made up of very terrific leaders, and they all have e-mail. But when I asked how many of them use it, only half of the hands went up, and some of those went up rather lamely. Rather haltingly.

I think that information technology will have profound consequences for how we organize in the future, and also for the sophistication that will be required by those of us who are leaders. The younger generation has been brought up in a high-tech world. I was born at a time when television was unheard of, when FM radio was virtually unheard of.

What will this mean for tomorrow's leaders? Let me draw an analogy. It's sort of like psychiatry and psychopharmacology. My wife is a psycho pharmacologist. She was trained as a psychiatrist, but she realized that talk therapy wasn't enough. And that many mental health problems can be dealt with effectively through medication and pharmaceuticals. But she realized that both are necessary. She still does talk therapy, but she also uses medication.

In a similar way, leaders are going to have to be both comfortable with advanced technology but at the same time probably even more hands-on than ever before. They will need more interpersonal competence.

## What Executives Can Do

What can you do to keep pace with the 'raplexity' and merit the incentive compensation you desire? Well, I suggest that you do three things.

**1.** *Seek feedback.* Arrange within your team, group, or family some form of "reflective backtalk." I learned this lesson when talking to one CEO who said: "I talk to my spouse for reflective backtalk, and I use her as a mirror. She acts as a psychological safety net." We all need to reflect on our experience, particularly negative experience, with someone we trust.

**2.** *Keep a diary or journal.* Record your reflections on your life experience in a journal. You will find this simple practice to be invaluable in your quest for wisdom.

**3.** *Read a few biographies and other books authored by your mentors.* You don't need a psychotherapist. Just look for inspiring examples—stories of successful people with whom you can relate. Make these people your models and mentors. Learn what you can from their inspiring examples and writings.

## What Organizations Can Do

Organizations can do 10 simple things to help people cope with "raplexity."

**1.** *Keep learning.* Send people to the best courses at the best universities and training companies. Make sure this learning is relevant and is applied on the job.

**2.** *Make changes in the organization to make it easy for people to grow.* Don't send a changed person back into an unchanged organization.

**3.** *Start coaching.* Identify people who are known to be good coaches and mentors and make them available and visible. If you walk around and ask: Who are the people here who have coached or mentored good leaders? you will get answers.

**4.** *Make it okay to tell the truth.* Encourage your mentors and others who supply you with feedback to speak up, to "speak truth to power."

**5.** *Reward the straight shooters.* The major reason why people don't speak truth to those in power is the history of the messenger being shot.

**6.** *Provide diverse experience within the organization.* Some of the best leaders I know of are people like the *Washington Post's* Ben Bradlee who have had a wide range of experience in the business. Ben, for example, has worked in production, reporting, editing, managing, and leading. In the best organizations, every senior executive spends substantial time in research, sales, manufacturing, marketing, management, and leadership assignments—so that they have a prismatic view.

**7.** *Give people more international assignments.* Many executives have to be convinced, almost coerced, to take an international assignment and be exposed to different languages and cultures. But you can't get a clear idea of how the world is changing just by talking to customers over the phone.

**8.** *Keep people surprised.* Senior executives, especially need to be surprised, even shocked, occasionally. Bertrand Russell, when asked about his favorite student, said: "He's my favorite because he always looks puzzled." All you can tell people is to keep their eyes open, embrace ambiguity, and not be frightened of surprise. One of my favorite questions to executives is: "In your company, what's the mean time between surprises?" How do you get people to improvise? Today, you must like the sound of jazz, and the sound of surprise.

**9.** *Make sure your name stays in the phone book.* The most important thing you could know about your business future is whether or not your name is still in the phone book. If it's not, you are probably out of business.

**10.** *Prize both masculine and feminine leadership attributes.* I agree that attributes more commonly associated with women will be in high demand among leaders in the next decade. But I hesitate to say that women leaders will be more in demand, because I don't want anyone to steal the female side of me. Many of the male leaders I admire give full expression to their feminine sides. In fact, some male leaders are almost bisexual in their ability to be open and reflective. Frankly, I don't believe that gender is the determining factor in leadership. What counts is the ability to be both tough and tender as the situation dictates.

# 7
## *The Leadership Advantage*

*The temptation is to reduce leadership to a simple for-
mula, perhaps requiring a touch of skill, a splash of
character, a pinch of diplomacy. My study of leaders
has given me a clear sense that the best ones do in fact
share certain qualities, many of which are discussed
here. But beyond the checklist of desirable qualities
lies the reality that the best leaders have all been masters of their experiences, the negative ones no less than
the positive ones. This is a double-edged sword: one
generally cannot take short-cuts to acquiring many of
the essential traits discussed in this essay; but if one
learns to master one's experiences, many of these traits
are within reach. That brings me back to one of the
central premises of my career: good leadership can
and should be taught.*

Never has the subject of leadership been of greater interest to managers, or to management writers. Richard Donkin,
writing in the *Financial Times,* describes "a fixation bordering on obsession [with] the qualities needed for corporate
leadership." It is, he adds, a "contagious" obsession, spreading in scope and intensity throughout out society, and sug-
gesting that Americans have lost their way.

If it is an obsession, it is a useful one for any organization
concerned about the future—but I understand the source of
the frustration Donkin and others display. For all the ink the
subject gets in scholarly, business, and popular journals,
leadership remains an elusive concept.

However, whether or not leadership is well understood,
its impact on the bottom line is dramatic, according to a
study by Andersen Consulting's Institute for Strategic
Change: the stock price of companies perceived as being

well led grew 900 percent over a 10-year period, compared to just 74 percent growth in companies perceived to lack good leadership. And *Fortune,* in its 1998 roundup of America's most admired companies, identifies the common denominator of exemplary organizations. "The truth is that no one factor makes a company admirable," wrote Thomas Stewart, "but if you were forced to pick the one that makes the most difference, you'd pick leadership. In Warren Buffet's phrase, 'People are voting for the artist and not the painting.'"

## Generating Intellectual Capital

My own observations of organizations and leadership lead me to two conclusions about what it will take to survive in the tumultuous years ahead:

The key to future competitive advantage will be the organization's capacity to create the social architecture capable of generating intellectual capital. And leadership is the key to realizing the full potential of intellectual capital.

Percy Barnevik, former chairman of ABB and one of Europe's most celebrated business leaders, says that "organizations ensure that [people] use only 5 to 10 percent of their abilities at work. Outside of work they engage the other 90 to 95 percent." The challenge for leaders, he adds, is "to learn how to recognize and employ that untapped ability." His assessment is supported by data on both sides of the Atlantic. Nearly two-thirds of companies surveyed by Kepner-Tregoe say they don't use more than half their employees' brainpower. And employees themselves are even less optimistic; only 16 percent said they use more than half their talents at work, according to a recent U.K. survey.

On the other hand, huge benefits accrue to organizations that, as Barnevik urges, learn to employ their collective brainpower, know-how, ideas, and innovation. A recent study of 3,200 U.S. companies, conducted by Robert Zemsky and Susan Shaman of the University of Pennsylvania, showed that a 10 percent increase in spending for workforce training and development leads to an 8.5 percent increase in productivity; a similar increase in capital expenditures leads to just a 3.8 percent increase in productivity.

Such findings explain why General Electric's Jack Welch says he has only three jobs as CEO: selecting the right people, allocating capital resources, and spreading ideas quickly. Welch typically asks the hundreds of GE managers he talks with not only about their ideas but who they've shared their ideas with, and who else has adopted them.

It is no accident that both Welch and Barnevik, two of the world's most accomplished business leaders, see their role in similar terms. In a knowledge economy, leaders cannot command employees to work harder, smarter, or faster. Knowledge workers, if they are earning their pay, know more about their work than the CEO does, and are in great demand. Without leaders who can attract and retain talent, manage knowledge, and unblock people's capacity to adapt and innovate, an organization's future is in jeopardy.

## Qualities of a Leader

Though Donkin implies that our search for the qualifies of leadership is futile, research points to seven attributes essential to leadership. Taken together they provide a framework for leading knowledge workers:

*Technical competence:* business literacy and grasp of one's field

*Conceptual skill:* a facility for abstract or strategic thinking

*Track record:* a history of achieving results

*People skills:* an ability to communicate, motivate, and delegate

*Taste:* an ability to identify and cultivate talent

*Judgment:* making difficult decisions in a short time frame with imperfect data

*Character:* the qualities that define who we are

Senior executives seldom lack the first three attributes; rarely do they fail because of technical or conceptual incompetence, nor do they reach high levels of responsibility without having a strong track record. All these skills are important, but in tomorrow's world exemplary leaders will be distinguished by their mastery of the softer side: people skills, taste, judgment, and, above all, character.

Character is the key to leadership—an observation confirmed by most people's personal experience as it is in my 15 years of work with more than 150 leaders, and in the other studies I've encountered. Research at Harvard University indicates that 85 percent of a leader's performance depends on personal character. Likewise, the work of Daniel Goleman makes clear that leadership success or failure is usually due to "qualities of the heart" (see "The Emotional Intelligence of Leaders," *Leader to Leader,* Fall 1998). Although character is less quantifiable than other aspects of leadership, there are many ways to take the measure of an individual (see "The Anatomy of Character," page 62).

## Demands of Followers

Power in the knowledge economy resides more with knowledge workers than with owners or managers. Serving the needs of those workers is a new leadership imperative. Research shows not only the characteristics of effective leaders but also the expectations that followers have of their leaders. Whether in a corporation, a Scout troop, a public agency, or an entire nation, constituents seek four things: meaning or direction, trust in and from the leader, a sense of hope and optimism, and results. To serve these constituent needs—and ultimately to unleash an organization's intellectual capital—leaders can foster four supporting conditions, which in turn can create four respective outcomes (see table).

• *Providing purpose.* Effective leaders bring passion, perspective, and significance to the process of defining organizational purpose.

EXEMPLARY LEADERSHIP
*To satisfy followers' needs and achieve positive
outcomes, leaders must provide four things.*

| In Service of Constituent Needs for: | Leaders Provide: | To Help Create: |
|---|---|---|
| Meaning and direction | Sense of purpose | Goals and objectives |
| Trust | Authentic relationships | Reliability and consistency |
| Hope and optimism | "Hardiness" (confidence that things will work out) | Energy and commitment |
| Results | Bias toward action, risk, curiosity, and courage | Confidence and creativity |

Every effective leader I've known is passionate about what he or she is doing. The time and energy devoted to work demand a commitment and conviction bordering on love. Michael Eisner, chairman of the Walt Disney Company, defines that quality as a strong point of view, or in Hollywood parlance, POV. In his company, he says, it is unfailingly the person with conviction who wins the day. "Around here," adds Eisner (we're talking about Hollywood, remember), POV is worth at least 80 IQ points."

One starts with passion; perspective is harder to come by—but is essential in a world of rapid change. For most people in organizations, the question is not only what happens next, but what happens *after* what happens next. As hockey great Wayne Gretzky explains, "It ain't where the puck is, it's where the puck will be." One Fortune 500 CEO puts it differently: "If you're not confused, you don't know what's going on." Because the fog of reality is so pervasive, constituents want not just a vision of where we're heading but also where they've been and where they are now. People want leaders to provide context.

Finally, knowledge workers—the best of whom have significant choice in the place and terms of their employment—want a sense of significance.

What is the meaning of our work?

What difference or larger contribution does it make to others?

How do we measure success?

And what are the positive outcomes of that success?

By making time for such reflection, leaders build support for organizational goals and objectives.

• *Generating and sustaining trust.* Since 1985, 20 percent of the American workforce has been laid off at least once. In a time when the new social contract makes the ties between organizations and their knowledge workers tenuous, trust becomes the emotional glue that can bond people to an organization.

These are the factors that generate trust—at work or in a partnership, a marriage, or a friendship: competence, constancy, caring, candor, congruity.

What I call congruity—or authenticity, feeling comfortable with oneself—is a further reflection of character. It is at the heart of any honest relationship. But congruity goes beyond simply knowing yourself; it is being consistent, presenting the same face at work as at home.

Candor is perhaps the most important component of trust. When we are truthful about our shortcomings or acknowledge that we do not have all the answers, we earn the understanding and respect of others.

Exemplary leaders create a climate of candor throughout their organizations. They remove the organizational barriers—and the fear—that cause people to keep bad news from the boss. They understand that those closest to customers usually have the solutions but can do little unless a climate of candor allows problems to be discussed. Especially during times of change, exemplary leaders share information about what's going on in the organization, the industry, and the world. They treat candor as one measure of personal and organizational performance, which can be gauged through employees' response to such statements as, "My organization encourages people to take the time to communicate openly, even about difficult questions." Or, "There is little fear of speaking openly about important issues."

Without candor there can be no trust. And by building trust, leaders help create the reliability and consistency customers demand.

- *Fostering hope.* Exemplary leaders seem to expect success; they always anticipate positive outcomes. The glass for them is not simply full but brimming.

Hope combines the determination to achieve one's goals with the ability to generate the means to do so. Hopeful people describe themselves with such statements as

I can think of ways to get out of a jam.

I energetically pursue my goals.

My experience has prepared me well for the future.

There are ways around any problem.

One example of a hopeful leader is Intel Chairman Andrew Grove, who told me 15 years ago that he grew up with a "Nobel complex." He emigrated from Hungary speaking little English, with no money, but his parents imbued in him a sense that he would succeed in whatever he attempted. If he went into science, he told me, he felt he could win the Nobel Prize. That psychological hardiness, the sense that things generally work out well, creates tremendous confidence in oneself and in those around one. And that kind of confidence influences others. It builds energy and commitment, and that in turn influences outcomes. In short, every exemplary leader that I have met has what seems to be an unwarranted degree of optimism—and that helps generate the energy and commitment necessary to achieve results.

- *Getting results.* As leaders we can provide meaning, build trust, and foster hope, but all of that counts for little unless an organization produces results.

Most leaders coming into a new position or facing a moment of truth are afforded some time and resources to deliver. That is what makes a collective sense of purpose, trust, and hope so important—they can carry people through what they know will be a difficult time. But these assets will dissipate if leaders do not get results. And, of course, we deliver results only by taking action.

That does not mean that every action will be successful. But, as Gretzky reminds us,"You miss 100 percent of the shots you don't take." Exemplary leaders never forget that they must ultimately take their best shots—and create a climate that tolerates missed shots yet demands that everyone continue to take them. Moving from talk to action is imperative, but especially in the times we live in, it requires commitment, enterprise, curiosity—and courage. It requires leadership.

Results-oriented leaders see themselves as catalysts. They expect to achieve a great deal, but know that they can do little without the efforts of others. They bring the zeal, resourcefulness, risk-tolerance—and discipline—of the entrepreneur to every effort of the organization. Nothing less will break through the noise, clutter, and competitive pressure of today's marketplace.

To be sure, we are paying unprecedented attention to the subject of leadership. We are also seeing the importance of intellectual capital to strategy, organizational design, leadership development, employee retention, and virtually every business practice that matters. Organizations that don't take such issues seriously, or that fail to make the connection between leadership and the quality of their intellectual capital, will probably not be in the phone book in 2001.

One CEO says, "We are making the topic of leadership an issue we have powerful conversations about. We encourage people to talk about it. We reward coaches. We want people to develop ways of getting feedback." They do so not as an exercise but as a way to compete. Exemplary leaders believe they have a responsibility to extend people's growth and to create an environment where people constantly learn. Those are the surest ways to generate intellectual capital and to use that capital to create new value. In the next century, that will be every leader's ultimate task.

## The Anatomy of Character

There are many definitions of character, but for exemplary leaders character goes beyond ethical behavior (although that is essential). The word itself comes from the Greek for *engraved* or *inscribed*. For the leaders I have studied, character has to do with who we are, with how we organize our experience. The great psychologist William James described it as "the particular mental or moral attitude [that makes one feel] most deeply and intensively active and alive, a voice inside which speaks and says, 'This is the real me.'"

Effective leaders—and effective people—know that voice well. They understand that there is no difference between becoming an effective leader and becoming a fully integrated human being.

Many aspects of character—such as our degree of energy or our cognitive skill—are probably determined at birth; others are influenced by our family life, our birth order, our relationships with parents, teachers, and friends. Yet, character develops throughout life including work life. Leaders can help others become more aware of their innate capacities. For example, by examining the kinds of decisions they make and don't make, senior executives and those they manage can develop their own character and cultivate new leadership throughout the organization.

For executive leaders, character is framed by drive, competence, and integrity. Most senior executives have the drive and competence necessary to lead. But too often organizations elevate people who lack the moral compass. I call them "destructive achievers." They are seldom evil people, but by using resources for no higher purpose than achievement of their own goals, they often diminish the enterprise. Such leaders seldom last, for the simple reason that without all three ingredients—drive, competence, and moral compass—it is difficult to engage others and sustain meaningful results.

# Part 2
*Organizing the Dream:*
*Social Architecture*
*for the New Global Village*

# 8

# Is Democracy Inevitable?

*Just over a quarter-century after this essay was originally published, it suddenly came true. The preface written for its republication in 1998's* Temporary Society *placed the piece in context and has been adapted here. When co-author Phil Slater and I first hypothesized that democracy would eventually triumph because it worked, we didn't instantly convert the world or even our editor. Our proposed title, "Democracy Is Inevitable," was changed to a more cautious "Is Democracy Inevitable?" When I saw, on CNN, the Berlin Wall begin to crumble, it was all I could do to keep from shouting, "Yes!"*

## Retrospective Commentary

Today the inevitability of democracy might seem obvious, but in the mid-sixties, when Phil Slater and I first argued that democracy would eventually dominate in both the world and the workplace, a nuclear war between the United States and the Soviet Union seemed more likely than a McDonald's in Moscow.

It all started because we had seen a common thread running through the most exciting organizations of that time: as the once absolute power of top management atrophied, a more collegial organization was emerging where good ideas were valued—even if they weren't the boss's ideas. We became convinced that democracy would triumph for a simple but utterly compelling reason: it was working. It was, and is, more effective than autocracy, bureaucracy, or any other nondemocratic form of organization. We went on later to develop these ideas more fully, I through my extensive work on leadership and organization, and Slater in an exploration of democracy's cultural and psychological underpinnings.

In international politics democratization is a very recent phenomenon, albeit a profound one. The democratization of the workplace has made fewer headlines but has been no less dramatic. In the sixties participative management was considered so radical that some of the Sloan Fellows at the Massachusetts Institute of Technology accused me of being a communist for espousing it. Today most major corporations couldn't live without it. A survey of 1,000 corporations conducted a few years ago by USC management expert Edward Lawler found that 80 percent used some form of participative management. And as we noted then, it is particularly common in companies engaged in inventions, such as electronics. Companies on the cutting edge of technological change today tend to be forced by their very nature to operate by democratic principles, and those that become bureaucratized and hierarchical usually find themselves quickly upstaged by fast-moving and egalitarian newcomers.

No longer a monolith, the successful modern corporation is less like a forbidding pyramid and more like a Lego set whose parts can be regularly reconfigured as circumstances change. The old paradigm that exalted control, order and predictability is giving way to a nonhierarchical order in which all employees' contributions are solicited and acknowledged and in which creativity is valued over blind loyalty. Sheer self-interest motivates the change. Organizations that encourage broad participation, even dissent, make better decisions. Rebecca A. Henry, a psychology professor at Purdue University, found that groups are better forecasters than individuals are. And the more the group disagrees initially, the more accurate the forecast is likely to be.

We said that adaptability would become the most important determinant of an organization's survival and that information would drive the organization of the future. This seems even truer today. The person who has information wields more power than ever before. But although we sensed how important processing technology would be, we didn't fully appreciate the extent to which the new technology would accelerate the pace of change and help create a global corporation if not a global village.

Our crystal ball let us down in a few other areas. We did not foresee, for example, the extraordinary role Japan would play in reshaping U.S. corporate behavior in the 1980s. The discovery that another nation could challenge U.S. domination in the marketplace inspired massive self-evaluation and forever disrupted the status quo. Nothing contributed more to the democratization of business than the belief—true or false—that Japanese management was more consensual than U.S. management. To meet Japanese competition, U.S. leaders were willing to try anything—even share their traditional prerogatives with subordinates. Again, what drove the victory of democracy was not democracy for its own sake but rather sheer self-interest. People were convinced that it worked.

Slater and I also did not foresee the prominent role women would begin to play in the rise of democracy. The women's movement was only embryonic in the early sixties, yet looking back we could have predicted a prominent role for women given our belief that those not overcommitted to the status quo would be the ones in the best position to take advantage of change, and this certainly applies to women.

Men have been committed to an individualistic, linear, competitive, atomistic, and mechanically conceptual world—one which they have dominated until more recently. But ironically, science—once the most extreme expression of this world—has now rendered it obsolete. Recent advances in physics and biology have opened up a new conceptual universe. The cosmos, scientists have begun to realize, is not a mechanism constructed of little particles that can be taken apart and put together—it is a gigantic unity of which the fundamental elements are relationships. It has been noted that one of science's greatest technological monuments— the Internet—may be the best illustration yet of the non-hierarchical, relational reality of global democracy. In this new reality, it must be recognized that women appear to have received better cultural training for the confusion and chaos that chronic change, democracy and the new sciences produce. Their control needs, on average, tend to be less exaggerated than those of men, who like to dominate their environment and make it simple and predictable.

In recent years our understanding of democracy has been enhanced by new data on early civilizations, particularly the work of Riane Eisler. Drawing on a wealth of archeological data, Eisler effectively demolished the popular assumption that authoritarianism and war are somehow "natural" to human beings. We may, in the end, simply be transitioning back to a non-authoritarian way of life better suited to us as human beings.

Transitions, of course, are difficult. The gradual shift from authoritarianism to democracy—from war to peace, from machismo to cooperation, from domination to attunement, from linear science to nonlinear science—is a paradigm shift of unprecedented magnitude. Such a change inevitably causes great strain and confusion for us poor human beings hungry for stability and familiarity. We reach excitedly toward the future with one hand and cling desperately to our old concepts with the other. Is it any wonder we feel pulled apart at times? We can see this strain in the so-called lack of civility in our daily lives today, in the frustration that produces so much ranting on the airwaves and so often leads to violence. We see our ambivalence in our high-tech science-fiction fantasies that begin with so much sophistication and end in some form of hand-to-hand combat. We see it in our many movies which depict brutal post-apocalyptic worlds created by the disastrous macho values, yet which attempt to render those same values newly meaningful and desirable.

Reality is less dramatic. Change is a gradual, two-steps-forward, one-step-back process, but we may reasonably be expected to muddle through. There will be plenty of disasters and atrocities along the way, for change never comes cheaply. Nobody likes becoming obsolete, and those who hold advantages seldom give them up without a struggle. But the process cannot be stopped without a global catastrophe; it gathers momentum every day. It will never be easy for us, but it may help a little to recognize what's happening and to admit that it all makes us a little uncomfortable, whether we think we welcome change or fight it tooth and nail.

*Warren G. Bennis*

Cynical observers have always been fond of pointing out that business leaders who extol the virtues of democracy on ceremonial occasions would be the last to think of applying them to their own organizations. To the extent that this is true, however, it reflects a state of mind that is by no means peculiar to business-people but characterizes all Americans, if not perhaps all citizens of democracies.

This attitude is that democracy is a nice way of life for nice people, despite its manifold inconveniences—a kind of expensive and inefficient luxury, like owning a large medieval castle. Feelings about it are for the most part affectionate, even respectful, yet a little impatient. There are probably few people in the United States who have not at some time nourished in their hearts the blasphemous thought that life would go much more smoothly if democracy could be relegated to some kind of Sunday morning devotion.

The bluff practicality of the "nice but inefficient" stereotype masks a hidden idealism, however, for it implies that institutions can survive in a competitive environment through the sheer good-heartedness of those who maintain them. We challenge this notion. Even if all those benign sentiments were eradicated today, we would awaken tomorrow to find democracy still entrenched, buttressed by a set of economic, social, and political forces as practical as they are uncontrollable.

Democracy has been so widely embraced not because of some vague yearning for human rights but because *under certain conditions* it is a more "efficient" form of social organization. (Our concept of efficiency includes the ability to survive and prosper.) It is not accidental that those nations of the world that have endured longest under conditions of relative wealth and stability are democratic, while authoritarian regimes have, with few exceptions, either crumbled or eked out a precarious and backward existence.

Despite this evidence, even so acute a statesman as Adlai Stevenson argued in a *New York Times* article on November 4, 1962, that the goals of the Communists are different from ours. "They are interested in power," he said, "we in community. With such fundamentally different aims, how is it possible to compare communism and democracy in terms of efficiency?"

Democracy (whether capitalistic or socialistic is not at issue here) is the only system that can successfully cope with the changing demands of contemporary civilization. We are not necessarily endorsing democracy as such; one might reasonably argue that industrial civilization is pernicious and should be abolished. We suggest merely that given a desire to survive in this civilization, democracy is the most effective means to this end.

## Democracy Takes Over

There are signs that our business community is becoming aware of democracy's efficiency. Several of the newest and most rapidly blooming companies in the United States boast unusually democratic organizations. Even more surprising, some of the largest established corporations have been moving steadily, if accidentally, toward democratization. Feeling that administrative vitality and creativity were lacking in their systems of organization, they enlisted the support of social scientists and outside programs. The net effect has been to democratize their organizations. Executives and even entire management staffs have been sent to participate in human relations and organizational laboratories to learn skills and attitudes that ten years ago would have been denounced as anarchic and revolutionary. At these meetings, status prerogatives and traditional concepts of authority are severely challenged.

Many social scientists have played an important role in this development. The contemporary theories of McGregor, Likert, Argyris, and Blake have paved the way to a new social architecture. Research and training centers at the National Training Laboratories, Tavistock Institute, Massachusetts Institute of Technology, Harvard Business School, Boston University, University of California at Los Angeles, Case Institute of Technology, and others have pioneered in applying social science knowledge to improving organizational effectiveness. The forecast seems to hold genuine promise of progress.

*System of Values*

What we have in mind when we use the term "democracy" is not "permissiveness" or "laissez-faire" but a system of values—a climate of beliefs governing behavior—that people are internally compelled to affirm by deeds as well as words. These values include:

**1.** Full and free *communication,* regardless of rank and power.

**2.** A reliance on *consensus* rather than on coercion or compromise to manage conflict.

**3.** The idea that *influence* is based on technical competence and knowledge rather than on the vagaries of personal whims or prerogatives of power.

**4.** An atmosphere that permits and even encourages emotional *expression* as well as task-oriented behavior.

**5.** A basically *human* bias, one that accepts the inevitability of conflict between the organization and the individual but is willing to cope with and mediate this conflict on rational grounds.

Changes along these dimensions are being promoted widely in U.S. industry. Most important for our analysis is what we believe to be the reason for these changes: *democracy becomes a functional necessity whenever a social system is competing for survival under conditions of chronic change.*

## Adaptability to Change

Technological innovation is the most familiar variety of such change to the inhabitants of the modern world. But if change has now become a permanent and accelerating factor in American life, then adaptability to change becomes the most important determinant of survival. The profit, the saving, the efficiency, and the morale of the moment become secondary to keeping the door open for rapid readjustment to changing conditions.

Organization and communication research at MIT reveals quite dramatically what type of organization is best suited for which kind of environment. Specifically:

- For simple tasks under static conditions, an autocratic, centralized structure, such as has characterized most industrial organizations in the past, is quicker, neater, and more efficient.
- But for adaptability to changing conditions, for "rapid acceptance of a new idea," for "flexibility in dealing with novel problems, generally high morale and loyalty . . . the more egalitarian or decentralized type seems to work better." One of the reasons for this is that the centralized decision maker is "apt to discard an idea on the grounds that he is too busy or the idea too impractical."[1]

Our argument for democracy rests on an additional factor, one that is fairly complicated but profoundly important. Modern industrial organization has been based roughly on the antiquated system of the military. Relics of this can still be found in clumsy terminology such as "line and staff," "standard operating procedure," "table of organization," and so on. Other remnants can be seen in the emotional and mental assumptions regarding work and motivation held today by some managers and industrial consultants. By and large, these conceptions are changing, and even the military is moving away from the oversimplified and questionable assumptions on which its organization was originally based. Even more striking, as we have mentioned, are developments taking place in industry, no less profound than a fundamental move from the autocratic and arbitrary vagaries of the past toward democratic decision making.

This change has been coming about because of the palpable inadequacy of the military-bureaucratic model, particularly its response to rapid change, and because the institution of science is now emerging as a more suitable model.

Why is science gaining acceptance as a model? Not because we teach and conduct research within research-oriented universities. Curiously enough, universities have been resistant to democratization, far more so than most other institutions.

Science is winning out because the challenges facing modern enterprises are *knowledge*-gathering, *truth*-requiring dilemmas. Managers are not scientists, nor do we expect them to be. But the processes of problem solving, conflict resolution, and recognition of dilemmas have great kinship with the academic pursuit of truth. The institution of science is the only institution based on and geared for change. It is built not only to adapt to change but also to overthrow and create change. So it is—and will be—with modern industrial enterprises.

And here we come to the point. For the spirit of inquiry, the foundation of science, to grow and flourish, there must be a democratic environment. Science encourages a political view that is egalitarian, pluralistic, liberal. It accentuates freedom of opinion and dissent. It is against all forms of totalitarianism, dogma, mechanization, and blind obedience. As a prominent social psychologist has pointed out, "Men have asked for freedom, justice, and respect precisely as science has spread among them."[2] In short, the only way organizations can ensure a scientific attitude is to provide the democratic social conditions where one can flourish.

In other words, democracy in industry is not an idealistic conception but a hard necessity in those areas where change is ever present and creative scientific enterprise must be nourished. For democracy is the only system of organization that is compatible with perpetual change.

## Retarding Factors

It might be objected here that we have been living in an era of rapid technological change for a hundred years, without any noticeable change in the average industrial company. True, there are many restrictions on the power of executives over their subordinates today compared with those prevailing at the end of the nineteenth century. But this hardly constitutes industrial democracy—the decision-making function is still an exclusive and jealously guarded prerogative of the top echelons. If democracy is an inevitable consequence of perpetual change, why have we not seen more dramatic changes in the structure of industrial organizations? The answer is twofold.

### Obsolete Individuals

First, technological change is rapidly accelerating. We are now beginning an era when people's knowledge and approach can become obsolete before they have even begun the careers for which they were trained. We are living in an era of runaway inflation of knowledge and skill, where the value of what one learns is always slipping away. Perhaps this explains the feelings of futility, alienation, and lack of individual worth that are said to characterize our time.

Under such conditions, the individual *is* of relatively little significance. No matter how imaginative, energetic, and brilliant individuals may be, time will soon catch up with them to the point where they can profitably be replaced by others equally imaginative, energetic, and brilliant but with a more up-to-date viewpoint and fewer obsolete preconceptions. As Martin Gardner says about the difficulty some physicists have in grasping Einstein's theory of relativity: "If you are young, you have a great advantage over these scientists. Your mind has not yet developed those deep furrows along which thoughts so often are forced to travel."[3] This situation is just beginning to be felt as an immediate reality in U.S. industry, and it is this kind of uncontrollably rapid change that generates democratization.

*Powers of Resistance*

The second reason is that the mere existence of a dysfunctional tendency, such as the relatively slow adaptability of authoritarian structures, does not automatically bring about its disappearance. This drawback must first either be recognized for what it is or become so severe as to destroy the structures in which it is embedded. Both conditions are only now beginning to make themselves felt, primarily through the peculiar nature of modern technological competition.

The crucial change has been that the threat of technological defeat no longer comes necessarily from rivals within the industry, who usually can be imitated quickly without too great a loss, but often comes from outside—from new industries using new materials in new ways. One can therefore make no intelligent prediction about the next likely developments in industry. The blow may come from anywhere. Correspondingly, a viable corporation cannot merely develop and advance in the usual ways. To survive and grow, it must be prepared to go anywhere—to develop new products or techniques even if they are irrelevant to the present activities of the organization.[4] Perhaps that is why the beginnings of democratization have appeared most often in industries that depend heavily on invention, such as electronics. It is undoubtedly why more and more sprawling behemoths are planning consequential changes in their organizational structures and climates to release democratic potential.

## Farewell to "Great Men"

The passing of years has also given the coup de grace to another force that retarded democratization—the "great man" who with brilliance and farsightedness could preside with dictatorial powers at the head of a growing organization and keep it at the vanguard of U.S. business. In the past, this person was usually a man with a single idea, or a constellation of related ideas, which he developed brilliantly. This is no longer enough.

Today, just as he begins to reap the harvest of his imagination, he finds himself suddenly outmoded because someone else (even perhaps one of his stodgier competitors, aroused by desperation) has carried the innovation a step further or found an entirely new and superior approach to it. How easily can he abandon his idea, which contains all his hopes, his ambitions, his very heart? His aggressiveness now begins to turn in on his own organization; and the absolutism of his position begins to be a liability, a dead hand on the flexibility and growth of the company. But the great man cannot be removed. In the short run, the company would even be hurt by his loss since its prestige derives to such an extent from his reputation. And by the time he has left, the organization will have receded into a secondary position within the industry. It might decay further when his personal touch is lost.

The "cult of personality" still exists, of course, but it is rapidly fading. More and more large corporations (General Motors, for one) predicate their growth not on "heroes" but on solid management teams.

*Organization Men*

Taking the place of the "great man," we are told, is the "organization man." Liberals and conservatives alike have shed many tears over this transition. The liberals have in mind as "the individual" some sort of creative deviant—an intellectual, artist, or radical politician. The conservatives are thinking of the old captains of industry and perhaps some great generals.

Neither is at all unhappy to lose the "individuals" mourned by the other, dismissing them contemptuously as Communists and rabble-rousers on the one hand, criminals and Fascists on the other. What is particularly confusing in terms of the present issue is a tendency to equate conformity with autocracy—to see the new industrial organization as one in which all individualism is lost except for a few villainous, individualistic manipulators at the top.

But this, of course, is absurd in the long run. The trend toward the "organization man" is also a trend toward a looser and more flexible organization in which the roles to some extent are interchangeable and no one is indispensable. To many people, this trend is a monstrous nightmare, but one should not confuse it with the nightmares of the past. It may mean anonymity and homogeneity, but it does not and cannot mean authoritarianism, despite the bizarre anomalies and hybrids that may arise in a period of transition.

The reason it cannot is that it arises out of a need for flexibility and adaptability. Democracy and the dubious trend toward the "organization man" alike (for this trend is a part of democratization, whether we like it or not) arise from the need to maximize the availability of appropriate knowledge, skill, and insight under conditions of great variability.

*Rise of the Professional*

While the "organization man" idea has titillated the public imagination, it has masked a far more fundamental change now taking place: the rise of the "professional." Professional specialists, holding advanced degrees in such abstruse sciences as cryogenics or computer logic as well as in the more mundane business disciplines, are entering all types of organizations at a higher rate than any other sector of the labor market.

Such people seemingly derive their rewards from inner standards of excellence, from their professional societies, from the intrinsic satisfaction of their tasks. In fact, they are committed to the task, not the job; to their standards, not their boss. They are uncommitted except to the challenging environments where they can "play with problems."

These new professionals are remarkably compatible with our conception of a democratic system. For like them, democracy seeks no new stability, no end point; it is purposeless, save that it purports to ensure perpetual transition, constant alteration, ceaseless instability. It attempts to upset nothing, but only to facilitate the potential upset of anything. Democracy and professionals identify primarily with the adaptive process, not the "establishment."

Yet all democratic systems are not entirely so—there are always limits to the degree of fluidity that can be borne. Thus it is not a contradiction to the theory of democracy to find that a particular democratic society or organization may be more "conservative" than an autocratic one. Indeed, the most dramatic, violent, and drastic changes have always taken place under autocratic regimes, for such changes usually require prolonged self-denial, while democracy rarely lends itself to such voluntary asceticism. But these changes have been viewed as finite and temporary, aimed at a specific set of reforms and moving toward a new state of nonchange. It is only when the society reaches a level of technological development at which survival is dependent on the institutionalization of perpetual change that democracy becomes necessary.

## Reinforcing Factors

The Soviet Union is rapidly approaching this level and is beginning to show the effects, as we shall see. The United States has already reached it. Yet democratic institutions existed in the United States when it was still an agrarian nation. Indeed, democracy has existed in many places and at many times, long before the advent of modern technology. How can we account for these facts?

### Expanding Conditions

First, it must be remembered that modern technology is not the only factor that could give rise to conditions of necessary perpetual change. Any situation involving rapid and unplanned expansion sustained over a sufficient period of time will tend to produce great pressure for democratization. Secondly, when we speak of democracy, we are referring not exclusively or even primarily to a particular political format. Indeed,

American egalitarianism has perhaps its most important manifestation not in the Constitution but in the family. Historians are fond of pointing out that Americans have always lived under expanding conditions—first the frontier, then the successive waves of immigration, now a runaway technology. The social effects of these kinds of expansion are of course profoundly different in many ways, but they share one impact: all have made it impossible for an authoritarian family system to develop on a large scale. Every foreign observer of American mores since the seventeenth century has commented that American children "have no respect for their parents," and every generation of Americans since 1650 has produced forgetful native moralists complaining about the decline in filial obedience and deference.

Descriptions of family life in colonial times make it quite clear that American parents were as easygoing, permissive, and child oriented then as now, and the children as independent and disrespectful. This lack of respect is not for the parents as individuals but for the concept of parental authority as such.

The basis for this loss of respect has been outlined quite dramatically by historian Oscar Handlin, who points out that in each generation of early settlers, the children were more at home in their new environment than their parents were— had less fear of the wilderness, fewer inhibiting European preconceptions and habits.[5] Furthermore, their parents were heavily dependent on them physically and economically. This was less true of the older families after the East became settled. But nearer the frontier, the conditions for familial democracy became again strikingly marked so that the cultural norm was protected from serious decay.

Further reinforcement came from new immigrants, who found their children better adapted to the world because of their better command of the language, better knowledge of the culture, better occupational opportunities, and so forth. It was the children who were expected to improve the social position of the family and who through their exposure to peer groups and the school system could act as intermediaries between their parents and the new world. It was not so much "American ways" that shook up the old family patterns as the demands and requirements of a new situation. How could the young look to the old as the ultimate fount of wisdom and knowledge when, in fact, their knowledge was irrelevant— when the children indeed had a better practical grasp of the realities of American life than did their elders?

### The New Generation

These sources of reinforcement have now disappeared. But a third source has only just begun. Rapid technological change again means that the wisdom of elders is largely obsolete and that the young are better adapted to their culture than are their parents.

This fact reveals the basis for the association between democracy and change. The old, the learned, the powerful, the wealthy, those in authority—these are the ones who are committed. They have learned a pattern and succeeded in it. But when change comes, it is often the *uncommitted* who can best realize it and take advantage of it. This is why primogeniture has always lent itself so easily to social change in general and to industrialization in particular. The uncommitted younger children, barred from success in the older system, are always ready to exploit new opportunities. In Japan, younger sons were treated more indulgently by their parents and given more freedom to choose an occupation since "in Japanese folk wisdom, it is the younger sons who are the innovators."[6]

Democracy is a superior technique for making the uncommitted more available. The price it extracts is uninvolvement, alienation, and skepticism. The benefits that it gives are flexibility and the joy of confronting new dilemmas.

## Doubt and Fears

Indeed, we may even in this way account for the poor opinion democracy has of itself. We underrate the strength of democracy because it creates a general attitude of doubt, skepticism, and modesty. It is only among the authoritarian that we find the dogmatic confidence, the self-righteousness, the intolerance and cruelty that permit one never to doubt oneself and one's beliefs. The looseness, sloppiness, and untidiness of democratic structures express the feeling that what has been arrived at today is probably only a partial solution and may well have to be changed tomorrow.

In other words, one cannot believe that change is in itself a good thing and still believe implicitly in the rightness of the present. Judging from the report of history, democracy has always underrated itself—one cannot find a democracy anywhere without also discovering (side by side with expressions of outrageous chauvinism) an endless pile of contemptuous and exasperated denunciations of it. (One of the key issues in our national politics today, as in the presidential campaign in 1960, is our "national prestige.") And perhaps this is only appropriate. For when a democracy ceases finding fault with itself, it has probably ceased to be a democracy.

## Overestimating Autocracy

But feeling doubt about our own social system need not lead us to overestimate the virtues and efficiency of others. We can find this kind of overestimation in the exaggerated fear of the "Red Menace"—mere exposure to which is seen as leading to automatic conversion. Few authoritarians can conceive of the possibility that an individual could encounter an authoritarian ideology and not be swept away by it.

More widespread is the "better dead than Red" mode of thinking. Here again we find an underlying assumption that communism is socially, economically, and ideologically inevitable—that once the military struggle is lost, all is lost. Not only are these assumptions patently ridiculous; they also reveal a profound misconception about the nature of social systems. The structure of a society is not determined merely by a belief. It cannot be maintained if it does not work—that is, if no one, not even those in power, is benefiting from it.

How many times in history have less civilized nations conquered more civilized ones only to be entirely transformed
by the cultural influence of their victims? Do we then feel less
civilized than the Soviet Union? Is our system so brittle and
theirs so enduring?

Actually, quite the contrary seems to be the case. For
while democracy seems to be on a fairly sturdy basis in the
United States (despite the efforts of self-appointed vigilantes
to subvert it), there is considerable evidence that autocracy
is beginning to decay in the Soviet Union.

## Soviet Drift

Most Americans have great difficulty in evaluating the facts
when they are confronted with evidence of decentralization
in the Soviet Union, of relaxation of repressive controls, or of
greater tolerance for criticism. We do not seem to sense the
contradiction when we say that these changes were made in
response to public discontent. For have we not also believed
that an authoritarian regime, if efficiently run, can get away
with ignoring the public's clamor?

There is a secret belief among us that either Khrushchev
must have been mad to relax his grip or that it is all part of a
secret plot to throw the West off guard: a plot too clever for
naive Americans to fathom. It is seldom suggested that "de-
Stalinization" took place because the rigid, repressive authoritarianism of the Stalin era was inefficient and that many additional relaxations will be forced upon the Soviet Union by the
necessity of remaining amenable to technological innovation.

But the inevitable Soviet drift toward a more democratic
structure is not dependent on the realism of leaders. Leaders
come from communities and families, and their patterns of
thought are shaped by their experiences with authority in
early life, as well as by their sense of what the traffic will bear.
We saw that the roots of democracy in the United States were
to be found in the nature of the American family. What does
the Soviet family tell us in this respect?

Pessimism regarding the ultimate destiny of Soviet political life has always been based on the seemingly fathomless capacity of the Soviet people for authoritarian submission. Their tolerance for autocratic rulers was only matched by their autocratic family system, which, in its demand for filial obedience, was equal to those of Germany, China, and many Latin countries. Acceptance of authoritarian rule was based on this early experience in the family.

But modern revolutionary movements, both fascist and communist, have tended to regard the family with some suspicion, as the preserver of old ways and as a possible refuge from the State. Fascist dictators have extolled the conservatism of the family but tended at times to set up competitive loyalties for the young. Communist revolutionaries, on the other hand, have more unambivalently attacked family loyalty as reactionary and have deliberately undermined familial allegiances, partly to increase loyalty to the state, partly to facilitate industrialization and modernization by discrediting traditional mores.

Such destruction of authoritarian family patterns is a two-edged sword that eventually cuts away political as well as familial autocracy. The state may attempt to train submission in its own youth organizations, but so long as the family remains an institution, this earlier and more enduring experience will outweigh all others. And if the family has been forced by the state to be less authoritarian, the result is obvious.

In creating a youth that has a knowledge, a familiarity, and a set of attitudes more appropriate for successful living in the changing culture than those of its parents, the autocratic state has created a Frankensteinian monster that will eventually sweep away the authoritarianism in which it is founded. The Soviet Union's attempts during the late 1930s to reverse its stand on the family perhaps reflect some realization of this fact. Khrushchev's denunciations of certain Soviet artists and intellectuals also reflect fear of a process going further than what was originally intended.

A similar ambivalence has appeared in China, where the unforeseen consequences of the slogan "all for the children" recently produced a rash of articles stressing filial obligations. As W. J. Goode points out, "The propaganda campaign against the power of the elders may lead to misunderstanding on the part of the young, who may at times abandon their filial responsibilities to the State."[7]

Further, what the derogation of parental wisdom and authority has begun, the fierce drive for technological modernization will finish. Each generation of youth will be better adapted to the changing society than its parents were. And each generation of parents will feel increasingly modest and doubtful about overvaluing its wisdom and superiority as it recognizes the brevity of its usefulness.

We cannot, of course, predict what forms democratization might take in any nation of the world, nor should we become unduly optimistic about its impact on international relations. Although our thesis predicts the democratization of the entire globe, this is a view so long range as to be academic. There are infinite opportunities for global extermination before we reach any such stage of development.

We should expect that in the earlier stages of industrialization, dictatorial regimes will prevail in all of the less developed nations. And as we well know, autocracy is still highly compatible with a lethal if short-run military efficiency. We may expect many political grotesques, some of them dangerous in the extreme, to emerge during this long period of transition, as one society after another attempts to crowd the most momentous social changes into a generation or two, working from the most varied structural baselines.

But barring some sudden decline in the rate of technological change and on the (outrageous) assumption that war will somehow be eliminated during the next half-century, it is possible to predict that after this time, democracy will be universal. Each revolutionary autocracy, as it reshuffles the family structure and pushes toward industrialization, will sow the seeds of its own destruction, and democratization will gradually engulf it.

We might, of course, rue the day. A world of mass democracies may well prove homogenized and ugly. It is perhaps beyond human social capacity to maximize both equality and understanding on the one hand, diversity on the other. Faced with this dilemma, however, many people are willing to sacrifice quaintness to social justice, and we might conclude by remarking that just as Marx, in proclaiming the inevitability of communism, did not hesitate to give some assistance to the wheels of fate, so our thesis that democracy represents the social system of the electronic era should not bar these persons from giving a little push here and there to the inevitable.

## Notes

1. W. G. Bennis, "Towards a 'Truly' Scientific Management: The Concept of Organizational Health," *General Systems Yearbook,* December 1962, p. 273.

2. N. Sanford, "Social Science and Social Reform," Presidential Address for the Society for the Psychological Study of Social Issues at Annual Meeting of the American Psychological Association, Washington, D.C., August 28, 1958.

3. *Relativity for the Millions* (New York: The Macmillan Company, 1962), p. 11.

4. For a fuller discussion of this trend, see Theodore Levitt, "Marketing Myopia," HBR July–August 1960, p. 45.

5. *The Uprooted* (Boston: Little, Brown and Company, 1951).

6. W. J. Goode, *World Revolution and Family Patterns* (New York: Free Press, 1963), p. 355.

7. Ibid., pp. 313–15.

# 9

# *The Coming Death of Bureaucracy*

*Originally published in 1966, this piece argues that bureaucracy is an institution whose time has past. The essay falters in some of its particulars—certainly General Motors is not the formidable empire it was thirty-five years ago. But the basic premise is truer today than it ever was. The wisdom of "destroying the pyramids," as Jan Carlzon called it, has become a First Principle of successful leaders ranging from Jack Welch to Percy Barnevik.*

Not far from the new Government Center in downtown Boston, a foreign visitor walked up to a sailor and asked why American ships were built to last only a short time. According to the tourist, "The sailor answered without hesitation that the art of navigation is making such rapid progress that the finest ship would become obsolete if it lasted beyond a few years. In these words which fell accidentally from an uneducated man, I began to recognize the general and systematic idea upon which your great people direct all their concerns."

The foreign visitor was that shrewd observer of American morals and manners, Alexis de Tocqueville, and the year was 1835. He would not recognize Scollay Square today. But he had caught the central theme of our country: its preoccupation, its *obsession* with change. One thing is, however, new since de Tocqueville's time: the *acceleration* of newness, the changing scale and scope of change itself. As Dr. Robert Oppenheimer said, ". . . the world alters as we walk in it, so that the years of man's life measure not some small growth or rearrangement or moderation of what was learned in childhood, but a great upheaval."

How will these accelerating changes in our society influence human organizations?

A short while ago, I predicted that we would, in the next 25 to 50 years, participate in the end of bureaucracy as we know it and in the rise of new social systems better suited to the twentieth-century demands of industrialization. This forecast was based on the evolutionary principle that every age develops an organizational form appropriate to its genius, and that the prevailing form, known by sociologists as bureaucracy and by most businessmen as "damn bureaucracy," was out of joint with contemporary realities. I realize now that my distant prophecy is already a distinct reality so that prediction is already foreshadowed by practice.

I should like to make clear that by bureaucracy I mean a chain of command structured on the lines of a pyramid—the typical structure which coordinates the business of almost every human organization we know of: industry, government, universities and research and development laboratories, military, religious, voluntary. I do not have in mind those fantasies so often dreamed up to describe complex organizations. These fantasies can be summarized in two grotesque stereotypes. The first I call "Organization as Inkblot"—an actor steals around an uncharted wasteland, growing more restive and paranoid by the hour, while he awaits orders that never come. The other specter is "Organization as Big Daddy"—the actors are square people plugged into square holes by some omniscient and omnipotent genius who can cradle in his arms the entire destiny of man by way of computer and TV. Whatever the first image owes to Kafka, the second owes to George Orwell's *1984*.

Bureaucracy, as I refer to it here, is a useful social invention that was perfected during the industrial revolution to organize and direct the activities of a business firm. Most students of organizations would say that its anatomy consists of the following components:

**1.** A well-defined chain of command.
**2.** A system of procedures and rules for dealing with all contingencies relating to work activities.
**3.** A division of labor based on specialization.
**4.** Promotion and selection based on technical competence.
**5.** Impersonality in human relations.
It is the pyramid arrangement we see on most organizational charts.

The bureaucratic "machine model" was developed as a reaction against the personal subjugation, nepotism and cruelty, and the capricious and subjective judgments which passed for managerial practices during the early days of the industrial revolution. Bureaucracy emerged out of the organizations' need for order and precision and the workers' demands for impartial treatment. It was an organization ideally suited to the values and demands of the Victorian era. And just as bureaucracy emerged as a creative response to a radically new age, so today new organizational shapes are surfacing before our eyes.

First I shall try to show why the conditions of our modern industrial world will bring about the death of bureaucracy. In the second part of this article, I will suggest a rough model of the organization of the future.

## Four Threats

There are at least four relevant threats to bureaucracy:
**1.** Rapid and unexpected change.
**2.** Growth in size where the volume of an organization's traditional activities is not enough to sustain growth. (A number of factors are included here, among them: bureaucratic overhead; tighter controls and impersonality due to bureaucratic sprawls; outmoded rules and organizational structures.)
**3.** Complexity of modern technology where integration between activities and persons of very diverse, highly specialized competence is required.
**4.** A basically psychological threat springing from a change in managerial behavior.

It might be useful to examine the extent to which these conditions exist *right now:*

### Rapid and Unexpected Change

Bureaucracy's strength is its capacity to efficiently manage the routine and predictable in human affairs. It is almost enough to cite the knowledge and population explosion to raise doubts about its contemporary viability. More revealing, however, are the statistics which demonstrate these overworked phrases:

**a.** Our productivity output per man hour may now be doubling almost every 20 years rather than every 40 years, as it did before World War II.

**b.** The Federal Government alone spent $16 billion in research and development activities in 1965; it will spend $35 billion by 1980.

**c.** The time lag between a technical discovery and recognition of its commercial uses was: 30 years before World War I, 16 years between the Wars, and only 9 years since World War II.

**d.** In 1946, only 42 cities in the world had populations of more than one million. Today there are 90. In 1930, there were 40 people for each square mile of the earth's land surface. Today there are 63. By 2000, it is expected, the figure will have soared to 142.

Bureaucracy, with its nicely defined chain of command, its rules and its rigidities, is ill-adapted to the rapid change the environment now demands.

### Growth in Size

While, in theory, there may be no natural limit to the height of a bureaucratic pyramid, in practice the element of complexity is almost invariably introduced with great size. International operation, to cite one significant new element, is the rule rather than exception for most of our biggest corporations. Firms like Standard Oil Company (New Jersey) with over 100 foreign affiliates, Mobil Oil Corporation, The National Cash Register Company, Singer Company, Burroughs Corporation and Colgate-Palmolive Company derive more than half their income or earnings from foreign sales. Many others—such as Eastman Kodak Company, Chas. Pfizer & Company, Inc., Caterpillar Tractor Company, International Harvester Company, Corn Products Company and Minnesota Mining & Manufacturing Company—make from 30 to 50 percent of their sales abroad. General Motors Corporation sales are not only nine times those of Volkswagen, they are also bigger than the Gross National Product of the Netherlands and well over the GNP of a hundred other countries. If we have seen the sun set on the British Empire, we may never see it set on the empires of General Motors, ITT, Shell and Unilever.

## Labor Boom

### Increasing Diversity

Today's activities require persons of very diverse, highly specialized competence.

Numerous dramatic examples can be drawn from studies of labor markets and job mobility. At some point during the past decade, the U.S. became the first nation in the world ever to employ more people in service occupations than in the production of tangible goods. Examples of this trend:

**a.** In the field of education, the *increase* in employment between 1950 and 1960 was greater than the total number employed in the steel, copper and aluminum industries.

**b.** In the field of health, the *increase* in employment between 1950 and 1960 was greater than the total number employed in automobile manufacturing in either year.

**c.** In financial firms, the *increase* in employment between 1950 and 1960 was greater than total employment in mining in 1960.

These changes, plus many more that are harder to demonstrate statistically, break down the old, industrial trend toward more and more people doing either simple or undifferentiated chores.

Hurried growth, rapid change and increase in specialization—pit these three factors against the five components of the pyramid structure described earlier, and we should expect the pyramid of bureaucracy to begin crumbling.

## Change in Managerial Behavior

There is, I believe, a subtle but perceptible change in the philosophy underlying management behavior. Its magnitude, nature and antecedents, however, are shadowy because of the difficulty of assigning numbers. (Whatever else statistics do for us, they most certainly provide a welcome illusion of certainty.) Nevertheless, real change seems underway because of:

**a.** A new concept of *man,* based on increased knowledge of his complex and shifting needs, which replaces an oversimplified, innocent, push-button idea of man.

**b.** A new concept of *power,* based on collaboration and reason, which replaces a model of power based on coercion and threat.

**c.** A new concept of *organizational values,* based on humanistic-democratic ideals, which replaces the depersonalized mechanistic value system of bureaucracy.

The primary cause of this shift in management philosophy stems not from the bookshelf but from the manager himself. Many of the behavioral scientists, like Douglas McGregor or Rensis Likert, have clarified and articulated—even legitimized—what managers have only half registered to themselves. I am convinced, for example, that the popularity of McGregor's book, *The Human Side of Enterprise,* was based on his rare empathy for a vast audience of managers who are wistful for an alternative to the mechanistic concept of authority, i.e., that he outlined a vivid utopia of more authentic human relationships than most organizational practices today allow. Furthermore, I suspect that the desire for relationships in business has little to do with a profit motive per se, though it is often rationalized as doing so. The real push for these changes stems from the need, not only to humanize the organization, but to use it as a crucible of personal growth and the development of self-realization.[1]

The core problems confronting any organization fall, I believe, into five major categories. First, let us consider the problems, then let us see how our twentieth-century conditions of constant change have made the bureaucratic approach to these problems obsolete.

*Integration*

The problem is how to integrate individual needs and management goals. In other words, it is the inescapable conflict between individual needs (like "spending time with the family") and organizational demands (like meeting deadlines).

Under twentieth-century conditions of constant change there has been an emergence of human sciences and a deeper understanding of man's complexity. Today, integration encompasses the entire range of issues concerned with incentives, rewards and motivations of the individual, and how the organization succeeds or fails in adjusting to these issues. In our society, where personal attachments play an important role, the individual is appreciated, and there is genuine concern for his well-being, not just in a veterinary-hygiene sense, but as a moral, integrated personality.

## Paradoxical Twins

The problem of integration, like most human problems, has a venerable past. The modern version goes back at least 160 years and was precipitated by an historical paradox: the twin births of modern individualism and modern industrialism. The former brought about a deep concern for and a passionate interest in the individual and his personal rights. The latter brought about increased mechanization of organized activity. Competition between the two has intensified as each decade promises more freedom and hope for man and more stunning achievements for technology. I believe that our society *has* opted for more humanistic and democratic values, however unfulfilled they may be in practice. It will "buy" these values even at loss in efficiency because it feels it can now afford the loss.

*Social Influence*

This problem is essentially one of power and how power is distributed. It is a complex issue and alive with controversy, partly because studies of leadership and power distribution can be interpreted in many ways, and almost always in ways which coincide with one's biases (including a cultural leaning toward democracy).

The problem of power has to be seriously reconsidered because of dramatic situational changes which make the possibility of one-man rule not necessarily "bad" but impractical. I refer to changes in top management's role.

Peter Drucker, over 12 years ago, listed 41 major responsibilities of the chief executive and declared that "90 percent of the trouble we are having with the chief executive's job is rooted in our superstition of the one-man chief." Many factors make one-man control obsolete, among them: the broadening product base of industry; impact of new technology; the scope of international operation; the separation of management from ownership; the rise of trade unions and general education. The real power of the "chief" has been eroding in most organizations even though both he and the organization cling to the older concept.

*Collaboration*

This is the problem of managing and resolving conflicts. Bureaucratically, it grows out of the very same process of conflict and stereotyping that has divided nations and communities. As organizations become more complex, they fragment and divide, building tribal patterns and symbolic codes which often work to exclude others (secrets and jargon, for example) and on occasion to exploit differences for inward (and always fragile) harmony.

Recent research is shedding new light on the problem of conflict. Psychologist Robert R. Blake in his stunning experiments has shown how simple it is to induce conflict, how difficult to arrest it. Take two groups of people who have never before been together, and give them a task which will be judged by an impartial jury. In less than an hour, each group devolves into a tightly-knit band with all the symptoms of an "in group." They regard their product as a "master-work" and the other group's as "commonplace" at best. "Other" becomes "enemy." "We are good, they are bad; we are right, they are wrong."

## Rabbie's Reds and Greens

Jaap Rabbie, conducting experiments on intergroup conflict at the University of Utrecht, has been amazed by the ease with which conflict and stereotype develop. He brings into an experimental room two groups and distributes green name tags and pens to one group, red pens and tags to the other. The two groups do not compete; they do not even interact. They are only in sight of each other while they silently complete a questionnaire. Only ten minutes are needed to activate defensiveness and fear, reflected in the hostile and irrational perceptions of both "reds" and "greens."

### Adaptation

This problem is caused by our turbulent environment. The pyramid structure of bureaucracy, where power is concentrated at the top, seems the perfect way to "run a railroad." And for the routine tasks of the nineteenth and early twentieth centuries, bureaucracy was (in some respects it still is) a suitable social arrangement. However, rather than a placid and predictable environment, what predominates today is a dynamic and uncertain one where there is deepening interdependence among economic, scientific, educational, social and political factors in the society.

## Revitalization

This is the problem of growth and decay. As Alfred North Whitehead has said: "The art of free society consists first in the maintenance of the symbolic code, and secondly, in the fearlessness of revision. . . . Those societies which cannot combine reverence to their symbols with freedom of revision must ultimately decay. . . ."

Growth and decay emerge as the penultimate conditions of contemporary society. Organizations, as well as societies, must be concerned with those social structures that engender buoyancy, resilience and a "fearlessness of revision."

I introduce the term "revitalization" to embrace all the social mechanisms that stagnate and regenerate, as well as the process of this cycle. The elements of revitalization are:

**1.** An ability to learn from experience and to codify, store and retrieve the relevant knowledge.

**2.** An ability to "learn how to learn," that is, to develop methods for improving the learning process.

**3.** An ability to acquire and use feed-back mechanisms on performance, in short, to be self-analytical.

**4.** An ability to direct one's own destiny.

These qualities have a good deal in common with what John Gardner calls "self-renewal." For the organization, it means conscious attention to its own evolution. Without a planned methodology and explicit direction, the enterprise will not realize its potential.

*Integration, distribution of power, collaboration, adaptation* and *revitalization*—these are the major human problems of the next 25 years. How organizations cope with and manage these tasks will undoubtedly determine the viability of the enterprise.

Against this background I should like to set forth some of the conditions that will dictate organizational life in the next two or three decades.

## The Environment

Rapid technological change and diversification will lead to more and more partnerships between government and business. It will be a truly mixed economy. Because of the immensity and expense of the projects, there will be fewer identical units competing in the same markets and organizations will become more interdependent.

The four main features of this environment are:

**a.** Interdependence rather than competition.

**b.** Turbulence and uncertainty rather than readiness and certainty.

**c.** Large-scale rather than small-scale enterprises.

**d.** Complex and multinational rather than simple national enterprises.

## "Nice"—and Necessary

*Population Characteristics*

The most distinctive characteristic of our society is education. It will become even more so. Within 15 years, two-thirds of our population living in metropolitan areas will have attended college. Adult education is growing even faster, probably because of the rate of professional obsolescence. The Killian report showed that the average engineer required further education only ten years after getting his degree. It will be almost routine for the experienced physician, engineer and executive to go back to school for advanced training every two or three years. All of this education is not just "nice." It is necessary.

One other characteristic of the population which will aid our understanding of organizations of the future is increasing job mobility. The ease of transportation, coupled with the needs of a dynamic environment, change drastically the idea of "owning" a job—or "having roots." Already 20 percent of our population change their mailing address at least once a year.

*Work Values*

The increased level of education and mobility will change the values we place on work. People will be more intellectually committed to their jobs and will probably require more involvement, participation and autonomy.

Also, people will be more "other-oriented," taking cues for their norms and values from their immediate environment rather than tradition.

### Tasks and Goals

The tasks of the organization will be more technical, complicated and unprogrammed. They will rely on intellect instead of muscle. And they will be too complicated for one person to comprehend, to say nothing of control. Essentially, they will call for the collaboration of specialists in a project or a team-form of organization.

There will be a complication of goals. Business will increasingly concern itself with its adaptive or innovative-creative capacity. In addition, supragoals will have to be articulated, goals which shape and provide the foundation for the goal structure. For example, one might be a system for detecting new and changing goals; another could be a system for deciding priorities among goals.

Finally, there will be more conflict and contradiction among diverse standards for organizational effectiveness. This is because professionals tend to identify more with the goals of their profession than with those of their immediate employer. University professors can be used as a case in point. Their inside work may be a conflict between teaching and research, while more of their income is derived from outside sources, such as foundations and consultant work. They tend not to be good "company men" because they divide their loyalty between their professional values and organizational goals.

## Key Word: "Temporary"

### Organization

The social structure of organizations of the future will have some unique characteristics. The key word will be "temporary." There will be adaptive, rapidly changing *temporary* systems. These will be task forces organized around problems to be solved by groups of relative strangers with diverse professional skills. The groups will be arranged on an organic rather than mechanical model; they will evolve in response to a problem rather than to programmed role expectations. The executive thus becomes a coordinator or "linking pin" between various task forces. He must be a man who can speak the polyglot jargon of research, with skills to relay information and to mediate between groups. People will be evaluated not vertically according to rank and status, but flexibly and functionally according to skill and professional training. Organizational charts will consist of project groups rather than stratified functional groups. (This trend is already visible in the aerospace and construction industries, as well as many professional and consulting firms.)

Adaptive, problem-solving, temporary systems of diverse specialists, linked together by coordinating and task-evaluating executive specialists in an organic flux—this is the organization form that will gradually replace bureaucracy as we know it. As no catchy phrase comes to mind, I call this an organic-adaptive structure. Organizational arrangements of this sort may not only reduce the intergroup conflicts mentioned earlier; they may also induce honest-to-goodness creative collaboration.

*Motivation*

The organic-adaptive structure should increase motivation and thereby effectiveness, because it enhances satisfactions intrinsic to the task. There is a harmony between the educated individual's need for tasks that are meaningful, satisfactory and creative and a flexible organizational structure.

I think that the future I describe is not necessarily a "happy" one. Coping with rapid change, living in temporary work systems, developing meaningful relations and then breaking them—all augur social strains and psychological tensions. Teaching how to live with ambiguity, to identify with the adaptive process, to make a virtue out of contingency, and to be self-directing—these will be the tasks of education, the goals of maturity, and the achievement of the successful individual.

## No Delightful Marriages

In these new organizations of the future, participants will be called upon to use their minds more than at any other time in history. Fantasy, imagination and creativity will be legitimate in ways that today seem strange. Social structures will no longer be instruments of psychic repression but will increasingly promote play and freedom on behalf of curiosity and thought.

One final word: While I forecast the structure and value coordinates for organizations of the future and contend that they are inevitable, this should not bar any of us from giving the inevitable a little push. The French moralist may be right in saying that there are no delightful marriages, just good ones. It is possible that if managers and scientists continue to get their heads together in organizational revitalization, they *might* develop delightful organizations—just possibly.

I started with a quote from de Tocqueville and I think it would be fitting to end with one: "I am tempted to believe that what we call necessary institutions are often no more than institutions to which we have grown accustomed. In matters of social constitution, the field of possibilities is much more extensive than men living in their various societies are ready to imagine."

### Note

1. Let me propose an hypothesis to explain this tendency. It rests on the assumption that man has a basic need for transcendental experiences, somewhat like the psychological rewards which William James claimed religion provided—"an assurance of safety and a temper of peace, and in relation to others, a preponderance of living affections." Can it be that as religion has become secularized, less transcendental, men search for substitutes such as close interpersonal relationships, psychoanalysis—even the release provided by drugs such as LSD?

# 10
## Corporate Boards

*Because of the radical changes in organizational life in recent years, corporate boards have become more important than ever. The old boys' club of the past, which did little more than rubber-stamp executive decisions, has given way to a diversified body that has both a legal and a moral obligation to scrutinize management and even to assume a leadership role, as the board of General Motors did a few years ago.*

## The Crisis of Corporate Boards

But I'd shut my eyes in the sentry-box,
So I didn't see nothin' wrong.
—*Rudyard Kipling*

The now famous McCloy report, undertaken as a result of corporate actions ranging in their seriousness from "ethical insensitivity" to criminally liable behavior, concludes: "It is hard to escape the conclusion that a sort of 'shut-eye sentry' attitude prevailed upon the part of both the responsible corporate officials and the recipients as well as on the part of those charged with enforcement responsibilities."

What *is* the proper role of a board of directors in the conduct of corporate affairs?

A former Penn Central director admitted shortly after the fall of that corporation, "I don't think anybody was aware that it was that close to collapse." And Gulf's directors were clearly embarrassed by their company's illicit payments and other criminal actions.

The lesson from the Gulf and Penn Central situations is simple: unless directors have the right information and know how to ask the right questions, they tend to see only what they are told to look at; when something "wrong" happens they are apt to be jolted out of their lethargy by unfriendly lawyers rapping loudly on their sentry box.

The spectacular embarrassments of boards of directors in recent years have been warning flares lighting up the corporate skies. But fireworks unfortunately block from view the deeper, more difficult issues. At the same time, they may tend to act as tranquilizers, falsely lulling the sentry into confidence that the criminals have been purged and further liability curbed.

These unfortunate incidents have led to a stream of discussion, some of it shrill and not altogether rational. The business community, most of all, has been reexamining the composition, operations, and procedures of boards of directors. While there are indications that procedures and operations have been tightened, the increased public expectations about corporate performance are a long and nervous distance from realization.

It is still the case that most board members are, in fact, willing dupes of management. They are expensive, impotent, and often frustrated rubber stamps. They are subject to major litigation and are selected solely by their subordinates. They seldom understand their function, because of lack of proper orientation or education, and therefore they often meddle in management affairs. Old-timers who have learned the function of a board find that they have no way to assume those functions, given the history, tradition, or make-up of the particular board on which they serve.

An example of board confusion and the consequent resistance to change can be found in the case of Arthur Goldberg, a former member of the Supreme Court and Ambassador to the United Nations, who resigned as a director of T.W.A. on October 18, 1976, in a dispute over the directors' proper role. Goldberg attempted to establish an independent committee of outside directors to review the actions and recommendations of management. He argued that this group should be allowed to meet independently, without interference from "inside" directors, officials, or administrators, and should benefit from an independent staff of technical specialists. His proposal was turned down by the board, and Goldberg resigned.

In the two years since then, three dozen suits have been filed by disgruntled shareholders of the Penn Central Transportation Co. against the directors who had served that company prior to its receivership. These suits are based on a law imposing ultimate legal responsibility for the management of a corporate enterprise on boards of directors. More recently, the Securities and Exchange Commission has rebuked two outside directors of Sterling Homex Corp. for allegedly falling to obtain "a sufficiently firm grasp of the administrative, organization, and financial practices of the firm," accepting, according to the S.E.C. report, "superficial answers to questions put to management."

*Players in a Chinese Baseball Game*

The fundamental point here is that a gap in the corporate directors system exists between what state statutes say are the responsibilities of boards of directors and the realities of any board's operations. Furthermore, these statutes vary from state to state and from country to country and are in constant flux, creating for all public corporations a situation on the order of Chinese baseball—a game in which players can move the bases anywhere they want to.

The effectiveness of boards of directors is impaired by at least eight specific predicaments which are at once the source and the manifestations of the gap between a board's legal responsibility and its actual operations.

• *Board Composition.* Though there is now a mix of "inside" and "outside" directors on most boards, charges of "clubbiness" still echo. Too often, people join boards because of the prestige it gives them or the stipend it pays, or because it provides an ideal activity for retired executives who want to keep busy but who understand they will exercise no control. Outside directors, chosen by the president or a few inside officers, become "angel's advocates" of top administration. On the other hand, diversity on a board may lead to a "devil's advocate" stance in questioning and often leads to a "Noah's ark" syndrome: filing into the board room one-by-one must be representatives of every type—one woman, one black, one Jew, one consumer—whose appointments are supposed to absolve everyone of guilt for years of neglect.

Knowledgeable, experienced women and minorities do have a place on boards, of course, but to pick them solely on the basis of prior neglect is an insult; and it is likely to lead to a board made up of people who know little about the enterprise and who raise so many single voices and write so many minority reports that conflicts cannot be resolved and progress is blocked.

The predicament, then, is how to create a board responsible to the shareholders without creating a political Noah's ark of dissident voices.

• *The Increasing Role of Law.* A board of directors cannot operate with a corporate management unless there is mutual trust and confidence. But today the law's increasing influence tends to erode this. Board members are now so vulnerable to and skittish about expensive lawsuits, for example, that they can no longer rely on the word of the chief executive officer in making decisions. They must have everything in writing, duly notarized, which often means that a corporation's legal counsel and chief financial officer play a more important role than the chief executive officer. Moreover, the law—which has difficulty distinguishing between deliberate wrongdoing and an honest mistake—punishes only acts of commission, not those of omission. Under these conditions, almost any board will encourage management to do nothing rather than introduce risky innovation. And innovation—the willingness to take risks in the marketplace—has been the genius of American enterprise.

• *Accountability.* At what precise location does the buck stop? Why should a chief executive officer be fired for a wrongdoing unless the entire board goes with him? Isn't the board equally culpable? How can board members be the ultimate arbiters, the pinnacle of corporate power, without being accountable as well? The demarcation lines of power, responsibility, and culpability are vague and subject to many different interpretations.

- *Diminished Executive Responsibility.* Every reform resulting from infractions of the law or from criminal behavior on the part of corporations has diminished the responsibility of the chief executive officer. Examples: a company's financial officer is required to report to an auditing committee; nominating committees are to be composed of outside directors reporting directly to the board; the required standing committees on corporate social responsibility are to report directly to the board, rather than through the chief executive officer. Requirements such as these have the effect of preventing the leader from leading.

- *The Double-Bind.* The chief executive officer's responsibility, on the one hand, is to maximize the return on the shareholders' investment. But the competitive practices by which this obligation is fulfilled—normally quite within the accepted norms of the enterprise—may now suddenly be made illegal by a law that is in flux. To the traditional conflict between risk-taking and corporate security there is thus now added subtle pressure of the chief executive officer to assure his personal immunity to legal action.

- *Conflict of Interest.* What is the position of a member of a bank board, for example, who serves also as financial adviser for an enterprise which is a customer of the bank, or of a lawyer on a university's board who represents a firm that does business with the university? Such relationships deserve careful scrutiny. But it is difficult to find knowledgeable, sophisticated candidates for boards of directors who have no ties whatever to other institutions. Indeed, if all board members with multiple obligations were forced to resign, we would end up bringing people with no knowledge, sophistication, or advisory capacity into positions of power.

- *The Ambiguity of State Statutes.* There is no uniformity in the state statutes under which corporations are chartered, and many are highly ambiguous. For example, no state statute distinguishes between outside and inside directors. This general ambiguity frustrates attempts to define precise roles for directors, and as a result it is virtually impossible to answer the question, "Who's in charge?"
- *The Education of Board Members.* It is not possible for board members to ask discerning questions, to understand their full legal and managerial prerogatives and responsibilities, or to fulfill their responsibilities without orientation and education; but most begin their terms completely naive about their roles. There is little or no orientation. New board members usually receive at best a glossy confection supposed to provide a description of the institution, but which in reality offers little more than the typical annual report. Given the many competing pressures for their time and attention, how can board members learn what they need to know about the enterprise they serve and the environment in which it operates?

### Confusion Rampant

There was a time when directors rarely had to dirty their hands or minds with anything but vague fiduciary responsibilities or the occasional selection of a president; today they find themselves surrounded by shrieking shareholders, lawsuits, and illicit practices, and they're confused. The major problem is the gap, more and more obvious, between their governing role as decreed by law and the reality of our complex, rapidly changing contemporary scene.

## Rx for Corporate Boards

Not since the early days of the New Deal has the field of corporate governance been so astir with proposals for reform. Everybody's in the act, it seems—not just Ralph Nader, who nags, hassles, and litigates on behalf of corporate social responsibility or the ubiquitous Lewis D. Gilbert, who presses for reform and sues corporations to make them more responsible to the shareholder. There are also such substantial, temperate people as the participants in the 52nd American Assembly (April 1977), whose conclusions on the "ethics of corporate governance" included a criticism that boards are "remote, insensitive, and not adequately reflective of the many publics they serve."

As a result of this growing clamor, two reforms are apparently being given serious consideration in Congress, state legislatures, and regulatory bodies:

- Federal chartering of corporations.
- Mandating certain proportions of public, independent (outside), and "special interest" directors, the latter including members of minority groups, to open up membership to broader constituencies and weaken the "clubhouse" atmosphere of board rooms.

That's all well and good. But I submit that these changes do not respond to the fundamental issues boards will have to confront in the coming years. These can be reduced to three:

- Restoring trust in the corporation. This can happen only if boards eliminate conflicts of interest; if board members make sure that the corporation they serve as the final repository of trust obeys the law; if they learn how to ask the right questions; and if they speak out on issues of public concern.
- Developing explicit guidelines regarding board and administrative accountability.
- Recruiting colleagues earnestly and well, making certain that the requisite combination of talents is present, and then providing a first-rate orientation program for new members as well as a plan for the recurring education of current members.

All the federal guidelines in the world will not improve the operations of boards until these rudimentary criteria are satisfied. Even if directors possess superior qualifications, no substantial change will occur unless they learn to ask discerning questions and to recognize and demand responsive, substantive answers. "Communication" or "dialogue" are not enough for dealing with important policy matters. Those require that directors ask questions, crystalize their views, and assert their informed opinions.

## More Regulation, More Transience

Consider J. Pfeffer's recent analysis of the three basic levels present in all organizations: the *technical* level assures the organization's capacity to produce some item or service; the *management* level coordinates and supervises the technical level; and the *institutional* level assures the organization's legitimacy, credibility, and success in coping with its environment. Most companies are now well equipped in technology and management. More and more, a firm's success will depend on its ability and sophistication at the institutional level.

That is because today's organizations are open systems, operating in an uncertain and unforecastable environment. We only know that there will be more regulations, more controls, more personnel movement from one organization to another, more joint ventures, more mergers, more independence. Corporate success will depend increasingly on being able to understand the political landscape, to deal with bureaucrats, to promote the right laws and regulations, to mobilize public opinion, and especially to know the strategy of all these. Retail price maintenance, tariff protection, and licensing to restrict entry into a field are prime examples of issues now entering the institutional environment.

Management is concerned with the technical and managerial levels, and most boards are drawn unwittingly into this same arena. But that is wrong. Only where the board plays a pivotal role in institutional management by helping management understand and meet its new environment can organizations succeed.

Instead of being drawn into arguments about cost effectiveness, the board should be concerned about changing markets so that they may see cost effectiveness in a new dimension. They should have ideas about new markets, new technologies, new hopes. They should understand publications and public affairs, realizing that there are many new constituencies and patronage structures out there upon which the organization can founder.

My concern with the effective operations of corporate boards reflects a broader concern which I share with Harold Williams, chairman of the Securities and Exchange Commission: "The issue [his words] of the very legitimacy of the corporation itself." A more specific expression of this concern came from Assistant U.S. Attorney General Robert H. Morse upon the conviction of a supermarket president on criminal charges involving rodent infestation in one of the company's sixteen warehouses: "Only through incarceration will the business community be dissuaded from such conduct." The fact that the president had been assured by a subordinate that the violation had been corrected carried no weight in court.

## Trading in the Marketplace of Ideas

How are we to re-establish the public's confidence in those who legally shoulder the responsibility for corporate America—the directors and top officials of the firm?

The most thoughtful and far-sighted chief executive officers and board directors are already striking out in new directions. Many of our top business leaders, men such as John deButts of A.T.&T., Reginald Jones of G.E., and Irving Shapiro of du Pont have long understood the role of political and social factors as major forces affecting business. Now they and many of their colleagues are spending ever-increasing amounts of time dealing with public affairs. And they do not take these responsibilities casually, for they realize that the marketplace of ideas, where business has not in the past fared especially well, may be as important as the marketplace of commodities.

Unfortunately, however, too many top managements remain oblivious to—or even resentful of—the new ball game.

Their ambivalence leads to policies and actions which are almost always too late and too little, a "muddling through" process: a Washington office, a high-priced speech writer, exhausting public appearance schedules for top executives, and a big sigh of relief that, now, the problem is taken care of.

These "remedies" barely touch the surface of the contemporary realities facing our corporations; they are nothing more than anxiety-reducing actions taken without understanding the scope of the problem. Perhaps no one understands this better than du Pont's Irving Shapiro, who has written in the *Wall Street Journal:*

> A new breed of manager is coming to the fore, no less competent on the basics of business, let us hope, but much more of a public person. This reflects the fact that big corporations have become quasipublic in nature. You see this in the increased regulations of business, in journalistic probings of the corporate interior, in labor relations and in other ways.
>
> Today you don't hear executives asking their trade industry associates to handle all of the relationships with Washington. What you see, increasingly, is company leaders doing the rounds in person, testifying, talking to congressmen in their offices, meeting with the regulatory agencies, meeting in the executive offices with people from the president on down.
>
> . . . This process is healthy for the political process, as well as business. The business leader learns that you don't reach decisions in government the way an engineer chooses the most efficient process for producing a product.
>
> An overwhelming majority of people in positions of responsibility in this country, whatever their walk of life, believes that we have a system that in practice works pretty well, and in principle is even better. What I see now within the ranks of business is a growing sensitivity, a growing sense of the possible and a growing set of talents to make the system work better.

# 11

## Our Federalist Future: The Leadership Imperative

*Today I have the same confidence in the inevitability of federalism that a third of a century ago I had in the triumph of democracy. James O'Toole is the senior author of this essay.*

The structure of the organization can then be symbolized by a man holding a large number of balloons in his hand. Each of the balloons has its own buoyancy and lift, and the man himself does not lord it over the balloons, but stands beneath them, yet holding all the strings firmly in his hand. Every balloon is not only an administrative but also an entrepreneurial unit.

—*E. F. Schumacher*

## The Geopolitical Solution: A Template for Corporations?

In these turbulent times prudent mapmakers work on Etch-a-Sketch pads. Political boundaries change almost weekly as new nations emerge with varying degrees of anguish from the disintegrating empires of yesterday. No part of the world is exempt. From the Balkans to the British Isles, from the banks of the St. Lawrence to Guangdong Province on China's muddy Pearl River, ethnic and linguistic groups are wrestling—often at the cost of their lives—with a fundamental challenge of our era: We'll call it the Iceland Dilemma. In a sentence, the horns of that dilemma are represented by the choice between the advantages of small-country autonomy, on the one side, and the benefits of big-country economies of scale, on the other.

Bleakly beautiful Iceland is being pulled and shaped by these two powerful but opposing forces. On one side is the Icelanders' fierce pride in their nation's Viking heritage. This pride has led the population of Iceland (in total, some 250,000 shivering souls) to form a committee to give Viking names to concepts that even their visionary national hero, Leif Ericksson, could never have imagined. Hence, in Iceland a computer screen is called a *skjar* (the ancient word for a "window" on a traditional turf house).

But that passion for what is uniquely theirs is only one side of modern Icelandic values. Even as Icelanders quote traditional sagas and support laws to require citizens to choose names for their children from an approved list of "pure" Icelandic origin, those same citizens are eager to enter into active participation in the global economy, to become a part of the highly competitive modern world of international technology, commerce, and finance.

Icelandic society is thus a vivid example of what philosophers once called the tension between the tribal and the universal. How to balance tradition with the desire for economic progress, how to be true to oneself while being a partner, and how to sing solo but be in the chorus at the same time—these are the essence of the Iceland Dilemma. Indeed, the entire world today is grappling with the need to strike a balance between nationalism and globalism. And that need is likely to grow more pressing as the new millennium unfolds, considering that there are more than 5,000 restless "nationalities" in the world but only 166 nation-states—so far. Clearly, the number of nations should be viewed as just penciled in, and can be expected to increase dramatically as countries divide and subdivide even further in coming years, all the while seeking simultaneously to be a part of the New Globalism.

Fortunately, there is a generic solution to the Iceland Dilemma: *federation.* Thus, many Icelanders would like to escape their own particular version of the dilemma through an exogamous marriage with the European Community (EC)—joining their fortunes to those of peoples who have little interest in the purity of the Icelandic tongue or the preservation of Icelandic culture but who can provide the political and economic clout Iceland needs to be a player in world markets. Indeed, the European Community is the surpassing model of the federalist future. With twelve member-states (and counting), the EC is now seen by some three score ethnic groups living in the twenty-five nations situated between Reykjavik and Riga as the best means for them to unify for overarching political and economic purposes, while at the same time maintaining their cultural integrity. As we shall see, not only is such confederation the most practical resolution of the Iceland Dilemma for nation-states, but it can be equally beneficial as a strategy for business corporations.

## Government (and Corporate) Federalism

Unlike monolithic forms of government, federations are alliances of more or less independent states, often with little in common but their desire to share in the benefits of swimming in a larger pond. The most durable example of confederation is Switzerland, where a workable union of divergent cultures has survived for more than seven hundred years. In modern Switzerland there are twenty-six semiautonomous cantons (and half-cantons), which together compose four major cultural groups, each with its own language and customs. Perhaps the most convincing argument in favor of federalism is that the Confederaziun Helvetica endures despite this remarkable diversity (tolerating even the reactionary values of one half-canton that is the last political body in the Western world to deny women the vote in local elections). In general, federations allow member units to pursue their unique—even quirky—interests, to realize their distinctive possibilities, and to address their special needs, as long as the units do not compromise the rights of other members or the needs of the alliance as a whole.

In that most successful of federations—our own resilient alliance of states—the whole is greater than the sum of Alabama, Alaska, Arizona, and the other disparate but essential components of the Union. In these rapidly changing times, such federations as the United States work better than monolithic nations (like the former, misnamed, Union of Soviet Socialist Republics) because they offer flexibility as well as strength. By their nature federal systems recognize the legitimacy of alternatives, of more than one possible response to a given challenge. If a federation were a poem, it would be not the epic saga of a single national hero but something like Wallace Steven's "Thirteen Ways of Looking at a Blackbird."

Committed to a single vision and course of action, a unitary government is often too slow to respond to changing conditions. In contrast to the singular stance of the monolithic state, federations are nimble by nature, accustomed to considering a full repertoire of responses. While the unitary nation goes for all or nothing, federations multiply the options and reduce the risk. In theory, at least, federations are also less prone to the ethnic animosities that are the ugliest aspects of hyperpatriotism. The very existence of a federation is implicit recognition that there is strength in diversity. In homogeneous groups outsiders are too often seen as monsters, devils, or obstacles on the road to "racial purity." But it is much harder to dehumanize outsiders in a heterogeneous alliance in which others are viewed as peers and partners (albeit ethnic vilification is not impossible in federations, as the former Yugoslav republics sadly demonstrate). James Madison, the guiding light of American federalism, argued that the true virtue of such a system lies in its recognition of the natural tendency toward the pursuit of self-interest—and in its built-in mechanism to counter that tendency by protecting the rights of minorities from "the tyranny of the majority."[1]

Because federalism allows constituent units to maintain their integrity while unifying for common purposes, it is not surprising that the form is now a major trend in business as well as in government. For if "centralization is the deathblow of public freedom," as Disraeli said, it is equally the death-blow of corporate innovation. For that reason, many of the world's most influential business leaders are creating new kinds of corporate confederations with numerous semi–autonomous units, often in far-flung countries, joined together only to allow them all to succeed better in an increasingly competitive global economy. Examples include Benetton, Coca-Cola, and the newly formed Asea Brown Boveri (ABB). These companies have become models for international orchestration, influencing the likes of General Electric's CEO Jack Welch. Welch is creating at GE a new corporate federalism which he describes as "boundaryless."

Significantly, the characteristics of successful national and corporate confederations are nearly identical. Moreover, the following characteristics of federalism have remained constant since they were first described by Madison in the late eighteenth century, and thus appear to possess almost universal validity.

• *Noncentralization.* In federations power resides in many semiautonomous constituent centers, deliberately diffused for the purpose of safeguarding the freedom and vitality of those units. This *non*centralization should not be confused with commonplace *de*centralization (typically characterized by an all-commanding central authority that unilaterally delegates specific, limited powers to its subordinate units). In sharp contrast, a true federal system is contractual and power cannot be rescinded unilaterally or arbitrarily by the central government (or central headquarters). For example, the corporate staff at one of America's most truly federalized corporations—Dayton-Hudson (DH)—cannot change the rules of the game that affect its Mervyn's and Target divisions. As with the Swiss confederation, such changes may occur only as the result of mutually respectful negotiations, a process that is prescribed in Dayton-Hudson's "constitution."

• *Negotiationalism.* In federations decisions are made in an ongoing process of bargaining between the units and the central authority—and often between the units themselves.

Thus there is shared decision making, and the units have a guaranteed voice in defining their financial, administrative, and other obligations to the central body. This doesn't mean that Coca-Cola's distributors and bottlers dictate terms to CEO Roberto Goizueta; nor, as we shall see, does Goizueta dictate to them either. Rather, it means that terms and conditions are negotiated and contractual.

• *Constitutionalism.* In federations there is a written (occasionally, unwritten) covenant that binds the allegiance of the units to the basic purpose, mission, philosophy, and principles of the overarching institution. Often this constitution spells out the mutual rights and responsibilities of all parties. Constituent units in turn may be free to have their own constitutions, as long as these do not violate the basic principles of the articles of federation. Much like the United States has its Constitution, ABB has a 21-page "bible" that lays out the principles by which the company operates, and Dayton-Hudson's 118-page "Management Perspectives" serves much the same purpose.

• *Territoriality.* In federations there are distinct boundaries between the constituent units. In the case of nations, these geographic boundaries may be based on ethnicity or tradition. In corporations the boundaries can be based on business or product line. (With franchisors like Coca-Cola and Benetton, the boundaries are often geographic.)

• *Balance of Power.* Federations seek balance not only between the central authority and the units but also between the units (the nineteenth-century confederation of German states failed, in no small measure, because Prussia over-dominated its weaker partners). Part of the negotiations that led to the 1980s merger of Dayton-Hudson and Mervyn's concerned the relative role the California chain would play in the established, Midwest-oriented pecking order of DH's other retail units.

• *Autonomy.* In a federation the units are free to experiment and be self-governing to the extent that they do not violate the fundamental principles necessary for the maintenance of the union. Of all the characteristics of federation, this is the most difficult to achieve and maintain. As students of the Civil War are aware, the American Union was nearly dissolved because of conflicting interpretations of this principle. Over far less morally significant matters, Benetton recently found itself sued by an angry franchisee who claimed that the corporation was imperiously dictating policies that ran counter to the spirit of the alliance. (We return to this important issue later.)

## The Necessity—and Fragility—of Federalism

Madison argued that these traits of federalism become necessities when an organization reaches a certain size. While the founders could imagine successful unitary republics on the scale of the Athenian city-state (or Renaissance Venice and Florence), they argued that even the original thirteen states were too big to function monistically. Their insight seems apposite to corporations as well. Small, well-managed companies like Ben and Jerry's, Herman Miller, and Chaparral Steel operate effectively within a unitary structure and culture and demonstrate little need for federalism. While Madison recognized that size alone is not the only relevant criterion for choosing federalism—diversity is another—it is clearly the single most important reason. Is it coincidental that almost all large social and economic institutions that find themselves in trouble today are unitary in form? From the People's Republic of China, to IBM, to the Los Angeles Unified School System, almost all such monolithic organizations could benefit from a heavy dose of federalism.

In this regard it is significant that many of history's most successful giant institutions—the Catholic church, the Roman Empire, the General Motors corporation, to cite three rather large examples—enjoyed their finest hours during periods when they were structured along roughly federal lines. For instance, GM reached its pinnacle in the late 1920s, when it briefly approached Alfred Sloan's original concept of six confederated divisions—and GM was never so *un*successful as it was in the late 1980s, when it had all but abandoned the last remnants of true divisionalization (even producing Buicks on Chevrolet assembly lines).

The GM example also illustrates the essential fragility of federalism, an inherent instability that stems from the aforementioned tension between (a) the needs of central authority to exert power and (b) the rights of the units to autonomy. The art of leadership in a federation is to preserve the balance between those evershifting forces. History shows how difficult that art is in practice. Like GM, most federations have a tendency—fatal in the long term—to overcentralize and homogenize. The old USSR is a classic political example of this pattern. And the root of the Soviet problem wasn't simply Communist dogma. Under Margaret Thatcher capitalist Great Britain also did not go far enough in the devolution of authority to the constituent parts of the United Kingdom (and the new democratic Russian "federation" seems to be regressing toward Soviet-style centralization). The former Union of South Africa was once a relatively effective (but undemocratic) federal state. Then, in the 1950s, power was centralized in order to impose apartheid on the reluctant English-speaking provinces. The result was the erosion of autonomy and the creation of a unitary (and even more undemocratic) republic.

At the other extreme, the United Arab Republic (a shortlived marriage of convenience between Syria and Egypt) had nearly none of the characteristics of successful federations listed earlier, and consequently crumbled as if constructed of Arabian sand. And conglomerate corporations—like Dart Enterprises in the 1970s—typically disintegrate (or degenerate into mere holding companies) when there is no unifying vision, constitution, or federal structure. As with so many conglomerates of the 1960–1970 era, the parts of Justin Dart's once mighty empire are now scattered across the Fortune 500.

The fundamental and continuing question facing all federations is this: What powers rightly belong with the central authority, and what powers should be reserved for the constituent units? Madison believed he had solved the question with the U.S. Constitution and Bill of Rights, which basically limited the power of Washington to matters of defense, foreign affairs, and regulation of interstate and international commerce. In theory he may have been on target, but in practice he failed to anticipate a slew of complex problems that could not be relegated simply to one box (federal responsibility) or the other (states' rights). The problem came to a head over a moral issue—slavery—and has recurred time and again, particularly in relation to other issues of human rights and, more recently, to environmental questions (for example, we are now agreed that no state has the right to pollute air that blows over neighboring territory). In fact, there has been a steady erosion of the power of the states, particularly in areas of fundamental moral principle. Until recently Americans had cherished the belief that setting educational policy was a state's right. Yet former President George Bush—an unapologetic opponent of centralization—argued that the education of the nation's youth is of such overarching importance that it cannot be left solely to the discretion of the states. Significantly, his solution to the problem was a classic example of federalist thinking: The national government will set performance standards, and the states and localities will be free to find the most effective ways and means of achieving those standards. This is a specific illustration of federalism's most basic playing rule: The central authority establishes the why and the what; the units are responsible for the how.

Significantly, it is this principle that has been violated, until recently, by almost every business corporation that has attempted to become a confederation. It was this "principle of coordination without losing the advantages of decentralization" that Alfred Sloan attempted, and failed, to define for GM in his classic 1921 "concept of the organization" study.[2] Some years later, in 1963, Sloan admitted he was "amused to see" that, in trying to simultaneously achieve coordination and specialization, his "language was contradictory." While

Sloan never abandoned his wish to resolve his corporate version of the Iceland Dilemma, in practice there was a steady erosion of "states' rights" at General Motors almost from the day he unveiled his federalist structure for the corporation.

In fact, Sloan, his colleagues, and their many generations of successors were never comfortable with the leadership style required for federalism to work. The system requires several things of those in central authority: faith in the power of people to solve their problems locally; willingness to forgo the satisfaction of exercising command and control; and understanding that, in complex systems and turbulent times, no one individual or group possesses enough knowledge to manage the jobs of everyone else in the organization. Sloan—and tens of thousands of managers around the world who were to become his disciples by way of the business school gospel of "specialization/differentiation" cases—was never comfortable with such basic assumptions about organizations and leadership. Indeed, the most famous practitioner of going-through-the-motions federalism was Harold Geneen, who had the form of confederation down pat at IT&T but lacked the essential "feel" for the technology of collaboration to make the system function entrepreneurially.

Therefore, in spite of the rhetoric of decentralization, neither GM nor IT&T (nor the countless giant corporations modeled after them) was ever a true confederation. At least not until the unprecedented turbulence of the late 1980s began to force corporate executives to reinvent Mr. Madison's (and Mr. Sloan's) marvelous notion . . . this time with feeling.

## Resolving the Big-Company versus-Small-Company Dilemma

Here's the circuitous path by which corporate America has finally arrived at federalism: Historically, America has been the land of the entrepreneur. In no other country have entrepreneurs been revered in legend the way they have been in the United States. Until midcentury the mythical Horatio Alger and the historical Henry Ford were genuine heroes (almost like Napoléon in France or Lenin in the Soviet Union). But by the end of World War II, the entrepreneur was an endangered species in this country. In the years immediately following the war, so-called organization men—the risk-averse children of the Great Depression—had little interest in chancy careers in the corporations they dominated. Surveying the structure of industry two decades after the war, the renowned Harvard economist John Kenneth Galbraith declared entrepreneurialism to be an anachronism and hailed the apotheosis of professional managerialism and giantism. "The planning system" (as he called the industrial form emerging in the 1960s) was to be dominated by a few monolithic corporations working in close concert with government ministries.[3] No longer would dozens of small firms compete within a given industry or for a given market. In Galbraith's brave new world, it would be USA, Inc. versus Japan, Inc. versus Germany, Inc. (or, more specifically, General Motors versus Toyota versus Volkswagen).

In fact, Galbraith was almost proved right: In the 1960s and 1970s, the big did get bigger and the number of competitors was reduced. For example, in the jet engine industry there were just three giants: GE, Pratt and Whitney, and Rolls-Royce—the first two of which built the largest factories in the Western world in pursuit of the holy grail of economies of scale. Similarly, by 1970 most major U.S. industries were dominated by one or two mammoth firms: GM (autos), U.S. Steel (metals), IBM (computers), Exxon (oil), Bank of America (finance), and Sears (retailing). In Europe the pattern was even more pronounced: The Italian government gobbled up scores of small companies and conglomerated them into giant, state-owned groups; in Britain nearly the entire auto industry was amalgamated into one giant firm. This "New Industrial State" was the right way to go, according to Galbraith—and most Europeans believed him: Witness Jean-Jacques Servan Schreiber's *Le Défi Américain.*

Everyone knows what happened next: Within a decade GM had been badly embarrassed not only by smaller Ford and Chrysler but also by a passel of even smaller Japanese and German firms; U.S. Steel was being chopped up by minimills; IBM had literally hundreds of smaller competitors; Exxon's megalomania had led it to acquire a bushel of small, successful, high-tech companies—and then to micromanage them into failures; and both Bank of America and Sears were being niched to death by, respectively, financial boutiques and numerous small competitors in the retailing industry. Thus, by the mid-1990s the entrepreneur was not only back from the brink of extinction; he (and now, she) was said to be in ascendancy. In the Reagan era the giant corporation seemed destined to the fate of the brontosaurus, and George Gilder was crowing (while Galbraith was eating crow).[4]

While there can be no doubt that the 1980s belonged to the entrepreneur, Mark Twain's oft-quoted line "News of my death has been greatly exaggerated" may be finding a parallel in the life cycle of large corporations. Today it seems wildly premature to join Gilder in assigning big business to the ash heap of history. This is not to defend the past behavior of the many complacent industrial giants who squandered America's precious assets in the 1960s and 1970s—their self-defeating human resources policies, suicidal customer relations, misguided planning, and faulty financial assumptions are beyond rational defense. Yet there is no evidence to suggest that the current denizens of the Fortune 500 are collectively about to go out of business—not next week, not next year, not in the next decade (and not even in the next century). There are several reasons that large corporations continue to survive—and it behooves the enthusiasts of small business to keep these in mind:

*Some Inherent Advantages of Large Corporations*
- They possess economies of scale in finance, purchasing, distribution, advertising, service, R&D (and, arguably, manufacturing).

- They are able to undertake *global* marketing.
- They have resources to protect themselves against cross-subsidization (dumping).
- They are able to maintain a large, diverse bank of skilled people (which allows them to invest in lengthy training for future assignments and to survive the loss of key individuals).
- They possess the organizational wherewithal and managerial know-how to bring more than one project at a time from the idea stage to full development.
- They provide key employees with a relatively high level of security and financial benefits.
- They are able to undertake the long-term planning and commitment of resources needed for giant, capital-intensive products (for example, a jet airplane).
- They have social clout with government and unions.
- They can afford to undertake basic research and to make slow, costly, incremental improvements in process technology.
- They have stability because they can afford to be integrated backward (to suppliers) and forward (to dealers).
- They tend to be diversified and hence less susceptible to vagaries of the economic cycle (and less vulnerable if one or two key products fail).

While such stability, security, predictability, synergy, and discipline are at best theoretical advantages of large business, sufficient examples can be supplied to support most of these claims. After all, what small firm would not want to have the financial, service, marketing, distribution, purchasing, and R&D punch of an IBM? Especially—and this is the key point—if those benefits of size could come without the *dis*benefits of bureaucracy.

Which brings us conveniently to the advantages of small- and medium-size businesses. Because there are so many static mom-and-pop firms that cannot serve as models of eminence, we have in mind here the characteristics of the fastest-growing entrepreneurial businesses cited recently by *Inc.* magazine:

*Some Inherent Advantages of Small Firms*

• They tend to be lean, agile, dynamic, and flexible (non-bureaucratic).

• They are close to their customers and thus sensitive to (and fast to react to) shifts in market demand.

• They are run by managers who often are owners and are therefore highly motivated by their equity positions.

• From top to bottom, nearly everyone in the company has direct, ongoing personal knowledge of most aspects of the business.

• Their employees are motivated by the human scale of the organization, by peer pressure, and by knowledge of how their roles contribute to overall company performance.

• They have excellent upward, downward, and lateral communications.

• They attract the most creative, energetic and risk-taking individuals (indeed, there is a "brain drain" from large to small companies).

• They have a focused orientation on a single product or related line of products.

• They have short production runs and can thus customize products and keep a constant watch on quality.

## The Big Mimic the Small

These impressive advantages are in fact the very characteristics of small firms that almost all large corporations today are attempting to capture through frantic attempts to alter their "corporate cultures." In order to "get close to customers," to "become people-oriented," and to "focus on quality," giant corporations around the world are experimenting with intrapreneuring, gain-sharing, team approaches, spin-offs, product-line focusing, specializing, downsizing, dis-integrating, subcontracting, and decentralizing—in effect, emulating what small companies do naturally.

Hence, in this paradoxical world we are faced with yet another fine irony: While entrepreneurs are trying to capture the advantages of large firms, managers of large corporations are at the same time attempting to behave like entrepreneurs! Therefore, it would seem as misguided today to speak of the decline of large organizations as it proved inaccurate twenty years earlier to speak of the fall of entrepreneurs. While smallness is *usually* more beautiful, bigness is simply a fact of life in a world where three billion people are increasingly linked by common technologies and markets.

It may be useful to think about this issue by way of analogy: Is the mega University of California going to give way to competition from hundreds of small colleges? Is the unitary government of France going to devolve all its power to the country's myriad *départements?* Is Boeing soon to give way to small-scale manufacturers of jumbo jets? While a reasonable answer to each of these questions is no, the most likely scenario is that the structures of giant universities, central governments, and colossal corporations will change to forms beyond our current ability to envision. Although we can't imagine exactly what these new structures will look like, it nonetheless seems reasonable to expect that almost all organizations that survive and thrive in the future will possess the best characteristics of today's big *and* small successes. That is why in so many well-led large organizations efforts are being made to overcome *dis*economies of scale by creating dozens of small, independent, manageable units.

## The Small Mimic the Big

While the giants attempt to avoid extinction by imitating the behavior of fast-moving small companies, the parallel challenge for entrepreneurs in coming years is to build global markets by capturing the advantages of gargantuan firms. Fortunately, meeting this challenge will be facilitated by emerging, computer-based technologies of production and distribution. Newly developed manufacturing tools give small companies the advantages of mass production while at the same time allowing them to customize products economically. New telecommunications technologies provide access to distant and specialized markets that were formerly out of reach for all but giant firms with global distribution networks. Sophisticated data bases provide even the smallest companies with marketing information that just yesterday was affordable only to the largest. And all this technology is currently available. At present American fabric and apparel manufacturers are linked by computer to hundreds of retailers, thus giving increased purchasing power to the small firms and faster inventory information to the manufacturers, all of which factors permit U.S. companies to use technology to help overcome Asia's competitive wage advantage.

By fine-tuning the federal strategy by which the small, semiautonomous American states combined and cooperated in order to gain the advantages of a large nation, small businesses around the world are creating networks, partnerships, consortia, and federations—all designed to give them the functional equivalent of bigness. The best-known company pursuing a federal strategy is Benetton, where finance, R&D, design, purchasing, and planning are centralized, while the activities of manufacturing and retailing are dispersed. The company is a unique confederation of hundreds of small, manager-owned manufacturers and franchised retailers all linked together by computer to form the United States of Benetton. Like Benetton, such companies as Nike and The Limited also have learned that it is better to achieve the benefits of forward and backward integration through confederation rather than through acquisition.

Importantly there is no single model of confederation. As Rosabeth Moss Kanter was the first to observe, companies around the word are "becoming PALs: Pooling, Allying and Linking" across corporate and national boundaries.[5] Small companies in particular are inventing all manner of joint ventures, subcontracting, franchising, R&D consortia, and strategic partnerships. These are taking the form of cooperation between customers and suppliers between domestic and foreign entities, between large and small organizations—and even among competitors: After all, entrepreneurs are willing to do whatever it takes in order to combine the advantages of big and small. Some examples: Small record and book publishers (and film producers) use the services of large distributors to gain economies of scale in marketing; small airlines form consortia to buy jet aircraft from brokers in order to gain economies of scale in purchasing; small "hollow" corporation design furniture, contract to have it made in Third World countries, and then wholesale it to large department stores in Europe and America (or market their products themselves-within-stores). As our colleague Jay Galbraith explains, the common thread in each of these examples is that small companies "buy the power of bigness"—that is, they have someone else provide the scale in marketing, purchasing, financing or manufacturing that is uneconomical for the small company to attempt itself.

The federal form has applications not only for manufacturing and retailing but for service industries as well. American Airline's SABRE system uses high technology to link the world-wide fortunes of numerous large and small competitors in the airline industry. In the United States nearly every service from real estate to plumbing has been successfully franchised, and international professional services firms like Arthur Andersen are in fact prime examples of the federal system. And Coca-Cola, with its global network of franchised bottlers and distributors, is the longest-standing—and most successful—example of the advantages of confederation.

## Federalism as a Revitalization Strategy

Of more recent origin—and less conventional structure—is the confederation ABB, which employs more people around the world than live in the entire country of Iceland. Although some components of the company are over a hundred years old, ABB's CEO, Percy Barnevik, has demonstrated the validity of federalism as a strategy to revitalize old-line manufacturing firms for competition in today's world markets. Barnevik explains that ABB "is a company with no geographic center, no national ax to grind. We are a federation of national companies with a global communications center."[6] Barnevik is not worried by the contradictions that led Sloan to abandon federalism: "ABB is an organization with three internal contradictions. We want to be global and local, big and small, radically decentralized with centralized reporting and control."

The managerial secret that allows ABB to turn these contradictions into what Barnevik calls "real organizational advantage" is federalism with a vengeance. ABB's operations are divided "into nearly 1,200 companies, with an average of 200 employees. These companies are divided into 4,500 profit centers with an average of 50 employees." With only 100 professionals in its Zurich headquarters, the company is not unified by the efforts of an all-powerful central staff à la GM. Rather, this *non*centralized confederation of semiautonomous units is held together by a common vision of globalism, excellence, and clearly enunciated responsibilities for performance. What is the role of central headquarters? "To operate as lean as is humanly possible," says Barnevik. And the role of leadership? To give managers "well-defined sets of responsibilities, clear accountability, and maximum degrees of freedom to execute."

## The Leadership Imperative

The sharpest image of the new federal leader that comes to mind is that of Coca-Cola's Roberto Goizueta at a recent meeting of the company's bottlers and distributors, where he was observed to implore those fiercely independent folks at least *three* times in *one* speech to "please paint your trucks red." How's that? In the year in which he earned some $80 million, the CEO of Coca-Cola had to plead with "his troops" to adhere to standards of corporate conformity? Clearly, something new is going on here. And that "something" is that leaders of federations don't think of their associates as troops—and the associates don't think of their leaders as generals.

Like ABB's, Coca-Cola's federalism is effective in a way that Sloan could never have imagined, because of a factor that emerged nearly three decades after the GM chief's death: a new concept of leadership. Sloan was a brilliant leader of GM, but therein lay the fatal flaw in his attempts to install federalism: Sloan was also the *only* leader at GM. In sharp contrast, the new leaders of the emerging federal corporations are *leaders of leaders* who, like Percy Barnevik and Roberto Goizueta, are willingly followed by other leaders who have subscribed to their "vision."

In the 1980s it became commonplace to regard the new leader as one who has the ability to generate a compelling, moving, and unifying vision. This means the ability to establish a climate and structure that give all members of the organization a clear sense of what they are doing and why. What has not been fully appreciated about "the vision thing" is that the purpose of a clearly communicated vision is to give meaning and alignment to the organization and thus to enhance the ability of *all* employees to make decisions and create change. The new leader does not make all decisions herself; rather, she removes the obstacles that prevent her followers from making effective decisions *themselves.* Thus, not only is the standard military leadership metaphor of generals and troops wrong; so is the classical peacetime metaphor of shepherds and sheep. The new leaders are no more shepherds than their followers are sheep. A more fitting metaphor is Schumacher's balloon man—now, a woman—who holds a fistful of strings attached to countless units, each tugging away because it is filled with the helium of entrepreneurial spirit.

Indeed, when we describe the emerging leadership relationship in today's federal organizations we come closest when we speak of *leaders of leaders.* In these organizations senior leaders are followed willingly by other leaders by virtue of the formers' vision, integrity, and courage (and not just by the organizational equivalent of a yank of the crook or the nipping of a sheepdog at the heels). Importantly, because people at *all* levels are leaders in their own right, there is little of the resistance to change that characterizes the middle ranks of most hierarchical organizations headed by a single commander in chief and staffed by layers of resentful sheep. In the emerging leadership relationship, it is far from easy for the outsider to identify *the* leader. As the chairman of Herman Miller, Inc., Max De Pree, explains, "The signs of outstanding leadership appear primarily among the followers. Are the followers reaching their potential? Are they learning? Serving? Do they achieve the desired results? Do they change with grace? Manage conflict?"[7] If so, the organization is blessed with an outstanding leader of leaders.

In the successful federal organization, a central—perhaps *the* central—task of the leader of leaders thus becomes the development of other leaders. At Dayton-Hudson Kenneth Macke spends about half of his time on the career development of the firm's top one hundred managers. With forty-five hundred employees in potential leadership positions, Percy Barnevik's job becomes one of creating the conditions in which all those people can succeed in their jobs. In effect, federalism provides a structural skeleton for the rhetorical goal of "empowerment." Thus, federalism does not obviate the need for leadership; instead, it focuses and redefines the task of the leader. The success of the current president of the European Commission of the EC, Jacques Delors, illustrates the necessity of federal leadership characterized by the provision of inspiring vision—coupled with the identification, nurturing, and development of future leaders empowered to carry out that vision.

Ultimately federalism may also pave the path toward more democratic organizations. When we ask, "Is democracy inevitable?" the answer is a more resounding and immediate

"Yes" in federal systems. For as Jefferson and Madison recognized, democracy is more natural in smaller units and less wieldy in large, unitary states. Lest this federalism sound like softheaded, "touchy-feely" management, it is worth noting that George Will has called for a marked return to federalism in the American system of government: "That is the future—congressional ascendancy and vigorous federalism. We can live with that. The Founders said we should."

## "A Pretty Good Alliance"

In essence federalism allows nations and corporations to have their organizational cake and eat it too. Given proper leadership, the New Federalism—whether in the guise of ABB or the EC—illustrates that it is possible to pursue innovation, self-governance, and autonomy, while at the same time enjoying the advantages of effective coordination, economies of scale, and the protection of cherished freedoms that only pluralism can provide. From a business perspective federalism erases the false "big-versus-small" dichotomy that has for too long preoccupied those engaged in debate about the essential traits needed for international competitiveness, much as it points the way toward variations on the theme of confederation that could lead to truly effective performance in the global economy.

Finally, we can imagine a time when corporations such as ABB—which are simultaneously global and deeply rooted in local cultures—serve as models for nations that aspire both to national self-expression and to survival in the world economy. These new confederations could resolve the Iceland Dilemma, and the only cost would be the loss of the jingoistic rhetoric of which national mottoes and state anthems have traditionally been composed. The slogans of the federations of the future probably won't be as stirring as the national slogans of the past. It is true that "My federation, a pretty good alliance" doesn't have the ring of "My country, right or wrong." But a world of overlapping and interwoven corporate and national federations would be a far better place in which to work and live.

## Notes

1. James Madison, "Federalist Paper #10."

2. Alfred E. Sloan, *My Years with General Motors* (New York, Doubleday Anchor, 1972).

3. John Kenneth Galbraith, *The New Industrial State* (Boston: Houghton-Mifflin, 1967).

4. George Gilder, *Wealth and Poverty* (New York: Bantam Books, 1982).

5. Rosabeth Moss Kanter, *When Giants Learn to Dance* (New York: Simon and Schuster, 1989).

6. William Taylor, "The Logic of Global Business: An Interview with ABB's Percy Barnevik," *Harvard Business Review*, March–April 1991.

7. Max De Pree, *Leadership is an Art* (New York: Doubleday, 1989).

# 12

## *The Secrets of Great Groups*

*Thomas Carlyle wrote that history's course is bent by the will of "The Great Man," the able and dedicated individual who stands above his (and, we should correct him by adding, "her") peers. Leo Tolstoy supposed that rulers and generals are merely slaves of historical forces. Perhaps both miss the mark. Over the course of my career, I've been astounded to discover the extent to which our world has in fact been the product of "Great Groups," teams of creative persons who banded together to achieve remarkable successes that would not have been possible through a traditional hierarchical approach. This article summarizes what I've learned about the style of leadership necessary to allow a Great Group to flourish.*

Personal leadership is one of the most studied topics in American life. Indeed, I have devoted a big chunk of my professional life to better understanding its workings. Far less studied—and perhaps more important—is *group* leadership. The disparity of interest in those two realms of leadership is logical, given the strong individualist bent of American culture. But the more I look at the history of business, government, the arts, and the sciences, the clearer it is that few great accomplishments are ever the work of a single individual.

Our mythology refuses to catch up with our reality. And so we cling to the myth of the Lone Ranger, the romantic idea that great things are usually accomplished by a larger-than-life individual working alone. Despite the evidence to the contrary—including the fact that Michelangelo worked with a group of 16 to paint the ceiling of the Sistine Chapel—we still tend to think of achievement in terms of the Great Man or the Great Woman, instead of the Great Group.

As they say, "None of us is as smart as all of us." That's good, because the problems we face are too complex to be solved by any one person or any one discipline. Our only chance is to bring people together from a variety of backgrounds and disciplines who can refract a problem through the prism of complementary minds allied in common purpose. I call such collections of talent *Great Groups*. The genius of Great Groups is that they get remarkable people—strong individual achievers—to work together to get results. But these groups serve a second and equally important function: they provide psychic support and personal fellowship. They help generate courage. Without a sounding board for outrageous ideas, without personal encouragement and perspective when we hit a roadblock, we'd all lose our way.

## The Myths of Leadership

Great Groups teach us something about effective leadership, meaningful missions, and inspired recruiting. They challenge not only the myth of the Great Man, but also the 1950s myth of the Organization Man—the sallow figure in the gray flannel suit, giving his life to the job and conforming to its mindless dictates.

Neither myth is a productive model for behavior, and neither holds up to current reality. In fact, I believe, behind every Great Man is a Great Group, an effective partnership. And making up every Great Group is a unique construct of strong, often eccentric individuals. So the question for organizations is, How do you get talented, self-absorbed, often arrogant, incredibly bright people to work together?

The impetus for my current work in groups was a meeting more than 40 years ago with anthropologist Margaret Mead. I had heard her speak at Harvard, and afterward I asked her whether anyone had ever studied groups whose ideas were powerful enough to change the world. She looked at me and said, "Young man, you should write a book on that topic and call it Sapiential Circles." I gasped, and she went on to explain that *sapiential circles* meant knowledge-generating groups. Like a lot of good ideas, it took a while to gestate, but over the years the power of groups became a recurrent theme for me. Recently, work by leading thinkers like Michael Shrage in the nature of technology and collaboration, Hal Leavitt and Jean Lipman-Blumen in *Hot Groups,* and Richard Hackman in the remarkable Orpheus Chamber Orchestra highlights the significance of this inquiry.

To see what makes Great Groups tick, I studied some of the most noteworthy of our time, including the Manhattan Project, the paradigmatic Great Group that invented the atomic bomb; the computer revolutionaries at Xerox's Palo Alto Research Center (PARC) and at Apple Computer, whose work led to the Macintosh and other technical breakthroughs; the Lockheed Skunk Works, which pioneered the fast, efficient development of top-secret aircraft; and the Walt Disney Studio animators. Every Great Group is extraordinary in its own way, but my study suggests 10 principles common to all—and that apply as well to their larger organizations.

- *At the heart of every Great Group is a shared dream.* All Great Groups believe that they are on a mission from God, that they could change the world, make a dent in the universe. They are obsessed with their work. It becomes not a job but a fervent quest. That belief is what brings the necessary cohesion and energy to their work.

- *They manage conflict by abandoning individual egos to the pursuit of the dream.* At a critical point in the Manhattan Project, George Kistiakowsky, a great chemist who later served as Dwight Eisenhower's chief scientific advisor, threatened to quit because he couldn't get along with a colleague. Project leader Robert Oppenheimer simply said, "George, how can you leave this project? The free world hangs in the balance." So conflict, even with these diverse people, is resolved by reminding people of the mission.

- *They are protected from the "suits."* All Great Groups seem to have disdain for their corporate overseers and all are protected from them by a leader—not necessarily the leader who defines the dream. In the Manhattan Project, for instance, General Leslie Grove kept the Pentagon brass happy and away, while Oppenheimer kept the group focused on its mission. At Xerox PARC, Bob Taylor kept the honchos in Connecticut (referred to by the group as "toner heads") at bay *and* kept the group focused. Kelly Johnson got himself appointed to the board of Lockheed to help protect his Skunk Works. In all cases, physical distance from headquarters helped.

- *They have a real or invented enemy.* Even the most noble mission can be helped by an onerous opponent. That was literally true with the Manhattan Project, which had real enemies—the Japanese and the Nazis. Yet most organizations have an implicit mission to destroy an adversary, and that is often more motivating than their explicit mission. During their greatest years, for instance, Apple Computer's implicit mission was, Bury IBM. (The famous 1984 Macintosh TV commercial included the line, "Don't buy a computer you can't lift.") The decline of Apple follows the subsequent softening of their mission.

- *They view themselves as winning underdogs.* World-changing groups are usually populated by mavericks, people at the periphery of their disciplines. These groups do not regard the mainstream as the sacred Ganges. The sense of operating on the fringes gives them a don't-count-me-out scrappiness that feeds their obsession.

- *Members pay a personal price.* Membership in a Great Group isn't a day job; it is a night and day job. Divorces, affairs, and other severe emotional fallout are typical, especially when a project ends. At the Skunk Works, for example, people couldn't even tell their families what they were working on. They were located in a cheerless, rundown building in Burbank, of all places, far from Lockheed's corporate headquarters and main plants. So groups strike a Faustian bargain for the intensity and energy that they generate.

- *Great Groups make strong leaders.* On one hand, they're all nonhierarchical, open, and very egalitarian. Yet they all have strong leaders. That's the paradox of group leadership. You cannot have a great leader without a Great Group—and vice versa. In an important way, these groups made the leaders great. The leaders I studied were seldom the brightest or best in the group, but neither were they passive players. They were connoisseurs of talent, more like curators than creators.

- *Great Groups are the product of meticulous recruiting.* It took Oppenheimer to get a Kistiakowsky and a Niels Bohr to come to his godforsaken outpost in the desert. Cherrypicking the right talent for a group means knowing what you need and being able to spot it in others. It also means understanding the chemistry of a group. Candidates are often grilled, almost hazed, by other members of the group and its leader. You see the same thing in great coaches. They can place the right people in the right role. And get the right constellations and configurations within the group.

- *Great Groups are usually young.* The average age of the physicists at Los Alamos was about 25. Oppenheimer—"the old man"—was in his 30s. Youth provides the physical stamina demanded by these groups. But Great Groups are also young in their spirit, ethos, and culture. Most important, because they're young and naive, group members don't know what's supposed to be impossible, which gives them the ability to do the impossible. As Berlioz said about Saint-Saens, "He knows everything; all he lacks is inexperience." Great Groups don't lack the experience of possibilities.

- *Real artists ship.* Steve Jobs constantly reminded his band of Apple renegades that their work meant nothing unless they brought a great product to market. In the end, Great Groups have to produce a tangible outcome external to themselves. Most dissolve after the product is delivered; but without something to show for their efforts, the most talented assemblage becomes little more than a social club or a therapy group.

## New Rules for Leaders

These principles not only define the nature of Great Groups, they also redefine the roles and responsibilities of leaders. Group leaders vary widely in style and personality. Some are facilitators, some doers, some contrarians. However, leadership is inevitably dispersed, sometimes in formal rotation, more often with people playing ad hoc leadership roles at different points.

Furthermore, the formal leaders, even when delegating authority, are catalytic *completers;* they take on roles that nobody else plays—cajoler, taskmaster, protector, or doer—and that are needed for the group to achieve its goal. They intuitively understand the chemistry of the group and the dynamics of the work process. They encourage dissent and diversity in the pursuit of a shared vision and understand the difference between healthy, creative dissent and self-serving obstructionism. They are able to discern what different people need at different times.

In short, despite their differences in style, the leaders of Great Groups share four behavioral traits. Without exception, the leaders of Great Groups:

• *Provide direction and meaning.* They remind people of what's important and why their work makes a difference.

• *Generate and sustain trust.* The group's trust in itself—and its leadership—allows members to accept dissent and ride through the turbulence of the group process.

• *Display a bias toward action, risk taking, and curiosity.* A sense of urgency—and a willingness to risk failure to achieve results—is at the heart of every Great Group.

• *Are purveyors of hope.* Effective team leaders find both tangible and symbolic ways to demonstrate that the group can overcome the odds.

There's no simple recipe for developing these skills; group leadership is far more an art than a science. But we can start by rethinking our notion of what collaboration means and how it is achieved. Our management training and educational institutions need to focus on group development as well as individual development. Universities, for instance, rarely allow group Ph.D. theses or rewards for joint authorship. Corporations usually reward individual rather than group achievement, even as leaders call for greater teamwork and partnership.

## Power of the Mission

It's no accident that topping both lists—the principles of Great Groups and the traits of group leaders—is the power of the mission. All great teams—and all great organizations— are built around a shared dream or motivating purpose. Yet organizations' mission statements often lack real meaning and resonance. Realistically, your team need not believe that it is literally saving the world, as the Manhattan Project did; it is enough to feel it is helping people in need or battling a tough competitor. Simply punching a time clock doesn't do it.

Articulating a meaningful mission is the job of leaders at every level—and it's not an easy task. In Shakespeare's *Henry IV, Part 1,* Glendower, the Welsh seer, boasts to Hotspur that he can "call spirits from the vasty deep," and Hotspur retorts, so can I, so can anybody—"but will they come when you do call for them?" That is the test of inspiring leadership.

I learned firsthand how critical a sense of mission—or its absence—can be to an employer. Several years ago, I had an assistant who handled the arrangements for my speeches and travel; at night she did volunteer work for a nonprofit, self-help organization. Her work for me was acceptable but perfunctory. It was clear that she was much more involved and committed to her unpaid work. Frankly, I was jealous. I came to resent the fact that I was not getting her best efforts; after all, I was paying her and they weren't. We talked about it, and she was very honest about the fact that it was her volunteer work that had real meaning for her; there she felt she was making a difference. So you can't expect every employee to be zealously committed to your cause. But you can accept the fact that part of the responsibility for uninspired work lies with the leader.

Great Groups remind us how much we can really accomplish working toward a shared purpose. To be sure, Great Groups rely on many long-established practices of good management—effective communication, exceptional recruitment, genuine empowerment, personal commitment. But they also remind us of author Luciano de Crescanzo's observation that "we are all angels with only one wing; we can only fly while embracing one another." In the end, these groups cannot be managed, only led in flight.

# 13

## The End of Leadership

*Am I perhaps exaggerating when I speak of "the end of leadership"? Actually, I would say not. But like a phoenix, a new and adaptive form of leadership is rising from the ashes wherever the old form has breathed its last. The cold, hard evidence is that organizations still using the "TOPdown" management approach won't survive much longer. This article offers some insights into what "the New Leadership," the successor to TOPdown leadership, will look like.*

I've never fully approved of formal debates. The very premise of a debate, where issues are egregiously over-simplified, can't help but lose the subtlely nuanced distinctions we academics relish and thrive on. So when I was asked not long ago to participate in this kind of foolishness, I was naturally resistant to participate. Especially when the "resolution before the house" was phrased as follows: "All successful organizational change must originate at the top." To make matters worse, the organizers of the debate insisted that I take the opposite position of the "resolution of the house," casting me "against type," so to speak. I would have felt far more comfortable being on the side of strong leadership, a position more compatible with most of my recent writing. I did agree, however, despite my strong reservations primarily because the organizers were colleagues and I wanted an expense paid trip to the East Coast. In accepting, I was reminded of an old *New Yorker* cartoon showing Charles Dickens in his publisher's office, being told rather sternly by his editor: "Well, Mr. Dickens, it's either the best of times OR the worst of times. It can't be both."

What I discovered was that getting impaled on the horns of a false dichotomy was rather more fun than I anticipated. More importantly in preparing for the debate, I arrived at an unexpected conclusion, close to an epiphanic event. I came to the unmistakable realization that TOPdown leadership was not only wrong, unrealistic and maladaptive but also, given the report of history, dangerous. And given certain changes taking place in the organizational landscape, this obsolete form of leadership will erode competitive advantage and destroy the aspirations of any organization that aims to be in the phone book beyond the year 2002.

*I think it is now possible to talk about the end of leadership without the risk of hyperbole.* Some of this change is organic and inevitable. But much of it is the legacy of our times ignited by that dynamic duo: globalization and relentlessly disruptive technology.

## The Encompassing Tendency

The idea of traditional TOPdown leadership is based on the myth of the triumphant individual. It is a myth deeply ingrained in the American psyche and unfortunately fostered and celebrated in the daily press, business magazines, and much of academic and popular writing. My own work, at times, has also suffered from this deification of the icons of American business: the Welches, the Barneviks, the Gateses—fill in your own hero. Whether it is midnight rider Paul Revere or basketball's Michael Jordan or, more recently, Mark McGwire, we are a nation enamored of heroes—rugged self-starters who meet challenges and overcome adversity. Our contemporary views of leadership are entwined with our notions of heroism, so much so that the distinction between "leader" and "hero" (or "celebrity," for that matter) often becomes blurred.

In our society leadership is too often seen as an inherently individual phenomenon. It's Oprah and Michael (Jordan or Eisner) and Bill (Clinton or Gates) and Larry and Hillary and

Monica. We are all victims or witnesses to what Leo Braudy calls the "frenzy of renown," the "peoplification" of society. Think of it: Can you imagine a best-selling magazine as popular as PEOPLE called SYSTEM?

And yet we do understand the significance of systems. After all, it is systems that encourage collaboration and systems which makes change not only effective but possible. A shrinking world in which technological and political complexity increase at an accelerating rate offers fewer and fewer arenas in which individual action, TOPdown leadership, suffices. And here is the troubling disconnect. Despite the rhetoric of collaboration, we continue to live in a "by-line" culture where recognition and status are conferred on individuals, not *teams of people* who make change possible.

But even as the lone hero continues to gallop through our imaginations, shattering obstacles with silver bullets, leaping tall buildings in a single bound, we know that that's a falsely lulling fantasy and that is not the way real change, enduring change, takes place. We know there is an alternative reality.

What's surprising is that this should surprise us. In a society as complex and technologically sophisticated as ours, the most urgent projects require the coordinated contributions of many talented people working together. Whether the task is building a global business or discovering the mysteries of the human brain, it doesn't happen at the top; TOPdown leadership can't hope to accomplish it, however gifted the person at the TOP is. There are simply too many problems to be identified and solved, too many connections to be made. So we cling to the myth of the Lone Ranger that great things are accomplished by a larger-than-life individual shouting commands, giving direction, inspiring the troops, sounding the tocsin, decreeing the compelling vision, leading the way and changing paradigms with brio and shimmer.

This *encompassing tendency* is dysfunctional in today's world of blurring, spastic, hyper-turbulent change, and will get us into unspeakable troubles unless we understand that the search engine, the main stem winder for effective change is the workforce and their creative alliance with top leadership.

A personal case in point. My colleague, David Heenan and I, wrote a book about the role of Number Twos in organizations, how they work and don't work. We thought it an original idea, one that was significant and astonishingly neglected in the literature. We entitled the book "Second Banana" and had chapters on some of the most famous and successful partnerships between Ones and Twos in corporate life; for example, the fabled relationship between Warren Buffet and his Number Two, Charles Munger, known for containing Buffet's enthusiasm about investments and referred to by Buffet as the "Abominable No Man." And there was a chapter called Banana Splits, on infamously unsuccessful partnerships such as the widely publicized split between Michael Eisner and Michael Ovitz. All twelve of the publishers who reviewed the book declined. One put it rather nicely. He said, "Warren, no one in America wants to be Number Two." He also quoted Leonard Bernstein who once proclaimed that "The hardest instrument to play in a symphony orchestra is second fiddle."

So David and I changed the title to *Co-Leaders* and added a subtitle, *The Power of Great Partnerships*. With that new title and a shift in emphasis away from being Number Two, it was published this year by John Wiley.

I give this example not to plug the book but to illustrate the power of this encompassing tendency of the Great Man which dominates our thinking and perverts our understanding of organizational life and how leading change really works.

## The Argument

I will present my argument in an unorthodox way by drawing on sources a little out of the ordinary for management scholars: examples and analogies from poetry, history and theater, as well as the more traditional sources of experimental studies and business anecdotes. I'll start with an excerpt from a poem by Berthold Brecht, the Marxist playwright.

## Questions from a Worker

Who built the town of Thebes of Seven Gates?
The names of kings are written in the books.
Was it the kings who dragged the slab of rock?
And Babylon, so many times destroyed,
Who built her up again so many times?

Young Alexander conquered India.
All by himself?
Caesar beat the Gauls.
Not even a cook to help him with his meals?
Philip of Spain wept aloud when his Armada
Went down. Did no one else weep?
Frederick the Great won the Seven Years War. Who
Else was the winner?

On every page a triumph.
Who baked the victory cake?

In ever decade a great man. Who picked up the check?

So many reports.
So many questions.

"In every decade a great man." That encompassing tendency again. And it shows up throughout history. In Plutarch's great biography of Cato the Elder, he wrote: "Rome showed itself to be truly great, and hence worthy of great leaders." What we tend to forget is that greatness lies within nations and organizations themselves as much, if not more, than their leaders. Could Gandhi achieve his greatness without staying close to the people representing their

greatness of spirit? So many questions. ... Now for a contemporary business example—I wrote an article in which I
quoted one of my favorite management philosophers, The
Great One, Wayne Gretzky, saying: "It's not where the puck
is, it's where the puck will be." Soon after I received a rather
sour letter from the Chairman and CEO of one of our largest
FORTUNE 100 companies who wrote: "I was particularly
interested in what you characterize as the Gretzky factor. I
think I know where the puck is going to be—the problem is,
we've got thousands and thousands of folk who don't want
the puck to go there, would rather that it wasn't going there,
and in the event that it is going there, aren't going to let us
position ourselves to meet it until after we've skated past. *In
plain English, we've got a bunch of people who want the world
to be the way it used to be—and are very disinclined to accept
any alternative forecast of the future.*" (Emphasis mine.)

Now what's interesting about this "leader" is that (a) he
was regarded as one of the most innovative and creative
CEOs in his industrial sector and (b) his unquestionable
"genius" was totally useless because he lacked a critical mass
of willing followers. And he had no followers because he was
unable to generate and sustain a minimum degree of trust
with his workforce, widely known to be resistant to and—no
exaggeration—*dyspeptic* with his pre-Copernican ego and
macho style.

If there is one generalization we make about leadership
and change, it is this: No change can occur without willing and
committed followers.

Let us turn now to social movements and how they are led
and mobilized. Mohammed Gandhi's singular American apos-
tle was Dr. Martin Luther King, Jr. who was introduced to his
teachings as a graduate student in Boston University's Divin-
ity School in the early 1950s. I had gone to college with
Coretta Scott and got acquainted with her future husband
while she attended the New England Conservatory of Music
and I was in graduate school at M.I.T. Recently, upon reading
John Lewis's book, *Walking with the Wind,* I recalled how
back then, light years ago, Coretta seemed the charismatic

one and Martin shy and bashful. Lewis, one of King's acolytes in the Civil Rights Movement of the '60s, now a Congressman from Atlanta and one of the most respected African-American leaders, tells us in his book how much of the movement was a team effort, a "band of brothers and sisters," and how Dr. King "often joined demonstrations late or ducked out early." (I should add that Lewis was and is a devoted admirer of King.) Gary Wills writes that "he tried to lift others up and found himself lifted up in the process. *He literally talked himself into useful kinds of trouble.* King's oratory urged others on to heroic tasks and where they went he had to follow. Reluctant to go to jail, he was shamed into going—after so many young people responded to his speeches and found themselves in danger." (Emphasis mine.)

Don't be misled here. I'm not just reiterating one of those well worn bromides about leadership; you know, where leaders carefully watch where their followers are going and then follow them. I'm saying something quite different. I'm saying that exemplary leadership and organizational change are impossible without the full inclusion, initiatives and cooperation of followers.

I mentioned earlier on that TOPdown leadership tendency is also *maladaptive* and I think it's time to return to that now. It's become something of a cliché to discuss the extraordinary complexity and ambiguity and uncertainties of our current business environment. As one of my CEO friends put it, "If you're not confused, you don't know what's going on." At the risk of oversimplifying his important work on leadership, Ron Heifetz asserts that with relatively simple, "technical problems," leadership is relatively "easy"; i.e. TOPdown leadership can solve them. But with "adaptive" problems, complex and messy problems, like dealing with a seriously ill cancer patient or cleaning up an ecological hazard, many stakeholders must be involved and mobilized. The truth is that adaptive problems require complex and diverse alliances. Decrees, orders, etc., *do not work.*

An elegant experiment dreamed up by one of the most imaginative, and least acknowledged social psychologists of his day, Alex Bavelas, dramatizes, if not proves, this point. Imagine a simple, wooden circular dining room table, about 10 feet in diameter with plywood partitions walling off the five participants from visible sight of each other. The table is constructed so that subjects can communicate only by passing messages written on 3 × 5 cards through narrow slots in the partitions. The cards are all color coded so that you can count how many messages were sent to whom and by whom. Also, the table was constructed so that different organizational forms can be simulated. For example, you can create a rough example of a typical bureaucratic, command-and-control organization by restricting the flow of messages to only one central person. We used three kinds of organizational models, the Wheel, which more or less resembles the typical organizational pyramid, the Chain, a slight modification of the Wheel and the Circle where everyone could communicate to the two participants adjacent to them. Not quite a completely connected network, but one of equality.

The problem to be solved was relatively simple. Each subject was given a pill box which contained six different colored marbles. They were what we used to called "purees," pure white, pure blue, pure green, red, etc., and easily identifiable. For each experimental trial, there was only one color that each subject had in common. On one trial, for example, it was the red, on another it was the green, and so on, randomly varied. There were 15 trials. As soon as the subject thought he had the correct color, he would drop the marble down a rubber tube in the table so that the experimenter could not only measure the accuracy for the group but also how long it took for all five subject to deposit the marble. Our predictions were not surprising and they were confirmed. The Wheel, the form most like the TOPdown leadership model was the most accurate and the most efficient; they were very, very quick. We did notice that in our post-experiment questionnaire, the central person reported having the highest morale and was wildly enthusiastic about his role while the other group members were, to be polite, pissed.

Expectable and not particular exciting results. So we decided to change the task to a more "adaptive" problem and substituted for the primary colors, the so-called "purees," ambiguously colored marbles: cat's eyes, ginger ale-ish, bluish-green or greenish blue, all sorts of dappled colored marbles. . . . Again, our predictions were confirmed. Now, under ambiguous and changing conditions, the Circle was the most efficient and accurate and all members claimed relatively high morale. On only one occasion, and we repeated this particular experiment about 50 times, did the Wheel perform better. In this one case, the central person was an exceptionally gifted artist and writer. She was also taking a minor in art history. Genius happens. Once in a blue moon.

The connection between that antidiluvian experiment and the messy, changing business environment barely needs stating. But it dramatically illustrates my point that none of us is as smart of all of us, that the TOPdown model, in the present business context, is dysfunctional, maladaptive and, as I'll get to now, dangerous.

The dangers of TOPdown leadership, vivid examples of colossal folly and disaster, are so numerous that one doesn't know where to begin. Stalin's communal farms? Niemeyer's Brasilia? Hitler's Holocaust? Chainsaw Al's Follies? Napoleon's Russian campaign? LBJ's VietNam? Mao's Cultural Revolution? Maggie Thatcher's poll tax? Perhaps the best source to turn to in this respect is Barbara Tuchman's *March of Folly,* an ignored treasure for students of organizational behavior.

She argues that folly occurs when a governmental leader pursues policies contrary to the self-interest of the nation. But to be real Folly, the policy must have been perceived as counter-productive *in its own time,* not merely by hindsight. Secondly, there are always feasible alternative means that were available. She takes her notion of folly and refracts it through the prism of four major epochal events: the Trojan Horse escorted through the gates of Troy, led innocently (and stupidly) by Priam's own warriors (who had heard from

Cassandra, among others, that it was probably a Greek ploy); the Renaissance Popes and how their actions brought about the Protestant Reformation; George III and the loss of the "colonies"; and LBJ and the Viet Nam War. Tuchman writes: "Wooden-headedness, the source of self-deception, is a factor that plays a remarkable role in individuals. It consists in assessing a situation in terms of preconceived fixed notions while ignoring or rejecting any contrary signs. It is acting according to wish while not allowing oneself to be deflected by the facts. It is epitomized in a historian's statement about Philip II of Spain, the surpassing wooden-head of all sovereigns: 'No experience of the failure of the policy could shake his belief in its essential excellence.'"

## The New Leadership

So where does all of this lead us in terms of the current organizational context? What should be clear by now is that post-bureaucratic organization requires a new kind of alliance between leaders and the led. Today's organizations are evolving into federations, networks, clusters, cross-functional teams, temporary systems, ad hoc task forces, lattices, modules, matrices—almost anything but pyramids with their obsolete TOPdown leadership. The new leader will encourage healthy dissent and values those followers courageous enough to say no. It will go to the leader who exults in cultural differences and knows that diversity is the best hope for long-term survival and success. The title of this article was deliberately provocative but, I hope, not too misleading. It's not quite the *end* of leadership, actually, but it clearly points the way to a new, far more subtle and indirect form of influence for leaders to be effective. The new reality is that intellectual capital, brain power, know-how, human imagination has supplanted capital as the critical success factor and leaders will have to learn an entirely new set of skills that are not understood, not taught in our business schools, and, for all of those reasons, rarely practiced. I am going to suggest that there are four competencies that will determine the success of New Leadership.

**1.** *The New Leader understands and practices the Power of Appreciation. They are connoisseurs of talent, more curators than creators.* We all pay lip service to acknowledgement and appreciation. To generalize just a tad, most organizations are woefully neglectful of bestowing either. And it is one of the most powerful motivators, especially for knowledge workers. To take only one example out of numberless cases, many years ago, I sent my first book to the Dean and, in turn, received a perfunctory, dictated note saying that he would take the book on his next plane trip and read it then. That was it. That was the last word I ever heard from him about something I had spent over three years working on. Not very motivating or energizing, to say the least.

What I'm also getting at is that the leader is rarely the best or the brightest in the new organizations. The New Leader has a smell for talent, an imaginative rolodex, unafraid of hiring people better than they are and are often more a curator than a creator. In my book, *Organizing Genius,* I looked at the leadership of Great Groups and in most cases, the leader was rarely the cleverest or the sharpest. Peter Schneider, president of Disney's colossally successful Feature Animation studio, leads a group of 1,200 animators. He can't draw to save his life. Bob Taylor, former head of the Palo Alto Research Center, where the first commercial PC was invented, wasn't a computer scientist. J. Robert Oppenheimer, head of the befabled Manhattan Project which produced the first nuclear device, while a brilliant physicist, never matched the accomplishments of the future Nobel Laureates working for him at Los Alamos. It goes on and on. Perhaps a story about two of Britain's most famous 19th Century Prime Ministers illustrates this point. It was said about William Ewart Gladstone that when you had dinner with Mr. Gladstone, you felt that he was the world's most brilliant and provocative, the most intelligent and wittiest conversationalist you have ever met. But when you were dining with Mr.

Disraeli, you felt that *you* were the world's most brilliant and provocative, the most . . . .

Max DePree put it best when he said that good leaders "abandon their ego to the talents of others."

**2.** *The New Leader keeps reminding people of what's important.* Organizations drift into entropy and the bureaucratization of imagination when they forget what's important. Simple to say, but that one sentence is one of the few pieces of advice I suggest to leaders: Remind your people of what's important. Even in my profession of teaching I will occasionally hear a colleague say, usually in half-jest, that the university would be a great place to work if only there weren't students around. What else is there but helping students to become successful at life? What can be more ennobling?

A powerful enough vision can transform what would otherwise be routine and drudgery into collectively focused energy—even sacrifice. Witness again the Manhattan Project. The scientists there were willing to put their careers on hold and to undertake what was, in essence, a massive engineering feat because they believed the free world depended on their doing so. Reminiscing about Los Alamos, Richard Feynman, the irreverent and future Nobel Laureate, told a story that illustrates how reminding people of "what's important" can give meaning and value to work. The U.S. Army had recruited talented engineers from all over the United States for special duty on the project. They were assigned to work on the primitive computers of the period (1943–45), doing energy calculations and other tedious jobs. But the Army, obsessed with security, refused to tell them anything specific about the project. They didn't know that they were building a weapon that could end the war or even what their calculations meant. They were simply expected to do the work, which they did slowly and not very well. Feynman, who supervised the technicians, prevailed on his superiors to tell the recruits what they were doing and why. Permission was granted to lift the veil of secrecy, and Oppenheimer gave them a special lecture on the nature of the project and their own contribution.

"*Complete* transformation," Feynman recalled. "*They* began to invent ways of doing it better. They improved the scheme. They worked at night. They didn't need supervising in the night; they didn't need anything. They understood everything; they invented several of the programs we used." Ever the scientist, Feynman calculated that the work was done "nearly ten times as fast" after it had meaning.

*Meaning.* Charles Handy has it right in his book *The Hungry Spirit.* We are all hungry spirits craving purpose and meaning at work, to contribute something beyond ourselves and leaders can never forget to stop reminding people of what's important.

**3.** *The New Leader Generates and Sustains Trust.* We're all aware that the terms of the new social contract of work have changed. No one can depend on life-long loyalty or commitment to any organization. Since 1985, 25% of the American workforce has been laid off at least once. That's about a half-million on average each year. In 1998, when the unemployment rate was the lowest in 30 years, roughly 110,000 workers were down-sized. At a time when the new social contract makes the times between organizations and their knowledge workers tenuous, trust becomes the emotional glue that can bond people to an organization. Trust is a small word with powerful connotations and is a hugely complex factor. The ingredients are a combination of competence, constancy, caring, fairness, candor and authenticity. Most of all the latter. And that is achieved by the New Leaders when they can balance successfully the tripod of forces working on and in most of us: ambition, competence and integrity. Authenticity, as Groucho joked, cannot be faked. To be redundant, it's real. The current cliché is "walk your talk." But it's far more than that. The best and perhaps the only way I know of to illustrate (as opposed to define) authenticity is to quote from Robert Bolt's Preface to his play, *A Man for All Seasons:*

"At any rate, Thomas More, as I wrote about him, became for me a man with an adamantine sense of his own self. He knew where he began and left off, what area of himself he could yield to the encroachments of his enemies, and what to the encroachments of those he loved. It was a substantial area in both cases, for he had a proper sense of fear and was a busy lover. Since he was a clever man and a great lawyer, he was able to retire from those areas in wonderfully good order, but at length he was asked to retreat from that final area where he located his self. And there this supple, humorous, unassuming and sophisticated person set like metal, was overtaken by an absolutely primitive rigor, and could no more be budged than a cliff."

**4.** *The New Leader and the Led Are Intimate Allies.* Earlier I referred to how Dr. King's followers shamed him into going to jail because so many young people responded to his speeches and found themselves in danger. They were the unsung heroes. People you've never heard of: James Bevel, Diane Nash, Otis Moss and many others. All heroes. John Lewis tells us in his book how much of the Civil Rights Movement was a heroic team effort, referring to Henry V "band of brothers."

It's not too much of a stretch to consider Jakob Schindler, the protagonist of an epochal story immortalized in the film *Schindler's List.* The power of Spielberg's film is the transformation of Schindler from a sleazy, down-at-the-heels small-time con-man who moves to Poland in order to harness cheap Jewish labor to make munitions which he can then sell to the Germans at low cost. His transformation is the singular compelling narrative of the film. And it comes about over a period of time where Schindler interacts with his Jewish workers, most of all the accountant, Levin, but also frequent and achingly painful moments where he confronts the evil of the war, of the holocaust, of the suffering, of the injustice. In the penultimate scene, when the war is over and the Nazis have evacuated the factory, but before the American troops arrive, the prisoners give him a ring, made for him, from the precious metals used by the workers. As he tries to put the ring on, he begins crying, "Why, why are you doing this? With this metal, we could have saved three, maybe four, maybe five more Jews." And he drives off in tears.

I find it hard to be objective about a scene that tears at my soul, but I want to argue that though this was a unique, singular event, it portrays what New Leadership is all about: that great leaders are made by great groups and by organizations that create the social architecture of respect and dignity. And, through some kind of weird alchemy, some ineffable symbiosis, great leadership brings that about. Without each other, the leader and the led are culturally impoverished. Only a poet could sum up the majesty of this alchemy:

We are all angels with only one wing.

We can only fly while embracing each other.

These New Leaders will not have the loudest voice, but the most attentive ear. Instead of pyramids, these post-bureaucratic organizations will be structures built of energy and ideas, led by people who find their joy in the task at hand, while embracing each other—and not worrying about leaving monuments behind.

## Selected Bibliography

There are several books I referred to in the article that would more likely be found on the book shelf of a history or English professor than a management scholar or practitioner but two of them, *Frenzy of Renown* by Leo Braudy, (Oxford, 1986) and Barbara Tuchman's *March of Folly* (Alfred Knopf, 1984), deserve to be. They are just terrific books on leadership. Braudy's is the first and only history of celebrity and is brilliantly written as might be expected but often found lacking in academic treatises. I've said enough about Tuchman in the text. I use it in my undergraduate leadership class and it's very useful. What historian Tuchman refers to as folly or wooden headedness, we might refer to as cognitive dissonance. John Lewis's book, *Walking with the Wind* (Simon & Schuster, 1998) is a splendid personal memoire of the civil rights movement, written by one of the most important African-American leaders. In Jim O'Toole's *Leading Change* (Jossey-Bass, 1995), the frontis piece of that book which I reproduced here underlines, with great wit and clarity, the basic premise of this important work; i.e. leaders better learn how to enroll willing followers. It could have also been written by a humanities professor, which he basically is, except with brio and a deep philosophical lens, he has written one of the most provocative and important books on leadership. Ronald Heifetz's book, *Leadership Without Easy Answers* (Belknap, 1994), more than lives up to its name and is not an easy read as the title suggests. But it is deep and complex and goes way beyond the domain of Corporate America, though he doesn't exclude that, into areas of community leadership, doctor/patient relationships among others. Gary Wills's book *Certain Trumpets* (Simon & Schuster, 1994) is already a classic. It has a lot in common with Howard Gardner's *Leading Minds* (Basic Books, 1995) which I should have referenced as well. Wills goes at leadership as a political scientist cum historian would, while Gardner is a cognitive psychologist. They both rely on fascinating narratives, but their choices of leaders, at the margins anyway, give away their world view, their range, and their informed biases. So while Wills chooses to focus on Cesare Borgia or King David, Gardner will take up Robert Maynard Hutchins or Jean Monet. At the same time, they often choose the same icon, like Martha Graham, Gandhi, Eleanor Roosevelt and Pope John XXIII. Two recent books I co-authored, one with Patricia Biederman, *Organizing Genius* (Perseus, 1997) and one with David Heenan, *Co-Leaders* (Wiley, 1999) provided some of the conceptual background for this article but tries to put the spotlight not so much on leadership but on Great Groups and Partnerships.

I'll end this bibliographic narrative with Berthold Brecht who always liked to have the last word anyway. He was incapable of collaboration or partnership except for his brilliantly wicked and bittersweet lyrics to Kurt Weill's *Threepenny Opera.* The poem I used came from Georg Tabori's book, *The World of Brecht* (Samuel French, 1964).

# 14
## Paradigm Shifts

*One of the best-received books I've been involved with is* Leaders, *which was co-written with Burt Nanus in 1985 and revised in 1996. This short essay briefly examined some of the organizational paradigm shifts that are now taken for granted before moving to a discussion of a paradigm shift that usually is overlooked: how the leader has used power in the past and how the leader can use it effectively in the future.*

The contexts of apathy, escalating change and uncertainty make leadership seem like maneuvering over ever faster and more undirected ball bearings. Dispiritedness has risen as we have traversed the wicked slalom of the last twenty years. But in spite of the mediocrities, travesties, trespasses, destructions and dislocations of the last two decades, we believe, with many contemporary thinkers, that it is not with stupor that the American people suffer anxiety and even nonallegiance. Rather, it is that we are approaching a major turning point in history—what Karl Jaspers referred to as an "axial point," where some new height of vision is sought, where some fundamental redefinitions are required, where our table of values will have to be reviewed. We seek lives not measured solely in terms of income, societies not assessed on gasoline consumption, and freedom from that most beguiling and misleading of all valuations, the GNP.

The fact is that as difficult, frustrating and fearful as these times are, they are also interesting, catalytic and crucial. "It is," as the fox said to the Little Prince, "not what it appears to be." A new paradigm is being born.

Survival in this seeming madness calls for great flexibility and awareness on the part of leaders and followers alike. Our larger objectives, peace and prosperity, must pivot on increased communication and broadened belief systems. We must fix our horizons not on the mandates of atrophying institutions but on the successes of burgeoning new enterprises. It is to the trends we should all look as we shape the future and as we shape ourselves.

Chronicler John Naisbitt isolated ten present and future persuasions in *Megatrends,* his bestselling description of the new paradigm.[3] The changes are as follows:

| From | To |
| --- | --- |
| Industrial Society | Information Society |
| Forced Technology | High Tech/High Touch |
| National Economy | World Economy |
| Short Term | Long Term |
| Centralization | Decentralization |
| Institutional Help | Self-Help |
| Representative Democracy | Participatory Democracy |
| Hierarchies | Networking |
| North | South |
| Either/Or | Multiple Option |

These changes have been examined, in one form or another, for some time. This includes "oldies" such as McGregor's "Theory Y,"[4] Townsend's *Up the Organization,*[5] Slater's "New Culture,"[6] and Salk's "Epoch B."[7] More recently, this paradigm shift can be observed in Prigogine's *Dissipative Structures,*[8] Peters's *Thriving on Chaos,*[9] Drucker's *The New Realities*[10] and Handy's *The Age of Paradox.*[11]

However, there is something missing—one issue that has been systematically neglected without exception: *POWER, the basic energy to initiate and sustain action translating intention into reality,* the quality without which leaders cannot lead. Just as the economists have painted themselves into a narrowing corner by failing to recognize the limitations and constraints of the free market, so too have students of organizations avoided the nucleus of leadership. Without any qualification, we can bluntly state that most of the current paradigms of organizational life, be they the "new age" variety or the older brands, have failed to consider *power*.*

Bertrand Russell once said, "The fundamental concept in social science is power, in the same sense in which energy is the fundamental concept in physics." Our ignorance of this, our forest-for-the-trees blindness, has led to human transactional short-circuitry. In short, we are a nation suffering from a serious power blockage.

Ironically, power is one of the most familiar forces in the universe. It is the pull and push we all experience and exercise from birth to death. It is implicit in all human interaction— familial, sexual, occupational, national and international— either covertly or overtly.

However, this basic social energy has been embroidered upon beyond recognition. It carries with it a host of connotations incurred over thousands of years. These implications— including avarice, insensitivity, cruelty, corruption—have led in aggregate to the disregard and disintegration of power across the board. In other words, power is at once the most necessary and most distrusted element exigent to human progress.

To understand this ambiguity, observe the ways in which power has been misused. Historically leaders have controlled rather than organized, administered repression rather than expression, and held their followers in arrestment rather than in evolution.

We *are* going forward, but we are doing so without affording power a place in our new vision. Our fear of confrontation—whether between lovers or friends or through crime, local injustices, the media or government—has slowed and in some cases stymied participation in a just future. Like homeowners who hesitate to call the exterminator because they're afraid when the termites stop holding hands the

---

* An important and seminal exception is Rosabeth Moss Kanter's book, *The Change Masters,* which deals directly and masterfully with power.[12]

house will fall down, *the paradox of any progress based on conflict is its ultimate fragility.*

We must learn to perceive power for what it really is. Basically, it's the reciprocal of leadership. Perhaps the best way to illustrate how we understand it is to use an illustration, and the best one that comes to mind is that of Lee Iacocca at Chrysler. He provided the leadership to transform a company from bankruptcy to success. He created a vision of success and mobilized large factions of key employees to align behind that vision. Almost exclusively because of Iacocca's leadership, by 1983 Chrysler made a profit, boosted employee morale, and helped employees generate a sense of meaning in their work. He empowered them. The effects weren't transitory, either—by 1995, Chrysler was the world's lowest-cost auto maker, with annual earnings of $2 billion and the highest profit margin of America's Big Three auto makers.

In fact, we believe that Iacocca's high visibility symbolizes the missing element in management today (and much of management theory) in that his style of leadership is central to organizational success. Our concept of power and leadership, then, is modeled on the Iacocca phenomenon: Power is the basic energy needed to initiate and sustain action or, to put it another way, the *capacity to translate intention into reality and sustain it.* Leadership is the wise use of this power: *Transformative* leadership.*

As we view it, effective leadership can move organizations from current to future states, create visions of potential opportunities for organizations, instill within employees commitment to change and instill new cultures and strategies in organizations that mobilize and focus energy and resources. These leaders are not born. They emerge when organizations face new problems and complexities that cannot be solved by unguided evolution. They assume respon-

---

* We are indebted here and throughout this book to the seminal work of James MacGregor Burns and especially want to note his contributions to our work.[13]

sibilities for reshaping organizational practices to adapt to environmental changes. They direct organizational changes that build confidence and empower their employees to seek new ways of doing things. They overcome resistance to change by creating visions of the future that evoke confidence in and mastery of new organizational practices. Over the next decade or two, the leadership we are talking about and will refer to throughout this book will become more evident in organizations able to respond to spastic and turbulent conditions.

We do face an uncertain and unsettling future, but not one without vision. Vision is the commodity of leaders, and power is their currency. We are at a critical point in our nation's history and we cannot go back as individuals or as a country to what we were ten, five or even one year ago. The future is now and it's our turn.

# 15
## *The Case for Co-Leaders*

*If a man aspires to the highest place, it is no dishonor
to him to halt at the second.*

—CICERO

*The publishing of* Co-Leaders: the Power of Great
Partnerships, *written by David Heenan, was a text-
book study in the resilience of the myth of the Great
Man. The book, originally titled "Second Bananas,"
explored the unrecognized and unsurpassed value of
outstanding deputies to leaders and to organizations.
A dozen publishers turned us away, one of whom
politely told me, "Warren, no one in America wants
to be Number Two."*

*When we changed the title and reframed the book to
avoid dwelling as much on the second banana concept, we were back in business. In "The Case for Co-
Leaders," drawn from the book, Heenan and I make
the case that, despite ongoing resistance in many
quarters to the idea that a person can make an important contribution and be fulfilled in anything other
than a top post, it is increasingly essential for Number
Ones to be in the business of developing and empow-
ering strong Number Twos. This approach was certainly evident when Bill Gates recently handed day-to-
day control of Microsoft over to Steve Ballmer, after
years of a productive partnership that fueled
Microsoft's growth and prepped Ballmer to take the
reins. It takes a certain kind of person to recruit a good
second banana and a certain kind of person to serve in
that role, but the results are more than worth the effort.*

An overseas visitor to our shores recently remarked: "If
beings from another planet were attempting to learn about
working in the United States by reading business magazines,

they would have to assume that everyone in America is either a CEO or about to become one."

The point is well taken. Ours is a culture obsessed with celebrity, and so we have made superstars of Bill Gates and other fascinating leaders, just as we have made legends of favored rock stars and screen actors. Nevertheless, even as we read yet another article that implies that Microsoft *is* Bill Gates, we know better. We know that every successful organization has, at its heart, a cadre of *co-leaders*—key players who do the work, even if they receive little of the glory.

Take Microsoft's Steve Ballmer. According to insiders much of the software giant's unprecedented success is due to Ballmer, its relatively unknown second in command. Ballmer is Microsoft's president and top tactician, the person responsible for everything from getting the first Windows operating system shipped to keeping the company supplied with top-notch personnel. Although the average person hears his name and wonders "Steve who?" Ballmer has created Microsoft as surely as has his more famous boss.

"Microsoft could lose Bill Gates," former staffer Adrian King told *Forbes,* "but it could not survive without Steve's sheer will to succeed. That's what makes the company unique."

This book reflects our conviction that you must look beyond the Bill Gateses of the world to understand what will make organizations succeed in the new millennium. In this first comprehensive study of co-leaders and their often quiet power, we challenge the time-honored notion that all great institutions are the lengthened shadows of a Great Man or Woman. It is a fallacy that dies hard. But if you believe, as we do, that the genius of our age is truly collaborative, you must abandon the notion that the credit for any significant achievement is solely attributable to the person at the top. We have long worshiped the imperial leader at the cost of ignoring the countless other contributors to any worthwhile enterprise. In our hearts we know that the world is more complex than ever and that we need teams of talent—leaders and co-leaders working together—to get important things done. The old corporate monotheism is finally giving way to a more realistic view that acknowledges leaders not as organizational gods but as the first among many contributors. In this new view of the organization, co-leaders finally come into their own and begin to receive the credit they so richly deserve.

Gates and Ballmer exemplify a relatively new type of alliance between a leader and his or her chief ally. In this scenario, so typical of Silicon Valley, the No. 1 and No. 2 associates seem more like buddies, or at least peers, than boss and subordinate. This new egalitarianism reflects a dramatic change in organizational life today. In Henry Ford's corporate America, the person at the top held all the power. He, and it was almost always a he, owned the company and all its assets. The workers were hired hands.

But on the cusp of the year 2000, economics is based on a very different reality. Microsoft and other high-tech companies are in the business of ideas. Good ideas belong, initially at least, to whoever has them, not to the company or the boss. Superior ideas can come from anyone in the organization, and they empower the people who have them, whether their business card says CEO or intern. If Microsoft is not a true meritocracy, it is nonetheless a company in which talent is valued and courted. Talent always has the power to walk (especially if, as in the case of Ballmer, the talent already has roughly $12 billion worth of Microsoft stock in its pocket). In such an environment, no chief executive would risk losing a key player by demanding unquestioning obedience or any of the other outdated hallmarks of the rigidly hierarchical corporation of yesterday. This new egalitarianism isn't just a matter of style. It's a question of survival. In the new climate, every leader knows that the organization's best minds will take major assets with them should they walk out the door.

## Co-Leadership Defined

*Co-leadership* is not a fuzzy-minded buzzword designed to make non-CEOs feel better about themselves and their workplaces. Rather it is a tough-minded strategy that will unleash the hidden talent in any enterprise. Above all co-leadership is inclusive, not exclusive. It celebrates those who do the real work, not just a few charismatic leaders, often isolated, who are regally compensated for articulating the organization's vision.

Although several leading companies from Citigroup to Daimler-Chrysler have restyled themselves around coequal CEOs, co-leadership should permeate *every* organization at *every* level. There are vivid demonstrations of successful power sharing from the Halls of Montezuma to the Hills of Silicon Valley. For example, the United States Marine Corps, with its fiercely proud tradition of excellence in combat, its hallowed rituals, and its unbending code of honor, personifies co-leadership. Despite its rigid command-and-control structure, the Corps' enduring culture screams togetherness: Semper fi. Esprit de corps. The few, the proud.

Such inclusive notions of leadership are not new. The Marines have been practicing their special brand of esprit for more than 220 years. But what is new are the changed realities of the twenty-first century. In a world of increasing interdependence and ceaseless technological change, even the greatest of Great Men or Women simply can't get the job done alone. As a result, we need to rethink our most basic concepts of leadership.

The prevailing winds blow in the direction of close-knit partnerships throughout the organization. In this new organizational galaxy, power doesn't reside in a single person or corner office. Rather power and responsibility are dispersed, giving the enterprise a whole constellation of costars—co-leaders with shared values and aspirations, all of whom work together toward common goals. As we look back at what we discovered in writing this book, one realization towers above all others: *Anyone* can be a co-leader—all he or she needs is talent and an organization that values and rewards co-leadership.

In researching this book, we spent five years scrutinizing dozens of gifted co-leaders, analyzing how they contributed to the greatness of their organizations. We studied how they related to the people above and below them and how they viewed the costs and rewards of being a costar. Because we believe personal stories are a lively, effective way to get important points across, we chose to make the case for co-leadership by telling the stories of a dozen outstanding adjuncts, from General George C. Marshall to Merrill Lynch's visionary Win Smith. Other co-leaders profiled range from Anne Sullivan Macy, Helen Keller's brilliant and devoted teacher, to legendary auto executive Bob Lutz.

*Co-Leaders,* then, is about truly exceptional deputies— extremely talented and dedicated men and women, often more capable than their more highly acclaimed superiors. No one illustrates this better than George Catlett Marshall. As important to his country as George Washington, Marshall brought unprecedented stature to a supporting role. With World War II looming, he rebuilt the United States Army despite extraordinary initial resistance. The architect of the Marshall Plan, he was President Truman's steady right hand as secretary of state and later secretary of defense. The first soldier to win the Nobel Peace Prize in peacetime, he was also a hero to the captains of his era. Truman, Eisenhower, and Churchill all said he was the greatest man they had ever known.

Routinely called on to do the work and forgo the credit, great partners sometimes have character where more celebrated leaders have only flash. Marshall is, again, the model. In retirement he turned down million-dollar offers to write his memoirs because he felt his reminiscences might trouble some of the people in his remarkable past. Such principled restraint is hard to imagine today when no tell-all memoir seems to go unwritten.

Again and again, *Co-Leaders* illustrates how the once yawning gap between the person at the top and the rest of the organization is closing because of rapid changes in the workplace and, indeed, the world. Although as a culture we continue to be mesmerized by celebrity and preoccupied with being No. 1, the roles of top executives are converging, the line between them increasingly blurred.

Called on to make more and more complex decisions more and more quickly, even the most da Vincian CEOs acknowledge that they can't do everything themselves. Farsighted corporations and other organizations require their leaders to do more than put effective systems in place. Future-oriented enterprises have to be able to spot the Next Big Thing and respond to it before the competition. Such organizations are like organisms, constantly adapting to shifts in the global environment. As a result, the CEO's job doesn't get easier the longer he or she is in place; it typically gets even more demanding.

In 1997 famously capable Intel chairman Andy Grove, beset by lawsuits, a bout with prostate cancer, a flaw in Intel's Pentium Pro chips, and a dip in second-quarter earnings, admitted that he was on the verge of being overwhelmed. "I don't think I've ever worked as hard," he told *Fortune.* "I've been feeling very sorry for myself the past six months. Things are running at borderline out of control inside the company and out. . . . I go home spent."

In such an environment, first-rate co-leaders are a necessity, not a luxury. In May 1998 Grove chose as his successor Craig Barrett, Intel's superbly fit chief operating officer (COO) and the person responsible for perfecting the chip maker's manufacturing processes. Grove was the first to praise Barrett for having done the operations job at Intel far better than he. And why shouldn't Grove seek a successor of Barrett's caliber? When you know you are going to be facing challenges at every turn, you want the best there is at your side.

Once a sinecure, the corner office has become a revolving door, as boards and shareholders become ever more demanding of CEOs. Increasingly, heading an important organization in America is like being one of the kings in ancient Crete who had extraordinary power and access to every perk and pleasure—but only for a time. After his year of absolute power, the king was put to death. For contemporary CEOs the pay and the perks are unbeatable while they are in office, but they can't count on being in office for long.

As the tenure of the average chief executive becomes shorter and shorter, the need for depth of leadership becomes even more crucial.

The untimely death in 1997 of Coca-Cola Enterprises, Inc. CEO Roberto Goizueta reminded the world that no complex organization can afford to rely too heavily on a single leader, however gifted and charismatic. Coke never stumbled in the days following Goizueta's death, largely because he had already groomed an able successor, M. Douglas Ivester, whom Goizueta had long referred to as "my partner." The company's major divisions were already reporting to Ivester, now CEO, when the Cuban-born chief became ill. The late chairman had also nurtured a dozen more key players under Ivester, who in turn had talented protégés of his own. In famed investor Warren Buffett's view, Goizueta's "greatest legacy is the way he so carefully selected and then nurtured the future leadership of the company."

Ivester has already gone far toward instituting a co-leadership culture at Coke. *Fortune* magazine's Betsy Morris recently described the atmosphere under Ivester: "Hierarchy is out—it slows everything down; he communicates freely with people at all levels. The conventional desk job is also out. Ivester prefers that employees think of themselves as knowledge workers—their office is the information they carry around with them, supported by technology that allows them to work anywhere. . . . A CEO on a pedestal is definitely out; a CEO as platoon leader is in." Ivester knows that co-leadership is a strategy for unleashing talent throughout the organization. Much more than rhetoric about teamwork, co-leadership is a commitment to partnering at every level, to serve the constantly changing needs of the organization. Yet even someone as committed to co-leadership as Ivester may be reluctant to share *all* his or her power. Ivester works closely with a team of 14 vice presidents but has not yet been willing to name a successor.

Contrast, too, China's smooth leadership transition with the sorry state of Russia, Cuba, and Malaysia. Deng Xiaoping's death quickly surfaced two talented co-leaders: President Jiang Zemin and Premier Zhu Rongji. Yet Russia, with ailing Boris Yeltsin acting more like a tsar than the country's first democratically elected president, desperately needs a succession plan. So, too, do autocratic Cuba and Malaysia.

Increasingly, corporations, countries, and other entities are realizing that top leaders and their co-leaders are not different orders of beings but essential complements: All are needed if the enterprise is to flourish. As college basketball's North Carolina Tar Heels were reminded in 1997, success, continuity, and survival depend on having a Bill Guthridge on board as well as a Dean Smith. Like athletic teams, all organizations need the bench strength, or deep leadership, provided by great co-leaders.

## Paths to Co-Leadership

In the course of studying outstanding lieutenants, we were constantly reminded that co-leadership is a *role,* not an identity and certainly not a destiny. There is no single personality type that consigns people to careers in a supporting role rather than a starring one (indeed most CEOs and other leaders have done both). True, some strong-willed individuals must run their own shows. It's hard—almost impossible actually—to imagine Donald Trump, George Steinbrenner, or Leona Helmsley finding happiness in the trenches. But they are the exceptions.

Because all leadership is situational, we are leery about categorizing co-leaders. The social world isn't nearly as orderly as the physical world. People—unlike solids, fluids, and gases—are anything but uniform and predictable. As you will see, the co-leaders described in these pages have distinguished themselves in very different fields of endeavor: Amy Tucker coaches women's basketball at Stanford, while Merrill Lynch's Win Smith helped democratize the ownership of stocks and bonds, perhaps the most important change in the U.S. economy in 50 years. And each of these great partners had or has a distinctive, often colorful personality. But in the course of our research, we found that, however they differed, each had taken one of three distinctive career paths to successful co-leadership. Each was either a fast-tracker, a back-tracker, or an on-tracker.

- *Fast-trackers* are deputies on the way up. For presidential hopeful Al Gore and others, co-leadership is a rite of passage. Indeed being No. 2 is a time-honored way to become top dog. According to a recent survey, 86 percent of the heads of Fortune 500 companies were previous seconds in command.

Upwardly mobile lieutenants understand that the route to the corner office is paved with achievement, loyalty, and luck. Savvy deputies also appreciate firsthand the need for superior bench strength. Fast-trackers tend to be good at what psychologist Erik Erikson terms "being generative"— that is, building their own cadre of talented lieutenants. Such co-leaders often understand, in the most visceral of ways, the value of sharing power.

- *Back-trackers* are former chiefs who have downshifted. One of history's most notable examples is Chou En-lai, who voluntarily relinquished command of the Red Army to a gifted junior officer, Mao Tse-tung. More recently, as few would have predicted, colorful cable pioneer Ted Turner seems to have found happiness as a vice chairman at Time Warner.

Some back-trackers disdain elements of the No. 1 role: deal making, strategizing, schmoozing with different interest groups, and the like. Some find the pressure and lack of privacy at the top to be major negatives. Others want to avoid the nerve-rattling revolving-door syndrome of today's executive suite. Generally speaking, these talented men and women find greater peace being the quiet power behind the throne.

- *On-trackers* are outstanding adjuncts who either didn't want the top slot or weren't promoted into it. These people find ways to prosper as supporting players. Passed over for CEO of Chrysler, Bob Lutz called his stint as second in command "absolutely the best period in my whole career." On-trackers have the ego strength to be a costar. If they are offered top billing, they will probably take it, as Harry Truman did a half century ago and as Bill Guthridge did at North Carolina in 1997. But they are also comfortable remaining part of a vibrant team of leaders.

Whatever their route to co-leadership, successful costars are consummate team players and, thus, valuable models for everyone interested in effective collaboration. Usually servant-leaders, they tend to be self-reliant, yet committed to organizational goals. Outstanding co-leaders "see themselves—except in terms of line responsibility—as the equals of the leaders they follow," says Professor Robert E. Kelley of Carnegie Mellon University. "They are more apt to disagree with leadership and are less likely to be intimidated by hierarchy and organizational structure."

We have excluded any discussion of unsuccessful partners, or off-trackers. These are people whose careers have derailed. Whereas fast-trackers are on the way up, these poor souls are on the way out.

What motivates great co-leaders? Why, in particular, are they willing to subordinate their egos, a sacrifice that seems all the more remarkable in an age that celebrates the star? We found three main reasons, which led us to classify co-leaders as follows:

**1.** *Crusaders,* like General George C. Marshall, who serve a noble cause

**2.** *Confederates,* such as Bob Lutz and Stanford assistant coach Amy Tucker, who serve an exceptional organization or enterprise

**3.** *Consorts,* like Helen Keller's teacher, Anne Sullivan Macy, and Win Smith of Merrill Lynch, who serve an extraordinary person.

Of course, there is some overlap among categories. George Marshall as *crusader* was driven by the cause of freedom and world peace. Yet he was also a staunch *confederate* of the U.S. military establishment (the army, in particular) as well as a loyal *consort* to his mentor, "Black Jack" Pershing, and later to presidents Roosevelt and Truman. At different stages in Marshall's life, these loyalties enabled him to find satisfaction in a supporting role.

## Critical Factors for Success

To be a successful co-leader, you need, above all, a champion who will allow you to succeed. Not every top gun is able to do that. Contrast Bob Lutz's success at Chrysler, thanks to the genuine partnership he had with CEO Robert Eaton, with Lutz's unhappiness at the auto giant when then CEO Lee Iacocca often undermined him. Great co-leaders are often born when leaders decide to do the one thing that most often distinguishes a great organization from a mediocre one—hire people who are as good or better than they are. As reserved as Lutz is flamboyant, Bob Eaton was perfectly comfortable with a partner who piloted his own jet fighter and who was a darling of the press. For Lutz's part, he long ago came to terms with being passed over for Chrysler's top job and found real happiness as Eaton's partner in everything but name. Indeed Lutz believes Eaton's willingness to share power was key to Chrysler's success. If Lutz had been made CEO in 1992, he said:"I would have had to have done it alone."

The ability to subordinate ego to attain a common goal is something both leaders and co-leaders need. Stephen Kahng built Power Computing Corp. into what *Business Week* described as the "fastest-growing computer startup of the 1990s." One of the industry's most respected technical experts, Kahng is also so nerdy and soft-spoken that his own staffers needle him about it. Knowing that he needed someone with different skills and a personality very different from his own to market the company's Apple clones and capture a greater share of the PC market, Kahng went after Joel Kocher, author of the winning marketing strategy, including direct sales, at Dell Computer Corp. Now Power Computing's president and COO, the exuberant Kocher is the antithesis of

Kahng—in everything but their shared vision of market domination. Kocher is head cheerleader as well as marketing strategist, fond of such stunts as having Power Computing's staff wear camouflage fatigues every Friday on Fight Back for the Customer Day. A colleague of Kocher's at Dell told *Business Week* that he "demands, inspires, attracts, and coaches greatness"—the sort of description most people associate with CEO, not second in command. But Kahng had the wisdom and confidence to hire his complement, where a lesser leader might have been put off by Kocher's stronger charisma.

True leaders also know that the only deputies worth hiring are the ones good enough to replace them. And for their part outstanding co-leaders know that they don't have to be at the top of the organizational chart to find satisfaction—that exercising one's gifts and serving a worthy cause are far more reliable sources of satisfaction than the title on one's office door. Such people have acquired the rare ability to distinguish between celebrity and success. As that unlikely philosopher, the late Erma Bombeck, once wrote, "Don't confuse fame with success. Madonna is one, Helen Keller is the other."

Courage is one of the attributes of all great co-leaders, and one we rarely associate with that role. Deputies have to be able to speak truth to power, even when it hurts. (Real leaders demand honesty from their adjuncts, knowing that good information, even when it's unpleasant, is the basis of good decision making.) It was young George Marshall's courage in publicly correcting General Pershing that caught Pershing's eye and launched Marshall's extraordinary career. And candor like his own was one of the attributes Marshall always sought in his staffers. Yes-men may feed the boss's ego, but they serve no other useful function. Indeed they guarantee that the boss's knowledge will be limited to upbeat information and whatever he or she already knows. Good co-leaders protect their bosses when possible, but good bosses are willing to endure occasional discomfiture in order to find out what they *need* to know.

Creativity is almost as important an attribute of co-leaders as courage. Deputies have to go beyond the manual to find what best serves the organization. When George Tenet was named director of the Central Intelligence Agency in 1997, his former boss, John Deutch, told an instructive story about Tenet's ability to think on his feet and act decisively.

"George is a tremendously loyal and devoted public servant," Deutch told the *Wall Street Journal*. "The time I really realized how devoted a deputy he was was in an extremely important meeting with important foreign dignitaries. He cleared the room to tell me I needed to zip up my fly."

Every chief has the right to the loyalty of his or her deputies. Working at a leader's side, a trusted co-leader is often privy to information that could seriously compromise the boss's position if it were shared. As candid as great partners are in private, they are equally discreet in public. They can keep the boss's secrets—as long as they can continue to reconcile them with their own consciences. To some extent, all No. 1s depend on an image of excellence to maintain their positions. Good co-leaders may know about personal flaws or weaknesses, but they don't feel compelled to reveal or underscore them. Especially in crises, leaders have to know that their first lieutenants will maintain the illusion of superiority, which makes leadership possible. An example of this is Vice President Al Gore's unswerving public loyalty to a bruised Clinton, despite the pressure on Gore to distance himself from the controverial president as Gore himself seeks the nation's highest office.

Co-leaders need unusually healthy egos. That's a paradox really, because it would seem that they would need less ego strength than their leaders. But, especially in a society as obsessed with winning as ours, it takes extraordinary confidence to be No. 2 or No. 3. No matter how great a contribution a great co-leader makes, the majority of the credit is going to accrue to the top individual. That's the nature of the organizationai beast. To some degree it may simply reflect the extent to which leaders function as symbols of their enterprises. But the fact is that even the best deputy will exist in the shadow of the boss. Bill Guthridge deserved considerable credit for Dean Smith's record-breaking 879 victories, but it was Smith whose name went into the record books, not the name of the man who spent 30 years as his assistant coach. As the self-effacing Guthridge told the press, "I knew my ego could take being lifetime assistant to the best coach around."

What does the organization get from a great partnership? A great many things. Two heads really are better than one when it comes to decision making. The psychological literature indicates that groups make better choices than do individuals. Last year Ford Motor's installation of the talented tandem of William Clay Ford, Jr., as nonexecutive chairman and Jacques Nasser as president and CEO was a ringing endorsement of co-leadership. "One of the nice things about this arrangement is that it does use the strength of two capable people," Ford told the *New York Times*. "Having watched how large this company has become, and how tough it is to manage, I think separating these jobs makes a lot of sense."

A first-rate deputy like Nasser can serve as an alternative model for the rest of the organization, one that other co-leaders may relate to more easily than to the person at the top. A great second can serve as institutional insurance in that he or she can quickly get up to speed to replace the person at the top. This is, tragically, one of the roles American vice presidents have had to play when presidents have died in office, and it is the role by which most people measure the vice president. Truman, whom as vice president FDR had kept in the dark about many important issues, including the development of the atomic bomb, proved surprisingly able in the nation's top job. The very thought of Dan Quayle succeeding George Bush so frightened many voters that it became a factor in Bush's failure to win a second term in office.

But heir apparent is just one of the many roles co-leaders play. Great partners may have strengths and skills that the boss lacks. The costar can compensate or complement. William Clark had superior cartographic abilities to Meriwether Lewis, for instance, that proved invaluable to the Corps of Discovery. Co-leaders can share the burden of leadership and lighten the workload. They routinely act as facilitators for their superiors. They almost always serve as advisers as well, at best providing the kind of candid, informed counsel that every leader needs. They are often conduits of critical information from elsewhere in the organization to the person in charge, and vice versa. They can also serve as sounding boards, counselors, confessors, and pressure valves. In bad times they may serve as lightning rods, even scapegoats. In the best of all possible organizations, they are genuine partners, though not necessarily equal ones, sharing responsibilities with the chief according to their individual skills and interests. Before Dean Smith's retirement in 1997, Bill Guthridge was responsible for the individual coaching at North Carolina, while Smith determined overall strategy—with Guthridge's quiet assistance. In the highly collaborative Clinton White House, Gore assumed major policy-shaping responsibility for several areas of national and international concern, including national security, environment, and technology.

## Just Rewards

Although service is the paradigmatic responsibility of co-leaders, there comes a time in everyone's career when he or she asks, "What's in it for me?" Although co-leaders usually lack the name recognition and enormous salaries of CEOs and others at the very top, there are rewards in being No. 2 or No. 3.

For starters serving under someone else can be a marvelous education. As a young deputy to Pershing, Marshall attended a superb military college of one, where he was able to study a first-rate soldier in the flesh, day in and day out. Vice President Gore has been in a unique position to study President Clinton during his two terms in office. What better curriculum for a presidential hopeful than the chance to see how the incumbent handles the duties and pressures of the nation's highest office? Clinton himself stumbled badly in his first months in office as he learned on the job. Six years later came the infamous Monica Lewinsky affair. How much better for Gore to be able to learn from someone else's mistakes—and successes—before assuming that demanding office?

Some of the greatest rewards of co-leadership grow out of the relationship with the person at the top. Some co-leaders have warm, sustaining relationships with the people they serve, as Win Smith had with Merrill Lynch cofounder Charlie Merrill. Merrill was a demanding taskmaster, but a superb mentor, and, over the decades, he and Smith became closer than many fathers and sons. Some of the letters they exchanged after illness forced Merrill into semiretirement are as tender as love letters. Accomplishing something together can forge a lasting bond. As profoundly troubled as Meriwether Lewis was, he and William Clark became close friends in the course of their epic journey and remained so afterward: Clark and his wife even moved into Lewis's house for a time.

The relationships that develop in executive offices are enormously varied. Some CEOs and COOs have healthy rivalries that energize both of them. Others have the professional equivalent of bad marriages that distract and drain them. Camaraderie grounded in shared accomplishment is one of the pleasures of any happy workplace, and it can be especially gratifying for the people who are most involved in setting the agenda and steering the enterprise.

Another frequent source of satisfaction for co-leaders is the opportunity to revel in interesting work and the pleasures of craft. CEOs often barter power and responsibility for truly engaging work. It can be hectic at the top, especially on days when one meeting follows another and even meals involve professional obligations. Many contented alter egos have talent or expertise that they are able to exercise undistracted by the top person's daunting calendar and sometimes tedious responsibilities. Amy Tucker seems to have found joy in her craft as associate head coach of the women's basketball team at Stanford, despite having tasted triumph as interim head coach. Bob Lutz was happy at Chrysler as the hands-on creator of such eye-catching vehicles as the Dodge Viper,

Plymouth Prowler, and Jeep Grand Cherokee. Successful co-leaders, especially those who have decided to remain No. 2, have often concluded that what they actually do is more important than making headlines.

As we shall see, some co-leaders find enormous satisfaction in serving a cause they believe in. Certainly Marshall is a superb example of someone who devoted his entire career to serving his country and indeed the world at large. For others, their work has many of the qualities of a religious vocation, and self-sacrifice is a price they are willing to pay. Born into island royalty, Bernice Pauahi Bishop believed that education could save her beloved fellow Hawaiians and devoted much of her life to creating the Kamehameha Schools. Eschewing the Hawaiian crown, she found another way to improve the condition of her people. As one observer said: "Refusing to rule her people, she did what was better, she served them."

Sometimes redefining power reflects a decision that there are more important things in life than other trappings of success. Princess Pauahi refused the crown because she believed accepting it would destroy her happy marriage to Charles Reed Bishop, who favored Hawaii's annexation by the United States. Amy Tucker is regularly offered head coaching jobs, especially now that women's basketball is booming, but she doesn't want to leave Stanford, a vibrant intellectual community in scenic Northern California.

As the happy buzz at visionary companies such as Steve Jobs's Pixar Animation Studios makes clear, the most exciting work being done today is collaborative, accomplished by teams of people working toward a common goal. Often there is still a Numero Uno, at least on the organizational chart. But in the growing number of global enterprises that trade in innovation, the real power is in the hands of the men and women who have the best ideas and the most valuable skills, whatever their job titles. In the workplaces of the new millennium, one of the leader's most important roles is to retain the necessary talent and unleash it. The rise of co-leadership reflects the fact that, despite the exalted terms in which we talk about No. 1s, they can actually accomplish things only when effectively teamed with other people.

## Leadership Redefined

If we still treat some CEOs like celebrities, we are increasingly beginning to see them more as stewards than kings. No one has been more articulate on this change in our traditional view of leadership than management sage Peter Drucker, who said in praise of such non-imperial leaders as Harry Truman and GE's Jack Welch: "They both understood executives are not their own masters. They are servants of the organization—whether elected or appointed, whether the organization is a government, a government agency, a business, a hospital, a diocese. It's their duty to subordinate their likes, wishes, preferences to the welfare of the institution."

To some degree this more egalitarian understanding of leadership reflects a backlash against CEOs who earn far more than they deliver. The surge in executive compensation in recent years has dismayed and infuriated the vast majority of people who work hard for modest pay. Thirty years ago the average chief executive in the United States earned 44 times as much as the average factory worker. According to the AFL-CIO, the ratio is now more than 300 to 1. Consequently, corporate boards as well as workers are beginning to question whether anyone deserves to make more than the budgets of some nations. Indeed Bob Eaton's $16 million annual compensation as CEO of Chrysler horrified German shareholder activists contemplating the 1998 merger of the Detroit automaker and Daimler-Benz AG. Eaton's German counterpart, Jürgen Schrempp, receives just $2 million a year.

Even *Business Week,* hardly a journal to foment revolution, huffed about the hubris of the chieftains of American business. "They are team leaders, not celebrities or one-man bands," the magazine editorialized. Yes, some extraordinary CEOs may deserve extraordinary compensation. "But usually, a chief executive works with a team of people who manage thousands of employees, each contributing to the success or failure of the company. A team leader requires respect to function. Making 200 times the average paycheck, simply because the market has a good year, doesn't generate respect."

That the American workplace needs to be rethought is increasingly obvious. The mounting anger over executive pay is only one piece of evidence. It is not a happy sign when the business best-seller list is topped by volumes devoted to Dilbert, the cartoon Everyworker, and the Orwellian hell in which he labors. This is organizational humor at its darkest, and one of its loudest messages is that it is time for sweeping change.

Although increasing numbers of firms are naming co-CEOs and showing other signs of embracing co-leadership, sharing power has its pitfalls. It will be interesting to see if Bob Eaton can work as comfortably with co-CEO Schrempp as Eaton once teamed with Lutz. The corner suite that houses incompatible executive peers can be an unhappy, unproductive place indeed. Boards can help keep the peace, but executive egos often make real partnerships impossible. You need only look at the vice presidency of the United States to see how hard it is for some No. 1s to share power. Even leaders who were abused as veeps had trouble treating their own vice presidents decently after becoming president. Truman, for example, was no better to Vice President Alben Barkley than FDR had been to him. Power is only shared by those who first choose to share it. In light of this first law of co-leadership, more and more organizations—and their governing boards—are realizing that willingness to share power is one of the criteria by which leaders must be judged.

As someone who knows both the executive experience and the subordinate one, the co-leader is a good model for a new, more egalitarian hybrid better adapted to the needs of the new millennium—people who can both command and follow, as the situation requires.

In American society the urge to be a star and the urge to achieve common goals as part of a community have always tugged us in different directions. As celebrity becomes less and less associated with genuine achievement, we need to think more clearly about what is best for our organizations and for ourselves. Great co-leaders remind us that we don't need to be captain to play on the team, that doing something we want to do and doing it well can be its own reward. That said, learning the secrets and skills of great No. 2s remains the surest path to becoming No. 1.

# Part 3
## *Embodying the Dream: Lessons in Character*

# 16

## An Invented Life: Shoe Polish, Milli Vanilli, and Sapiential Circles

*I wrote this short autobiography some years ago at the request of a colleague who had solicited similar sketches from others in the field of the study of leadership and management. Writing it was one of those heartening experiences, like a successful high school reunion, in which looking back made me not nostalgic for the past but grateful for the present and hopeful for the future. Elsewhere in this book I have recounted in greater detail some of the more significant periods of my career that are touched on in this chapter. This particular version of my life is intended to be candid rather than exhaustive. And it illuminates such mysteries as why I hate the accordion.*

Not long after I sat down to write this brief intellectual autobiography, I had a small epiphany: I realized that what I was doing was actually *biography,* imagining a narrative about someone named myself. The result is a selection of stories, some called memories, that I—and to some extent others— have created to give coherence and meaning to my life.

What I'm talking about is self-invention. Imagination. That's basically how we get to know ourselves. People who cannot invent and reinvent themselves must be content with borrowed postures, secondhand ideas, fitting in instead of standing out. Inventing oneself is the opposite of accepting the roles we were brought up to play.

It's much like the distinction I made in my last book, *On Becoming a Leader,* between "once-borns" and "twice-borns."* The once-born's transition from home and family to independence is relatively easy. Twice-borns generally suffer as they grow up; they feel different, even isolated. Unsatisfied with life as it is, they write new lives for themselves. I'm one of those twice-born.

I believe in self-invention, have to believe in it, for reasons that will soon enough be clear. To be authentic is literally to be your own author (the words derive from the same Greek root), to discover your native energies and desires, and then to find your own way of acting on them. When you've done that, you are not existing simply to live up to an image posited by the culture, family tradition, or some other authority. When you write your own life, you have played the game that was natural for you to play. You have kept covenant with your own promise.

## Shoe Polish

Samuel Beckett is my favorite playwright. Among the major writers of the twentieth century, he perhaps alone understood the relative insignificance of human existence in a vast, indifferent universe. His stage settings were virtually empty, an abyss without a timepiece, a space on the cusp of a precipice. Beckett dismissed the ordinary subject matter of the theater—social relations, struggles for power, and the like—as diversions masking the anguish and despair that are the essential human condition. Instead he asked bleak, existential questions: How do we come to terms with the fact that, without having asked for it, we have been thrown into being? And who are we? What does it mean when we say "I"?

In the 1958 play *Krapp's Last Tape,* Beckett continues his lifelong exploration of the mystery of self. An old man listens to the confessions he recorded in earlier years. To the old

---

*I am indebted to Abraham Zaleznik for this idea.

Krapp, the voice of the younger Krapp is sometimes that of a total stranger. In what sense, then, can the two Krapps be regarded as the same human being? In this essay I will try to bring the younger Bennis into some uneasy connection with the older one. But don't forget: I'm writing about a person who invented himself.

As I see it now, the landscape of my childhood was very like a Beckett stage set—barren, meager, endless. A little boy waited there for someone who might not, probably would not, show up. There were walk-ons occasionally: twin brothers ten years my senior, a father who worked eighteen hours a day (when he took off his shoes and soiled socks, the ring of dirt around his ankles had to be scrubbed off with a stiff-bristled brush), and a mother who liked vaudeville and played mah-jongg with her friends when she wasn't helping my father eke out an existence.

I was withdrawn, sullen, detached, removed from hope or desire, and probably depressed—"mopey," my father called it. I was also left pretty much alone. I had no close friends. I can't remember how I spent my time, except I know that I made up improved versions of my life that ran like twenty-four-hour newsreels in my mind.

I didn't much like school, and barely remember most of my teachers. Except for Miss Shirer. I liked Miss Shirer enormously. She taught the eighth grade, and she was almost famous because her older brother, William Shirer, was broadcasting from Berlin on CBS. I leaned into the radio whenever Shirer was on. That he was anti-Hitler was thrilling to a kid who, in 1938, often felt like the only Jew in Westwood, New Jersey, a town that richly deserved its reputation as a major stronghold of the German Bund.

On one psychically momentous occasion, Miss Shirer asked us to spend about ten minutes telling the class about our favorite hobby. I panicked. After all, I liked Miss Shirer a lot, but the truth was that I didn't have anything remotely like a favorite hobby. My efforts to develop recreational interests like those of the other guys had failed miserably. I was mediocre at sports. I was bored with stamps. I was too clumsy to tie dry flies, too nervous to hunt, too maladroit to build model airplanes out of balsa wood. What I finally decided to do, in a moment of desperate inspiration, was to bring a shoe box full of shoe polish, different colors and shades in cans and bottles, since the only palpable physical activity I regularly engaged in was shining the family shoes.

And so when it was my turn in the spotlight, I revealed the arcane nature of a new art form. I described in loving detail the nuances of my palette (I was especially good on the subtle differences between oxblood and maroon). I discoursed on the form and function of the various appliances needed to achieve an impressive tone and sheen. I argued both sides of the debate on solid versus liquid wax and wrapped it all up with a spirited disquisition on the multiple virtues of neat's-foot oil. It was a remarkable performance, if only because it was, from start to finish, an act of pure imagination. I could tell from her smile that Miss Shirer thought it was terrific. Even the class seemed impressed in a stupefied way. And there, in a flourish of brushes and shoe polish, a new Warren Bennis was born.

You should know a few other things about me before we draw any conclusions about my intellectual or academic contributions. My favorite essayist, Isaiah Berlin, once remarked that his reputation was based on systematic overestimation of his abilities. ("Long may this continue," he added merrily.) Over three decades I have written a great deal. A small portion of that work has had a life outside the pages of the journals in which it originally appeared. The most enduring examples are the work on planned change, the study of the stages of groups, the essay on the inevitability of democracy that almost miraculously came true twenty-six years after it was written, and the more recent work on leadership, particularly the ongoing analysis of why leaders can't lead. I am proud of that body of work, some written with distinguished colleagues. But there are moments when I look back and have my doubts. Where is the irrefutable masterpiece, the systematic application, the great theoretical treatise? When I think about the achievements of some of my peers, I sense a depth and continuity that is majestically alien to my own. In an essay on Tolstoy, Berlin notes the distinction Tolstoy makes between foxes and hedgehogs. Foxes know many things of various degrees of importance, while hedgehogs know one big thing. Foxes are conceptualists. While the critics are fussing about the latest vulpine theory, the fox is already working on the next one. Hedgehogs, at their best, produce Darwins; at their worst, pedants. Foxes occasionally can claim an Einstein or an Oppenheimer but more often are simply dilettantes. I'm clearly a fox with a sneaking admiration for the hedgehog.

There's another aspect of my intellectual development that can't be dismissed: that is empathy and the role it has played in both my temperament and my work. I think the ability to read and respond to others has to do with my Jewishness and the sense of marginality that goes with it. Minorities have to be good at picking up subtle cues of rejection. Our moral radar is always switched on, ready to detect what is and what is not acceptable to the majority community. As Lionel Trilling once said, this enables us to understand the mind of the enemy. But Trilling also felt, as did Berlin and as do I, that empathy, or at least that part of it that involves eternal vigilance—the stethoscope always probing for danger—can also undermine one's critical abilities. There is what Berlin called the "fatal desire to please." Over the years I've come to value the ambivalent gift of empathy, but it did lead me, earlier on, to work on projects that a friend once described as "good boy" work—solid books of readings that cited everyone and his or her colleagues and left no idea unturned or fully developed.

Arthur Lovejoy, the historian of ideas, once wrote that every writer possesses, and often tries to hide, his or her distinctive "metaphysical pathos," those subterranean, often unconscious impulses and values that govern our choice of intellectual work. My way of putting it would be less metaphysical and abstract, although it makes the same point. It seems to me that the issues we select to study are almost always the underground churnings of unresolved conflicts—that our ideas stem from an attempt to solve our existential predicaments and that the unlikely force behind all rational problem solving is the need to quiet our demons. (We are all children of our time, and, needless to say, mine includes the golden age of psychoanalysis.)

These, then, are some of the early forces that shaped me:

• A family structured like a double helix, my brothers, bonded in unimaginable ways, in one strand, and a mother and father who rarely connected, in the other. I felt outside this structure, almost invisible, a nonparticipant observer. Growing up in a Jewish family in a gentile community, I rejected both. Talk about marginal.

• A search for power and potency born out of what I perceived as an unsuccessful father, who, prodded by my mother, moved from town to town, opening and soon closing a series of candy stores, malt shops, and soda stands. Like so many of my depression-era generation, I remember the day my father lost his last regular job as one of the most wretched and despondent of my life. Without realizing it then, I vowed never again to feel such utter hopelessness. Understandably, given the disappointments of his own working life, my father kept urging me to learn a trade, by which he meant carpentry or printing or tailoring. My mother, whose unrelenting forcefulness frightened me even more than my father's passivity, thought I should be a child movie star, on the order of Bobby Breen, who sang, on the brink of adolescence, like a castrated cantor. Recognizing that my voice was at best croaky and had a range of about half an octave, she insisted that I take ten accordion lessons from Pietro Agostino of Hackensack, New Jersey, sincerely believing that what my voice lacked, the 120 bass Hohner accordion could easily redeem. I did finally master "The Sharpshooters' March" and "Over the Waves." But even the professionally optimistic Pietro Agostino, who probably needed the $1.50 an hour I paid for my lesson and claimed to admire my "drive" (I schlepped the accordion on the Rockland County bus, ten miles from Westwood and back again, twice a week), felt that I lacked what he charitably described to my mother as "touch." Go figure.

• A terrible sense of uncertainty, which may be the human condition for non-grown-up humans. My only early certitudes were my ability to observe and an insatiable hunger to learn. The latter arose not out of anything as neutral as curiosity but because I needed the illusion of understanding in order to feel safe. After the shoe polish affair, I developed a growing sense of the power of the imagination, which may be the only real power children have.

I emerged from boyhood sure of only two things: that I never wanted to get on another bus carrying an accordion and that I didn't want to grow up to be like the people I already knew. It was almost time to invent a life of my own.

## The U.S. Army: 1943–1947

The Army Specialized Training Program, better known as ASTP, beckoned. To qualify you had to pass a physical and demonstrate an IQ of 125 or so. Camp Hood, Texas (now Fort Hood), was the venue for its seventeen weeks of basic training. Following my stint at Camp Hood, I was shipped to UCLA for the collegiate portion of my army career. The army had no trouble matching my many incompetencies with a career track: I was assigned to major in "sanitary engineering." Fortunately, ASTP was dismantled in order to prepare for the D-day invasion of Normandy. And I was sent to Fort Benning, Georgia, to attend the infantry school there.

The so-called Benning School for Boys was the best possible education for combat. If education is supposed to prepare you for what you will confront in real life, then the training there was near perfect: German villages and cities were reproduced on the base, and we were drilled in what we were likely to encounter as the Germans desperately resisted the end of the war. While it's fair to say no one is every truly prepared for combat, Fort Benning came pretty damned close.

In 1944 I was commissioned as a second lieutenant and sent almost immediately to the European theater of operations, first as a platoon commander and later as a company commander. I was nineteen. (Later I learned I had been the youngest infantry officer in the ETO.) The company I joined had been savaged during the Battle of the Bulge. Out of 189 men and six officers, the normal size of an infantry company, only 60 men and two officers remained. One of the two, Claude Williams, had graduated from Benning just two months before I did. The other, the CO, Captain Bessinger, had in civilian life been the caretaker of the Vanderbilt mansion in Asheville, North Carolina. He was old, I thought, almost thirty-five, and half deaf because of the incessant roar of German antitank guns. He was also one of the finest leaders I've ever met.

As noted earlier, I had first become interested in leadership watching my twin brothers, one of whom effortlessly initiated activities that attracted other kids (including a rather tame teenage gang), while the other couldn't influence his way into a stickball game. My army experience affirmed my lifelong interest in the topic.

In the army I saw firsthand the consequences of good and bad leadership in the simplest and starkest terms—morale, tank support that would or would not be where it was supposed to be, wounds, body counts. The army was the first organization I was to observe close-up and in-depth. And although I have been in pleasanter classrooms, it was an excellent place to study such organizational realities as the effects of command-and-control leadership and the paralyzing impact of institutional bureaucracy.

Captain Bessinger was a wonder. Despite his poor hearing, he really listened to the men, inspired them, and protected them from the whims of the brass. In every way Bessinger embodied what Doug McGregor, my mentor later in college, immortalized as a "Theory Y" orientation.

Bessinger was also my first role model, although I didn't know that phrase then and even now the banality of the term doesn't do justice to the man. A high school dropout, Bessinger literally kept me alive. He taught me how to identify different kinds of German artillery by their sound. He taught me how and when to duck. He also had a quality I deeply respect but have never been able to emulate—the courage to be patient.

After a month or so in combat, I became weakly confident that I wasn't going to bolt or go nuts (I was less sure I wasn't going to die). And in the time-honored army fashion, I began grumbling about the conditions we were fighting in. We had inadequate air cover and tank support, incompetent "forward observers" from the artillery, delays in getting reserves, unspeakable rations, and so on. Each day my voice would grow more strident, and each day Captain Bessinger would chew his tobacco and listen, with less and less of his legendary patience. One day (only a few weeks before the war ended, as it happened) I blurted out, "I, for one, don't know how the hell we're going to win this f—ing war unless. . . ." Finally, the captain spat out his plug of Red Man, looked at me through sad, beagle eyes, and said, "Shit, kid, they've got an army too."

Bessinger had given me exactly the useful truth I needed. The Germans did have an army, an army composed largely of hungry fourteen- and fifteen-year-old kids, shooting wooden bullets because they had run out of metal casings (the wooden bullets exploded hideously on contact). They were even more frightened than I was and had to contend with a bureaucracy that was at least as bad.

I wonder how much that story conveys to someone who wasn't there. The army in wartime was an organization, unlike most I've studied since, in which miscommunications and errors in judgment could kill you. I was a teenager, desperately trying to make sufficient sense of the general chaos to stay alive, and along came a person who listened, as empathically as possible, and who, despite coming from a totally different culture from my own, was able to transcend age, rank, and ethnic and religious background to help me cope with our mutual dilemma. Bessinger, whom I haven't seen since he was wounded in 1945, wasn't just a leader; he was the kind of leader you read about in the Bible.

I came very close to signing up for a career in the army once the war ended. My division, the Sixty-third, was dismantled, and I was eventually sent to European headquarters in Frankfurt, where I served in the transportation corps. I had a Jeep and a driver, an apartment in the Frankfurt compound, and membership in the officer's club. I was twenty. The army had already served me well, if only by giving me an honorable way to leave my family. It had taught me self-reliance and the extraordinary power that comes of being organized and using your time efficiently. Frankfurt was a kind of finishing school. I learned what fork to use and how dry a martini should be. I took weekend trips to Luxembourg City, Wengen, Switzerland, and Bad Homburg with a sweet "older woman" (she was going on twenty-six), a captain in the WACS. Among the heady things she taught me was how to eat an artichoke.

The main reason I didn't sign up for an army career was that my runner, Gunnar, had beguiled me with stories about the college he had been attending before the war. He loved the school, located in bucolic-sounding Yellow Springs, Ohio, in large measure because it allowed him to work part of the year and attend classes the rest of the time. The college had a strange name: Antioch.

Gunnar told me he wanted to become a clinical psychologist, and he had already worked for the Psychological Corporation, validating tests, and in the personnel department of Macy's, testing job applicants. He said that the courses he had taken had prepared him for the jobs and that the jobs had enhanced his classroom experience. I was fascinated by Gunnar's tales of Antioch. No one in my entire family had gone to college—no one. But Antioch intrigued me, and I figured I could afford it, given both the GI Bill and the co-op job system.

Gunnar was killed by an errant canister of white phosphorus on the last day of fighting in the town of Budesheim, Germany. And I, after serving two more years in Europe, was accepted as a freshman at Antioch.

## Antioch College: 1947–1951

I took the train to Antioch. (It actually stopped at Springfield, and I hitchhiked the last ten miles to Yellow Springs.) As we neared my destination, my seatmate couldn't resist asking me why I wanted to go to a "Commie school," with its "nigger-lovers, pinkos, and people who believe in free love." (What, I have wondered ever since, is the opposite of free love—expensive love?)

Antioch was progressive. Even then we called it "politically correct," although without the ironic tone we use today. In many ways it was an ideal community. The campus heroes were intellectuals. There were no Greek societies or social clubs. People of color were celebrated, the Young Communist League and followers of Henry Wallace were taken seriously, and the talk was ferocious, utopian, and unending.

But for all its commitment to diversity and independent thought, Antioch had a definite subculture, an unwritten Antioch way. We ordered our organically grown wheat from Deaf (pronounced Deef) County, Texas; our Telemann from Sam Goody in New York; and Dwight MacDonald's *Politics* and *The Nation* from Greenwich Village. The books we read were Erich Fromm's *Escape from Freedom,* Bertrand Wolfe's *Three Who Made a Revolution,* Edmund Wilson's *To the Finland Station* and *Axel's Castle,* Marquis Child's *Sweden: The Third Way,* Djuna Barnes's *Nightwood,* Malcolm Lowrey's *Under the Volcano* (we all knew that it was his one and only novel and that he had died too young from booze), T. S. Eliot's *The Cocktail Party,* and the complete works of Thomas Mann, Hemingway, Fitzgerald, Dos Passos, Ford Madox Ford, and Virginia Woolf.

We uniformly vilified the literary upstarts: Norman Mailer, Irwin Shaw, Herman Wouk, and James Jones.

The army taught me the value of being organized. At Antioch I learned to have opinions. That may not sound very important, but it amounted to a personal paradigm shift. Before college, I had been like Olenka in Chekhov's story "The Darling." Olenka, Chekhov writes, "saw the objects about her and understood what was going on, but she could not form an opinion about anything and did not know what to talk about. You see, for instance, a bottle, or the rain, or a peasant driving his cart, but what the bottle is for, or the rain, or the peasant, and what is the meaning of it, you can't say, and could not even for a thousand rubles."

What freedom, what liberation, to have opinions, sometimes based on reason and evidence, sometimes based on nothing more than the liberal campus zeitgeist. There were times at Antioch when a particular politically correct opinion would run through the entire population like a flu epidemic (vegetarianism and the superiority of home weaving were two I recall). But all the same, having opinions was, at least for me, tantamount to developing a personal identity.

Later on, as I became a nimbler, more seasoned Antiochian, I developed a whole set of counter-opinions. I began tweaking, sometimes reviling, the campus's more doctrinaire positions in a series of pseudonymous satires in the college literary magazine, writing under the name Dr. Gruppen Ausgefundener (Dr. Group Finder-Outer). The satires caused George Geiger, our venerable professor of philosophy, to compare me with S. J. Perelman (what a coup!) and made just about everybody look at me differently.

As a result, I was "tapped" (informally, of course) by the campus intellectuals, despite my philistine interest in social psychology and economics. The cognoscenti were easy to spot at Antioch. They wore army fatigues (the women especially); smoked Camels in long black cigarette holders; drank beer at night at Com's, a black bar in town; listened with closed eyes to Johnny Coltrane keening on the jukebox;

played esoteric games like Botticelli; regularly threatened to transfer to Columbia or Chicago; and constantly said "fug," emulating James Jones's queer contraction in *From Here to Eternity,* a book everyone claimed to loathe. I trembled with delight when I was invited to join them at Com's.

Henry Broude was one of the Brahmins, then a senior (I was a junior, or, as we, finding all labels of rank offensive, said, "a third-year student"). He was Waldemar Carlson's teaching assistant in Fiscal Policy, which introduced me to Keynes. Henry, now a distinguished economist at Yale, probably doesn't remember this, but after he read my term paper for the course, he said I might want to consider graduate school and mentioned in particular Harvard or MIT. The Nobel laureate John Franck once said that he always knew when he had heard a good idea because of the feeling of terror that seized him. I was seized.

There were at least three other things that influenced me during those Antioch years. First was the famous co-op program, pioneered by one of the college's great presidents, Arthur Morgan, an engineer who was Roosevelt's first head of the Tennessee Valley Authority. Antioch's program was mandatory, complex, and extraordinary. You came to campus for eight weeks; then, with the counsel of an adviser, decided on a job somewhere in the world—usually a fairly large urban center—and worked for twelve weeks; then returned to campus for sixteen weeks. It normally took five years to finish Antioch, decades before that became the national norm. I did it in four because, in classic Antioch fashion, I got co-op credit for my four years in the army.

Splicing classroom experience with real-world work was a wonderful way to explore the relationship or lack thereof between theory and practice, word and act, those who make history and those who study it. There was an exquisite tension between the idealistic tilting at windmills that went on on campus and the inevitable compromises of the workplace.

Second, Antioch forced me to confront, for the first of innumerable times, both my desire to achieve personal satisfaction and the often conflicting urge to live up to the motto of Antioch's founding president, Horace Mann: "Be ashamed to die until you have won some victory for humanity." That tension between self-expression and civic responsibility continues to trouble me, perhaps even more now than it did then.

Third, Antioch deserves credit for teaching me to beware of totalized explanations of life and other mysteries. Despite the campus's sometimes unfortunate tendency toward groupthink, there were so many competing ideas poking at you that you couldn't help developing a healthy skepticism about commissars of thought. The quest for a Parnassian truth, a rule or rules for everything, was what my heart wanted but my mind rejected. The Spanish film director Luis Buñuel used to say, "I would give my life for a man who is looking for the truth, but I would gladly kill a man who thinks he has found the truth." Although there were a few "true believers" on the faculty, most of the professors were skeptics with little patience for universal systems. Certainly the great lesson of the first half of the twentieth century has been that overarching systems or theories that eliminate the opportunity for independent thought lead to totalitarianism. We had experienced the savagery of Nazism, the horrors of Stalinism, the limits of Marxism and Freudianism. We were sufficiently adolescent to continue to seek the grail of grails. But we also knew, in our disappointed hearts, that the Truth could be fatal to millions.

But my most important influence at Antioch by far was its president, Doug McGregor. He came there in 1948 at the age of forty-two, open, broad-grinned, and tweedy from MIT, where he had started an industrial psychology department. I don't think there was a search committee in those days, or else Arthur Morgan simply ignored it. Morgan visited McGregor at MIT, liked him enormously, and asked him to become college president.

Doug was at Antioch for six years and turned the school on its head. At his very first assembly, he announced, while our collective jaws dropped, that he valued his four years in analysis more than his four years as an undergraduate, that he hadn't the faintest idea what the students or faculty wanted, and that maybe the campus should shut down for a week while we had some "goal discussions" in small groups. Soon after, goal discussions were initiated (much to the consternation of the Brahmins, who thought they amounted to "pooling ignorance"). Those sessions redefined our collective aspirations, focused our vision for our education, and constituted a superb example of how change is facilitated by involving those who will be most affected.

In a foreword to a book of Doug's essays, published after his death at the tragically early age of fifty-eight, I described Doug as "a born innovator, a born experimenter. He refused to accept what was, or the traditional, uncritically, and it may be that his greatest and most permanent achievement was to create an atmosphere in which students, as well as faculty, were stimulated to question and challenge continually in an effort to create an educational program that had a relationship to the whole life of the individual. . . . If there was anything he was trying to overcome or destroy, it was the institutional habit of talking about the virtue of democracy while running affairs autocratically."

By the time Doug returned to MIT in 1954 to start a new program in organizational studies, he had already laid the groundwork for what today is called organizational behavior, human relations, or personnel management. As Mason Haire, one of his colleagues at MIT in the 1940s, pointed out, Doug created much of the professional field in which he operated: "Much of the work that goes on now couldn't have happened if he had never been."

If Captain Bessinger saved my life, Doug McGregor surely shaped it. In my final year at Antioch, I took a tutorial with him on "superior-subordinate relationships and leadership" and several courses on group dynamics, taught by his MIT colleague, the maverick psychologist Irving Knickerbocker.

I liked everything about Doug and tried to be like him in every conceivable way. I started smoking a pipe, tried to dress the way he did (though I was a 38 short and he was at least a 42 long), and applied to MIT for graduate work, although I had little idea what it would entail or even that it would funnel and focus my later choices. The truth is that I wouldn't have gotten into MIT without his recommendation; nor would I have gotten tenure there without his full-throated endorsement (he threatened to quit if it wasn't granted unanimously); nor would I have sought a university presidency; nor, in short, would my life have taken the direction it has.

In a recent interview a British journalist, David Oates, talks about my dissociation of myself from my family and quotes me as saying, "I was brazen in getting teachers at school to make me the favorite son. I kept being adopted by intellectual father figures and was shameless at sucking up to mentors." Sounds awful, doesn't it? The phrase "sucking up" is appalling, I know. Without repudiating that confession, I'd like to reframe it: I did cultivate major figures in my field—Doug McGregor, Carl Rogers, Abe Maslow, Erik Erikson, Peter Drucker, and others. While I was not unmindful of what their patronage might mean professionally, the truth is that I couldn't resist the power of their ideas and their personalities. I was so drawn to genius, perhaps, because I felt so ordinary myself.

## MIT and Milli Vanilli: 1951–1956

MIT was as different from Antioch as Cambridge from Yellow Springs. My straight-A performance at Antioch and Doug's three-page letter of recommendation were the sole reasons I was admitted to the MIT Economics Department. In college I had taken algebra and introductory physics, and that was about it. Most of my new MIT classmates had taken advanced calculus, knew at least the rudiments of set theory, understood Markov chains, and had mastered Boolean algebra. At my first interview, the then-admissions officer, economist Charles P. Kindleberger, outlined the courses I'd have to take to catch up and confessed, "We didn't exactly throw our hats in the air when we saw your application." It was a daunting revelation.

MIT was a confusing cocktail of makeup mathematics; philosophy of science; microeconomics from a great teacher, Bob Bishop; more economics from a great mind, Paul Samuelson; industrial statistics from Bob Solow; consumer economics from Franco Modigliani; and economic history from Walt Rostow (my only honest A). A pop quiz: Three of the above are Nobel laureates. Who are they?

But there were also George Shultz, who taught labor economics, and Alex Bavelas, who was the most brilliant designer of small-group experiments who ever lived. And then there was another early mentor, the most playful professor during my MIT days, Herb Shepard, who taught me that groups are real, even if they don't have spinal cords, and introduced me to Harry Stack Sullivan, Karen Horney, Erving Goffman, Norbert Wiener, L. J. Henderson, Elton Mayo, Walter Cannon, and a raft of people who were developing networks—not the human networks I was familiar with but electronic ones. In other words, a raft of people who were inventing the present day.

What a dazzling group! I was sometimes befuddled, routinely intimidated, and thoroughly outclassed by these new colleagues of mine, including my fellow graduate students (there were no women in the department then, and the only minority group was Canadians). It is probably true that I was the least prepared, the least mathematically inclined (Samuelson put it charitably when he said I lacked "mathematical flair"), and the only one who really wondered why he was there. The painful truth is that in Samuelson's seminar, whenever he was summing up, saying something like, "Well, that's the theory of duopoly," he would look over at me and ask, "Warren, are you with me?" If I nodded yes, he knew he was free to go on to the next unfathomable point (perhaps the Stackleburg point!), certain that everyone else in the class had got it hours before.

To get through the Ph.D. program, a sometimes uneasy amalgam of economic theory and social science, I began to memorize and mimic. I don't think I really understood what the Walrasian General Theory of Equilibrium was all about, but I was perfectly capable of memorizing the equations. I imitated my professors and the brightest of my fellow graduate students. For roughly two years I lip-synced what I heard, Milli Vanilli style. Eventually the words I formed on my lips came more naturally, but I often wondered whether I was kidding myself and should try my hand at something else (tailoring, Dad?).

Perhaps most of us learn through a form of lip-syncing, but I often found the process terribly confusing. Sometimes I would identify with Herb Shepard, cuddly, empathic, and warm, and at other times with Bob Solow, Brooklyn-tough, caustic, and wonderfully lucid. Sometimes my model was Talcott Parsons, who taught sociology at Harvard (I took up to half my social science courses at Harvard under an agreement between MIT and Harvard that may still be in effect today) and was unfathomable in ways that Samuelson couldn't dream of. Parsons was a Weberian sociologist prone to neologisms whom the graduate students dubbed "Talk-a-Lot" Parsons in our Christmas play. Sometimes my model was Alex Bavelas, with his Gretsky-like touch in setting up small-group experiments, so subtle and brilliant and utterly charming.

I lip-synced all of them. When I began teaching undergraduates, I didn't always know who I'd be that day or what I would sound like. On some days I thought of myself as a total fraud. Especially the day I bought an expensive, nonrequired book on microeconomics at the Harvard Coop after Paul Samuelson had casually mentioned it in class. Written by Stanford professor Tibor Scitovsky, it was called *Competition among the Few*. It cost $5.95 (the rent on my small apartment on Gray Street was only $9.00 a week), and when I handed the clerk my Coop credit card, I became woozy with self-doubt. What was I doing, lip-syncing idols and going broke buying books I could hardly understand?

After completing my thesis in less than a year and a half—something of a miracle, given my state of mind—I taught social psychology for one year (1955–1956) as an assistant professor and then left because the department had a policy against hiring its own until they had taught elsewhere for at least five years.

Actually, I was glad to leave. I still couldn't pass Paul Samuelson in the corridor without stammering over his first name, and I had begun to suspect that the MIT approach to truth, mathematical and quantitative, was not only beyond me but limited as well. Logical positivism had stormed the social sciences in the 1950s with its belief that all certifiable truths about human behavior could be predicted with scientific certainty. I wasn't sure about that then and am even more dubious about it today. However meticulously obtained, facts are rarely unassailable. And I was tired of fighting my natural impulse, revealed as long ago as Miss Shirer's eighth-grade class, to poeticize the materials at hand and give them a distinctive shape.

The thing I feared most, even beyond incompetence (which I thought about constantly), was that I would become an anemic heir to the majestic but alien minds of my teachers. And I was terribly tired of moving my lips to someone else's tune.

## Bethel, Boston, and Sapiential Circles: 1955–1967

Life picked up steam that last year at MIT. It's a jumble of memories now, but a nascent career seemed to be taking shape. A career as what was less obvious. While officially my degree was in economics, I knew in my heart I was a generalist. At Cambridge dinner parties, where one's discipline was an identity card, I sometimes blushed when I described myself as an economist. Often I would simply say that I taught at MIT and a respectful hush would fall over the group, as if those letters sufficed for station identification.

The lack of a clear-cut professional identity had its advantages. I was an inkblot on which others could project their needs. Once, for instance, the editor of a mildly radical journal published at Brandeis called and asked if I would join the editorial board. I did so gladly. Later the editor, Lew Coser, told me that the key reason for the invitation was that the journal needed a gentile on its masthead and thought one from MIT would look especially good. Actually, I enjoyed the editing involved, but, more important, our editorial board meetings put me in touch with a group of scholars more interested in ideas than in their measurement—people like Coser and his wife, Rose; Kurt Wolff; and Maury Stein. My Brandeis circle thought of me as an economist, whereas at MIT I was generally regarded as a social psychologist. Not having to be pinned down was fine with me.

In 1955 I was invited to Bethel, Maine, the summer headquarters of the National Training Laboratories. At Bethel, as we all called it, everyone was buzzing about a new social invention called T-groups (the T stood for training). Established in 1947 by the redoubtable refugee psychologist Kurt Lewin, NTL crackled with intellectual energy and the heady sense that some major discovery about the real nature of groups was taking place.

Bethel was singularly fortunate in having three genuine social revolutionaries on hand to help it weather Lewin's tragically premature death at the age of forty-seven. Ronald Lippitt, Kenneth Benne, and Leland Bradford each brought their own special gifts to bear. A distinguished young social psychologist, Ron Lippitt contributed intellectual rigor and methodological sophistication. No one could articulate the extraordinary spirit of the place better than Ken Benne, Bethel's resident philosopher. He was a dazzling intellectual "fox" who has taught me much. And holding it all together was Lee Bradford, who was both a visionary and a first-rate manager, a man who continued to dream even as he kept an institution full of dreamers running smoothly.

Leading a T-group at Bethel was a wild, exhilarating experience—"a trip," as the nation would begin to say a decade later. For a period of two weeks a group of strangers was brought together and asked to leave behind the roles, constraints, and norms of everyday life. People screamed, people guffawed, people wept, people talked: You never knew what would happen next. In the micro-utopias of Bethel, I discovered what life could be like when the usual mechanisms that govern our quotidian lives are absent. As the group developed and evolved, I saw how we search for structure and support and how we recoil from some individuals and align ourselves with others. I also realized how deeply our attitudes toward authority are buried and how stubborn they are.

In the supercharged atmosphere I was sometimes overwhelmed by what I saw and felt. When a group really came together, when the communication was free and telling and truthful, you could practically feel the bonds between us expanding and deepening like the intertwined roots of enormous trees. Once in a while I felt that our bodies were somehow actually joined, like those of Siamese twins, so that the emotions circulated between the members of the group, creating some superior new social organism. It was heady stuff that made what took place in the typical academic small-group lab look as drab as a black-and-white movie.

Later that year Herb Shepard and I wrote two articles on "natural groups" in which we described the stages of group growth that I had experienced so vividly at Bethel. The articles were published back to back—an unusual move—in *Human Relations,* then the most prestigious journal in social psychology. No mention was made, needless to say, of merging roots or Siamese twins.

Although I was unaware of it at the time, it seems clear to me now that the study of group dynamics that flourished after World War II was as much a response to the recent past as a leap into the future. And in large part, I now believe, it was a reaction to Hitler.

At least two of the giants in the field, Kurt Lewin and Fritz Redl, were Jewish refugees from Hitler's reign of terror. It seems almost inevitable that they would have developed a profound faith in democratic groups, given their firsthand experience of the destructive power of charismatic leaders, including their ability to enslave their followers. Lewin's early experiments, as well as those of his students, seem now almost foreordained to demonstrate that democratic groups are not only more fulfilled psychologically but more efficient, especially under complex and changing conditions. The theory that democratic groups are superior struck a sympathetic chord with a whole generation that had heard the ominous roar of a nondemocratic group cheering Hitler at Nuremberg.

Interestingly, those Americans who were drawn to Kurt Lewin's theories were almost all midwestern populists with a homegrown anti-authoritarian tradition of their own. I'm referring to Bradford, Benne, and Lippitt, of course, but also to Herb Thelen, Ren Likert, Doug McGregor, and many others. In that postwar period social scientists and related researchers, myself included, tended to view all authority with deep-seated skepticism, if not suspicion. We adopted much the same stance toward leaders that Baudelaire took toward newspapers: that you might learn from them if you read them with the proper contempt.

The three years between the time I left MIT and returned there in 1959 were spent teaching at Boston University. I worked mainly with Ken Benne and Bob Chin, as well as with the head of BU's Psychology Department, Nathan Maccoby. I also taught at Harvard with Freed Bales, Phil Slater, and Ted Mills and did research on groups with Will Schutz and Tim Leary (both at Harvard in the antediluvian age before Esalen and LSD, respectively) and with the psychoanalyst Elvin Semrad at what was irreverently called Boston Psycho.

At that time I was also undergoing six years of psycho-analysis with a Boston-trained analyst. That means, for those of you uninitiated in the therapeutic and intellectual folklore of the 1950s, a real, orthodox Freudian analysis. My analyst changed the pillow case for each analysand, every fifty-minute hour.

That was a rich, tumultuous, enchanting time in my life. Only my mother seemed unwowed by all I was experiencing. I remember telling her in 1959 that I had been psychoanalyzed. I sensed that she didn't like the thought of me untangling my psyche in the presence of a non-Bennis, but her only response was to ask how much I had paid the doctor. I told her—$3.00 an hour for the first three years, $15.00 an hour after that. "And you went how often?" she asked. I told her—five days a week for the first three years and four days a week for the next three. She was silent for several minutes and then said, "Hmmm . . . that comes to quite a bit of money." Another pause, and she said, "Son, I wish you had taken that money and spent it on yourself."

In 1959 Doug McGregor invited me to return to MIT, where he was heading up a department in the new Sloan School of Management. He had already recruited a formidable team: Don Marquis and Ed Schein, in particular, and later Bill Evan, Per Soelberg, Tom Allen, Mason Haire, Harry Levinson, Bob Kahn, Dave Berlew, and Fritz Steele.

Those years at BU and MIT were my best in academic terms. My output was prodigious—everything from tightly designed experiments in small-group communications to psychoanalytic exegeses of the schism between C. P. Snow's "Two Cultures." With Benne and Chin I produced my first book, a selection of readings titled *The Planning of Change* (1961). I also did another book of readings in interpersonal dynamics, in collaboration with Ed Schein, Dave Berlew, and Fritz Steele.

Both books eventually went into four editions, but even more thrilling than their success was the experience of working as part of an intellectual team. Sometimes when a group of talented people comes together, even if only for a short time, something wonderful happens. Each individual energizes the others, teaches them and learns as well. When everything goes right, this creative collaboration produces something new and important. Twenty-five years ago I mentioned this phenomenon—which has led to such diverse

achievements as the Bauhaus School and the atom bomb—
to Margaret Mead, who was giving a speech at Harvard. I
asked her whether much had been written about it. She said
no. "You write about it," she said. "And call the book *Sapiential Circles.*" And that, finally, is what I am doing now.

## SUNY Buffalo: 1967–1971

I made the pilgrimage to Buffalo, as did many others, largely
under the spell of Martin Meyerson's bold dreams and blandishments. I visited the western New York campus, and later,
in my Beacon Hill home in Boston, I asked Martin what his
own goal for Buffalo was. Always thoughtful, he hesitated a
moment and said, "To make it a university where I would like
to stay and be a professor after finishing my administrative
responsibilities."

Over the next six weeks I spent most of my time trying to
decide whether or not I should leave Boston for Meyerson's
grand experiment on the shores of Lake Erie. It was an
excruciating period, made even more tense by the fact that
my wife had had a miscarriage after her first trip to Buffalo
and had to spend most of the time in bed. My memory of that
late-winter trip to Buffalo is one of exhaustion. And God, was
it cold! As I walked down the roll-away stairs into the white
swirl of the runway at Buffalo International Airport, all I could
think of was someone's bitchy observation that summer in
Buffalo was three weeks of bad iceskating. (Actually, summers there are lovely—as summers are only in places where
you fully understand the alternative.)

My colleagues at the Sloan School were unsympathetic
when I announced I was considering an offer to be provost at
the State University of New York at Buffalo. Their attitude
toward administrative jobs at any university bordered on
contempt "God," one asked, "why do you want to spend your
time shuffling papers?" And then, of course, there were the
snowblower jokes. It was difficult to explain to them what I
was going through, but now I realize it was a genuine crisis.

I was haunted, almost obsessed, by the need not just to teach and research management and leadership but to experience it firsthand. I wanted, as Shakespeare put it, to know "a hawk from a handsaw."

I turned to everyone I could think of for advice. I remember calling David Riesman at Harvard one day early in March 1967. He had taught at the law school at Buffalo when it was still a private university and was advising Meyerson on social science matters. David gave me a realistic assessment of the academic state of the university (many mediocre departments; some first-rate ones, including the quirky, creative English Department). He also put in a perversely good word for the industrial landscape, with its "chartreuse and black and mauve smoke against the steel-gray sky."

Still perplexed, I approached a friend at the Harvard Business School who studied mathematical models of decision making. He said he had once been in a similar position and had gone to his dean for advice. "Why don't you work it out mathematically?" the dean asked him. My friend howled when he recalled his indignant response: "But this is important!"

Meyerson kept up his dignified campaign of persuasion. His great gift as a recruiter was his ability to transmogrify all the highly visible drawbacks of Buffalo and make them reappear in the guise of exhilarating challenges. What a pleasure it was to be with him! Meyerson has a wonderfully agile, broad-ranging mind; he can think of nine things at once. Moreover, he seemed to know everybody. (It's from him that I learned the importance of the Rolodex.)

In recruiting, Meyerson's ace in the hole was a truly monumental vision for transforming Buffalo from a conventional university to an academic New Jerusalem—"the Berkeley of the East," as he liked to say. The ideas were stunning: decentralization of authority; dozens of new colleges that would function as intimate "intellectual neighborhoods"; universitywide research centers to grapple with urban studies, higher education, and other major issues; a new campus to be built from the ground up—the list went on and on. It was a seductive dream that tended to drive out any trivial-seeming qualms I had about the weather and the number of good bookstores in Buffalo compared with Boston.

While I was pondering the Buffalo offer, I was also considering two others—one from the Salk Institute and the other, ironically, to be vice-president for academic affairs at USC. As I weighed and reweighed alternatives, real life intruded one morning when I discovered that someone had broken into our house and stolen the family's winter coats from the vestibule.

The Boston winter ended that day. Drawn outside by the sweet air of early spring, I took a brisk, pleasant stroll over to Filene's Basement, where I bought a new overcoat—the heaviest alpaca snowcoat in the store.

Obviously, without realizing it I had made up my mind.

Two other provost candidates handpicked by Meyerson accepted about the same time. Eric Larrabee, a suave and brilliant New York editor *(Harper's, Horizon),* became provost of arts and letters, and Karl Willenbrock agreed to leave his post as an associate dean at Harvard to head Buffalo's engineering faculty. Four other provosts were recruited from the existing faculty.

Larrabee, Willenbrock, and I—Meyerson's chief outside recruits—arrived on campus that fall with all the optimism and confidence of young princes joining a crusade. Though only Willenbrock was a seasoned administrator, our relative inexperience didn't deter us in the least. We were sure that in this academic Great Good Place, creativity would count for more than traditional training and ordinary credentials. Meyerson had emphasized this point repeatedly. If in fact his idea of unorthodox training was a degree from Harvard in a field other than the one you were appointed to teach in, then so be it. We had no doubt we could set Buffalo free.

We certainly looked the part. Buffalo is a town where you don't have to make fashion statements. Swathed in down, everybody looks pretty much like the Michelin man for most of the winter. But we three had style, even panache. I remember the entrance we made at the first provosts' meeting. Karl invited me to have breakfast with him before the meeting at the Frank Lloyd Wright–designed house he had picked up for a song on his arrival in Buffalo. Afterward he and I climbed into his white Porsche convertible (a sure sign of an out-of-towner—people in upstate New York tend to favor cars with front-wheel drive in colors that will stand out against the snow, not disappear in it). As we were about to drive away, Karl's wife, Millie, came out to say good-bye and handed us berets to protect us from the wind.

We drove from Willenbrock's Frank Lloyd Wright house to Larrabee's Frank Lloyd Wright house (which was adjacent to Meyerson's Frank Lloyd Wright house). Eric was waiting for us, a homburg perched on his aristocratic head, his umbrella furled. I remember the sense of euphoria I had as we drove toward campus in the warm September sun and my complete confidence that, if nothing else, we epitomized Buffalo's new look. God only knows what the natives thought as we drove onto the tree-lined campus. To some, I'm sure, we must have looked like the vanguard of a particularly spiffy occupying force.

During my first year as provost at Buffalo, I recruited nine new chairs and two new deans, changing about 90 percent of the leadership structure of the social sciences. The faculty gained forty-five new full-time faculty (almost 75 percent of the present Buffalo faculty were appointed under Meyerson). I personally interviewed more than thirty candidates for various jobs. The newcomers were a largely self-selected group who shared the commitment to innovation, risk taking, and excellence that was the credo of the Meyerson presidency.

For that first year Buffalo was a kind of academic Camelot. When we provosts gathered around the president's conference table, we were ready to work miracles. Occasionally, however, signals reached me that not everyone took us quite as seriously as we took ourselves. One morning I found that on my coatrack someone had hung a Batman cape (I eschewed the down parka that was the winter uniform of the campus and wore a Tyrolean cape that I thought was quite dashing). The anonymous critic had a point. Omnipotent fantasy was the delusion of choice that year in the administration building.

The occasional doubt crept in. In my end-of-the-year provost's report, I ticked off the high points of the ambitious reorganization we were undertaking but cautioned that "each of these virtues could be transformed overnight into obstacles and problems." But such reservations were rare.

The commitment to transforming the university shaped my home life as well. Our house was constantly filled with academic superstars and promising newcomers we were desperately trying to recruit and with Buffalonians with whom we were frantically getting acquainted. As one local wag observed, my wife and I were always entertaining "two hundred of [our] closest friends." That first year we had sixty-five parties—brunches in the garden, afternoon wine-and-cheese parties, but mostly large dinner parties where everyone who mattered was invited to meet whoever was being wooed.

Sometime late in that first spring, my four-year-old daughter, Kate, came into the garden while I was reading the newspapers in a rare moment of stillness. She looked pensive. I asked her what she was thinking. She said she was thinking about what she wanted to do when she grew up.

"What have you decided?" I asked.

She paused for a long time and then said, "When I grow up, I want to be a guest."

I picked her up and laughed. And then later, when I was by myself, I cried. At four Kate was like the psychiatrist's child who wants to grow up to be a patient. Her remark wasn't so much clever as it was true—and terribly sad.

I learned a great deal at Buffalo, but one thing I did not learn was how to integrate intimacy with ambition. I still haven't learned at sixty-eight. Yeats writes that "the intellect of man is forced to choose / Perfection of the life, or of the work, and / if it take the second must refuse / A heavenly mansion, raging in the dark." In real life the dilemma is even more excruciating, because it is often the people we love who are left raging in the dark.

Like John Kennedy's Camelot, our academic utopia lasted roughly a thousand days. By 1970 our attempt to transform the university was interrupted by the campus unrest that was sweeping the country. At one point six hundred police officers in full riot gear appeared on campus, ready to use force if protesting students got too uppity. It was not academic life as any of us had known it. A student filmmaker at Buffalo put it nicely when he titled his cinema vérité record of that turbulent semester *Andy Hardly Goes to College*. The halls of ivy were no longer filled with the optimism of a few years earlier but instead were filled with the lingering smell of tear gas.

In the final analysis the Meyersonian spirit at Buffalo was defeated by a changed political and economic reality. Yet there were ways in which we contributed, however unwittingly, to that failure.

Examining what went wrong at Buffalo altered forever the way I think about change. Martin Meyerson had the first thing that every effective leader needs—a powerful vision of the way the organization should be, a vision he was able to communicate to me and many of his other recruits. But unless a vision is sustained by action, it quickly turns to ashes.

The Meyersonian dream never got out of the administration building. In ways that only later became clear, we undermined the very thing we wanted most. Our actions and even our style tended to alienate the people who would be most affected by the changes we proposed. Failing to appreciate the importance to the organization of the people who are already in it is a classic managerial mistake, one that new managers and change-oriented administrators are especially prone to make. We certainly did. In our Porsches and berets, we acted as if the organization hadn't existed until the day we arrived.

There are no clean slates in established organizations. A new administration can't play Noah and build the world anew with two handpicked representatives of each academic discipline. Talk of new beginnings is so much rhetoric—frightening rhetoric to those who suspect that the new signals the end of their own careers. At Buffalo we newcomers disregarded history. But without history, without continuity, there can be no successful change. A.N. Whitehead said it best: "Every leader, to be effective, must simultaneously adhere to the symbols of change and revision and the symbols of tradition and stability."

What most of us in organizations really want (and what status, money, and power serve as currency for) is acceptance, affection, self-esteem. Institutions are more amenable to change when the esteem of all members is preserved and enhanced. Whatever people say, given economic sufficiency they stay in organizations and feel satisfied in them because they feel competent and valued. Change carries the threat of loss. When managers remove that threat, people are much freer to identify with the adaptive process and much better equipped to tolerate the high degree of ambiguity that accompanies change.

When I think of Buffalo, I think of that joke "How many psychiatrists does it take to change a light bulb?" The answer is "One, but the light bulb really has to want to change." Organizations change themselves when the members want to. You can't force them to change, even in a Batman cape.

## The University of Cincinnati: 1971–1978

The logical next step after Buffalo was a college presidency. My name began to surface at the meetings of presidential search committees, short-lived organizations I would come to know well over the next two decades. During 1970–1971 my name appeared on several short lists, and in the fall of 1971 I became president of the University of Cincinnati.

Less than a year into my tenure, I had a moment of truth. I was sitting in my office on campus, mired in the incredible stack of paperwork on my desk. It was four o'clock in the morning. Weary of bone and tired of soul, I found myself muttering, "Either I can't manage this place, or it's unmanageable."

As I sat there, I thought of a friend and former colleague who had become president of one of the nation's top universities. He had started out full of fire and vision. But a few years later, he had quit. "I never got around to doing the things I wanted to do," he explained.

Sitting there in the echoing silence, I realized that I had become the victim of a vast, amorphous, unwitting conspiracy to prevent me from doing anything whatsoever to change the status quo. Unfortunately, I was one of the chief conspirators. This discovery caused me to formulate what I thought of as Bennis's First Law of Academic Pseudodynamics, which states that routine work drives out nonroutine work and smothers to death all creative planning, all fundamental change in the university—or any institution, for that matter.

The evidence surrounded me. To start, there were 150 letters in the day's mail that required a response. About a third of them concerned our young dean of education, Hendrik Gideonse. His job was a critical one—to bring about change in the way the university taught teachers and to create a new relationship between the university and the precollege students in the deprived and deteriorating neighborhood around us, the neighborhood from which we drew an increasing number of students.

But the letters were not about education. They were about a baby, Gideonse's ten-week-old son. The young dean was committed to ensuring that his wife had the time and freedom to develop her potential as fully as his own. And so he was carrying the baby to his office twice a week in a portable bassinet that he kept on the desk while he worked. The local paper had run a story on Gideonse and his young office companion, with picture, on page one. National TV had picked up the story. As a result, my in-basket had begun to overflow with letters urging me to dismiss the dean or at least have him arrested for child abuse. My response was to say that if Gideonse could engage in that form of applied humanism and still accomplish the things we both wanted in education, then I, like Lincoln with Grant's whiskey, would gladly send him several additional babies for adoption. But there was no question that Hendrik and his baby took up quite a bit of my time.

Also on my desk was a note from a professor, complaining that his classroom temperature was down to sixty-five degrees. Someone once observed that trying to lead faculty is like herding cats. What did this man expect me to do—grab a wrench and fix the heating system myself? A parent complained about a four-letter word in a Philip Roth book being used in an English class. The track coach wanted me to come over and see for myself how bad the track was.

And that was the easy stuff. That year perhaps 20 percent of my time had been taken up by a problem at the general hospital, which was owned by the city but administered by the university and which served as the teaching hospital of the UC medical school. A group of terminal-cancer patients had, with their consent, been subjected to whole-body radiation as a possible beneficial therapy. The Pentagon, interested in gauging the human effects of nuclear warfare, had helped subsidize the study.

Like Hendrik's baby, this too became a major story, one in which irresponsible comparisons were made between the cancer study and Nazi experiments on human guinea pigs. The flap eventually subsided after a blue-ribbon task force recommended changes in the experiment's design. But by then I had invested endless time in a matter only vaguely related to the primary purposes of the university—and wound up being accused of interfering with academic freedom in the bargain.

In my cluttered office that morning, I grew up in some fundamental way. I realized that, from now on, my principal role model was going to have to be me. I decided that the kind of university president I wanted to be was one who led, not managed. That's an important difference. Many an institution is well managed yet very poorly led. It excels in the ability to handle all the daily routine inputs yet never asks whether the routine should be done in the first place.

My entrapment in minutiae made me realize another thing: that people were following the old army game. They did not want to take responsibility for the decisions they properly should make. "Let's push up the tough ones" had become the motto. As a result, everybody was dumping his or her "wet babies" (as old hands at the State Department call them) on my desk. I decided then and there that my highest priority was to create an "executive constellation" to run the office of the president. The sole requirements for inclusion in the group were that the individual needed to know more than I did about his or her area of competence and had to be willing to take care of daily matters without referring them back to me. I was going to make the time to lead.

I realized that I had been doing what so many leaders do: I was trying to be everything to the organization—father, fixer, policeman, ombudsman, rabbi, therapist, and banker. As a CEO who was similarly afflicted put it to me later, "If I'm walking on the shop floor and see a leak in the dike, I have to stick my finger in." Trying to be everything to everyone was diverting me from real leadership. It was burning me out. And perhaps worst of all, it was denying all the potential leaders under me the chance to learn and prove themselves.

Things got better after that, although I never came close to the ideal. As I look back at my experience at UC, I compare it with my psychoanalysis: I wouldn't have missed it for the world, and I would never go through it again. In becoming a leader I learned a number of important things about both leadership and myself. As Sophocles observes in *Antigone,* "But hard it is to learn the mind of any mortal, or the heart, 'til he be tried in chief authority. Power shows the man."

Having executive power showed me three personal truths. First, I was, as the song says, "looking for love in all the wrong places." Intellectually I knew that leaders can't, shouldn't, count on being loved. But I seriously underestimated the emotional impact of angry constituents. I believed the false dream that people would love me if only they really got to know me. I call it the Lennie Bernstein syndrome. Ned Rorem, Bernstein's friend and colleague, recalls how "Lennie" was furious about a negative review in the *New York Times*. "He hates me," Bernstein said of the critic. Rorem suggested gently that Bernstein really couldn't expect everyone to love him. Bernstein was stunned for a moment by his friend's insight. "Oh, yeah," Bernstein finally conceded, "that's because you can't meet everybody."

Even worse than not being loved was not being understood. I found that so dispiriting that I began to develop a whole new theory about the social determinants of depression. It came to me sometime in 1976. I was flying back from a fund-raising trip to Washington, D.C., and idly skimming through the pages of the American Airlines magazine *American Way,* when I came across a fascinating feature about the items various famous Americans would leave in a time capsule to symbolize America on its two hundredth anniversary. The first celebrity was the astronaut Neil Armstrong. I had helped recruit Armstrong to UC and was floored by his response. He chose a credit card (I forget what it was supposed to symbolize).

I was simply amazed that Armstrong thought the credit card was emblematic of the United States in 1976. It seemed so remote from the technological triumph the country had accomplished in space or what Armstrong himself was famous for. By sheer happenstance, when I got back to Cincinnati that night I attended a party to which Armstrong had also been invited. I couldn't resist asking him about the magazine article. I told him I couldn't understand why he hadn't brought up his famous moonwalk or something else about his historic space flight. Why hadn't he chosen the

American flag he planted on the moon or his fabled camera instead of a credit card?

He looked at me sadly and answered as if from the Slough of Despond. "You too," he said. "Isn't there any way I can escape the astronaut image? Do you realize that I've been teaching aeronautical engineering at your university for the past five years, getting decent student ratings, working on a few important bioengineering projects at the medical school, and still, all you think of me as is Neil Armstrong, astronaut? No wonder I'm depressed."

Anyone in authority, astronaut or baseball player, university president or national leader, is to some extent the hostage of how others perceive him or her. The perceptions of other people can be a prison. For the first time I began to understand what it must be like to be the victim of prejudice, to be helpless in the steel embrace of how other people see you. People impute motives to their leaders, love or hate them, seek them out or avoid them, and idolize or demonize them independently of what the leaders do or are. Ironically, at the very time I had the most power, I felt the greatest sense of powerlessness.

Finally, at UC I began to work out the relationship every leader must resolve between the self and the organization. One university president I knew took his own life because, according to his best friend, "he cared too much for the institution."

Secretly I had doubts about how much I loved UC. I felt that my predecessor had cared too much for the university, so much so that he thought, in the manner of de Gaulle, "UC, *c'est moi.*" I think it's dangerous to identify so strongly with an institution that your own self-esteem can be affected by the outcome of the campus Big Game.

Ultimately, I think, a leader should love the organization enough to help create a self-activating life for it. He or she has to love it enough to try to turn it into an environment in which others can understand and care for it, even in difficult times. A leader has to care enough about the organization to want it to be autonomous, able to function very nicely without him or her.

And I realized an important personal truth. I was never going to be completely happy with positional power, the only kind of power an organization can bestow. What I really wanted was personal power, influence based on voice.

## The Rest So Far

In February 1979 I joined forty other scholars, executives, and futurologists at Windsor Castle for a colloquium on the evolutionary forces at work in society and the ways in which rapid change was likely to affect management.

I learned more about change that week than I had bargained for. At the age of fifty-three I experienced a myocardial infarction, a heart attack that landed me in a fifteen-bed ward at historic Middlesex Hospital, with a glamorous society photographer on my right and an engaging tramp on my left. It was probably the most crucial event of my adult life. I eventually spent three months in England, recuperating. And during that period I had nothing to do but think about what I had learned in the course of five decades and what I wanted to do with the rest of my life.

During the avoidance phase of my recovery, while I was groping for distractions, I learned that Rudyard Kipling had been taken to Middlesex Hospital with a perforated duodenum. When his physician asked Kipling what was the matter, he explained, "Something has come adrift inside" (he died in Middlesex a week later).

I too was acutely aware that something had come adrift inside. Forcibly removed from the overbooked professional life I had created for myself, I began to write poetry for the first time ever. Once again I was discovering what I had learned by putting it into words. My favorite of the poems was one called "Plea Bargaining." In it an authoritative voice asks, "How soon would you like to visit your grave? Answer Not for a long, long time."

During my recuperation at Windsor Castle, I received a call from Jim O'Toole, a management professor at USC, wondering if I would be interested in a professorship there. In June 1979 I visited the campus. I was intrigued by then-dean Jack Steele's vision for the School of Business Administration (I'm a sucker for a vision every time) and astonished by the quality of the faculty he had assembled.

I am now in my twentieth year at USC—my longest continuous tenure at any institution. In many ways it has been the happiest period of my life. USC has provided me with exactly the right social architecture to do what seems most important to me now: teaching in the broadest sense.

At USC I have the leisure to consolidate what I've learned—about self-invention, about the importance of organization, about the nature of change, about the nature of leadership—and to find ways to communicate those lessons. Erik Erikson talks about an eight-stage process of human development. I think I have entered Erikson's seventh stage—the generative one—in which self-absorption gives way to an altruistic surrender to the next generation. Although writing is my greatest joy, I also take enormous pleasure in people-growing, in watching others bloom, in mentoring as I was mentored.

USC has provided me with several other structures for transmitting what I know, including a new Leadership Institute that will be an international center for the study of leadership and the development of leaders in every field. Recently I was also able to apply the sometimes painful lessons I learned as a university president, in the course of heading the committee that chose Steven Sample to be the new USC president.

My father died when he was fifty-nine and Doug McGregor died at fifty-eight. Abe Maslow was barely sixty. When I was growing up, that was the norm. But now, at seventy-five, I find that I need a new role model for the last third of my life, which is shaping up to be the most challenging of all. In a recent television commentary, writer John Leonard praised his mother and his mother-in-law, two remarkable women in their eighties. He said of them that in the course of their lives, they had been pushed out of the windows of a lot of burning buildings. "I need to know," said Leonard, "how they learned to bounce."

I am learning how to bounce from my closest friend, Sam Jaffe, who will be ninety-two this year. (When in his fifties Sam was the Academy Award–winning producer of *Born Free*.) What I have already discovered is that the need to reinvent oneself, to "compose a life," as Mary Catherine Bateson puts it, is ongoing. Three years ago Sam and I took a summer course on Dickens at Trinity Hall, Cambridge. Sam, who recently tried to buy the film rights to a book I had given him, continues to scrimmage in the notoriously competitive subculture of Hollywood. He gives me hope.

I find that I have acquired a new set of priorities. Some of the old agonies have simply disappeared. I have no doubt that my three children are more important than anything else in my life. Having achieved a certain level of worldly success, I need hardly think about it anymore. Gentler virtues seem terribly important now. I strive to be generous and productive. I would hope to be thought of as a decent and creative man.

I think Miss Shirer would be proud.

# 17

# The Years of Scholarship:
# An Intellectual Memoir

*I was honored when USC's Marshall School of Business organized a conference to mark my 75th birthday in the spring of 2000. For the occasion, I was asked to create an "intellectual memoir" which would chronicle in some detail the academic journey I began in MIT in 1951. Just as writing "An Invented Life" was a wonderfully cathartic encounter with my past, so too was writing this memoir an exhilarating experience. It will hopefully offer readers some valuable insights into the milieu which gave rise to a generation of influential colleagues who reshaped American organizational behavior.*

*Language, and thought like the wind*
*and the feelings that make the town;*
*[man] has taught himself, and shelter against the cold*
*refuge from the rain. He can always help himself,*
*He faces no future helpless.*

—Antigone of Sophocles

The arc of events that have shaped my intellectual passions, all of which Sophocles describes—language, thought, feelings, community, change, human advancement and a promising future—still remain obscure to me, perhaps easier to describe than understand. I remain as confused as my students when we argue the age-old dispute between those who think history is determined by events, that we are all, a la Tolstoy, "slaves of history," or those who favor Carlyle and believe that history is simply a succession of biographies, that every great institution, in his words, is "the lengthened shadow of a Great Man." (It never occurred to Carlyle that there could be a Great Woman.) On the face of it, my path has seemed more Tolstoyean than Carlylean. It's as if I've careened, or *careered*, into one zone of intellectual opportunity after another, a sort of an academic ziggurat, or, what I suppose many years later Karl Weick would have referred to as a set of "eccentric precursors." The only thing I am certain about at this point is that history has favored my career.

There was a young soldier I got to know in Germany in late 1944 who had his mind set on attending Antioch College in Yellow Springs, Ohio, after the war because of its co-op program where students divided their time between the classroom and a job. It sounded appealing to me because it was affordable. (Word of the G.I. Bill of Rights had not reached me.) Yellow Springs did sound a bit rural to a city boy; on the map, the two closest "metropolises" were Xenia and Springfield. But it still sounded attractive because of some vague idea that the life of the mind should have some connection to the so-called "real life" I had been experiencing in the Army. So, in 1947, at the advanced age of 22 and after 4 years in the Army, I ventured to Yellow Springs, Ohio.

At the beginning of my sophomore year there, in 1948, a new president was appointed, a 40-something, rather dashing professor from M.I.T., Douglas McGregor. He announced at his first student-faculty "assembly" that he found his 4 years of psychoanalysis more important than his entire undergraduate education. This explosive and unexpected admission was taken in a variety of ways. Most of the faculty were disapproving and cynical and wondered "what have we gotten ourselves into?" There were a few, at the other extreme, who thought, "Gosh, what a candid and brave thing to say!" There were no opinions in the middle, a rather common Antioch response to just about anything. McGregor brought along with him a brilliant and fascinating Merlin, one Irving Knickerbocker, an early pioneer at Black Mountain College, an institution perhaps even more supremely radical than Antioch. Their main interest was in what appeared to be a new field of study, group dynamics.

In the first year of his tenure at Antioch, McGregor, along with his sidekick, Knickerbocker, decided to suspend all classes on Fridays (for the full academic year) for community-wide discussion groups that were to come up with a set of "goals" for the college, what nowadays we would refer to as a mission statement. There were "trained facilitators" and "process observers" and panelists and position papers and *rapporteurs* and spokespersons and God knows what else to coordinate this campus-wide creative bedlam. Most of the faculty were either disapproving and cynical of what they bitterly referred to as "examining our own navels" or worse, and the students were somewhat stupefied but also somewhat excited about getting Fridays off. For any number of reasons, it turned out to be something of a "learning experience," as we Antiochians learned to call virtually everything. And it was a helluva lot of fun.

Another ridiculously creative idea McGregor floated (and for which he raised $1 million dollars from the Kettering Foundation) was for Antioch faculty to also take advantage of the co-op program by taking a year off to do real work in a non-academic setting. Like a mini-co-op program for faculty. The faculty once again were disapproving and cynical. (I learned later that being disapproving and cynical is in our blood.) One hapless assistant professor, an art historian I seem to recall, did advantage himself of this opportunity and took a year off for a job at what was then called Standard Oil of New Jersey. Nothing's been heard from him since.

Without any critical hesitation, I was enthralled with McGregor and his ideas, especially his concern for integrating theory and practice and his belief that the behavioral sciences could lead to a better understanding of organizational and group life and which in turn could lead to more enriching lives. After all, the motto of Antioch's founder, Horace Mann, burned into the limbic zone of our brains, was, "Be ashamed to die until you have won some victory for humanity!" So, Candide-like, innocent and wondrous, I started on my academic odyssey, totally unaware that the career I was about to enter would turn out to be one long, adventurous co-op program. As it has had the character of a three-act play, I'll present it as such.

## Act I: The Early Academic Journey (1951–67)

*This entire act is set in Cambridge, Massachussetts, in three locations: M.I.T., Boston and Harvard Universities. All of the action takes place within W.B.'s memory. He is 26.*

Keep in mind the *zeitgeist* of the 50s and 60s. World War II had ended only 6 years earlier and remained deep in our collective memory. Between the ghost of Hitler and the victory of democracy and its close relative, science, there was hope in the air. Everywhere. Science and Technology made us supremely confident that we were entering a new age. The "shadow of Hitler's ghost"* dominated our thinking and those of us interested in social and political research were committed to the idea of democratic leadership, with an urgent need to understand more about the horror of collective pathology of groups and organizations such as those we witnessed in Germany and the other Axis Powers as well as the Soviet Union.

Keep in mind also that the behavioral sciences came of age during the war. The Office of Strategic Service, (OSS), the precursor to the CIA, the Office of War Information (OWI), The U.S. Army statistical branch, the Operations Research Group, plus hundreds of intellectuals who escaped Hitler's wrath developed a hugely successful behavioral science. The four volumes of *The American Soldier*, edited by S. Stouffer and F.A. Mosteller, *The Authoritarian Personality* by Adorno, Frenkel-Brunswik et al., which purported to measure the "authoritarian personality" with its F-scale (for Fascist), the robust statistical and experimental methods created by the Operations Research Group, led by the likes

---

*As noted earlier, this phrase is borrowed from Barbara Kellerman's seminal essay on this topic.

of P. Morse, G. Kimble R. Ackoff and C.W. Churchman, the seminal work of the Tavistock Institute in the UK, directed by A.T.M. Wilson, working with E. Trist, F.E. Emery, E., Jaques, et al., the psychological testing of the OSS, with at least two future presidents of the American Psychological Association, D.Katz and J.G. Miller, R. Likert of the eponymous scale, the work of C. Hovland and I. Janis on persuasion and influence and Margaret Mead on propaganda at the OWI, all led to the creation of a truly scientific ethos for social research. Wars are a golden opportunity to re-structure societies and to this extent, WWII was a Good War.

*Scene 1 (1951–55)*

On Doug McGregor's advice, I went to the mecca of the scientific studies of group dynamics, M.I.T. By the time I got there, alas, most of the researchers I came to study with had gone; Lewin had died and his students who would shape a fair amount of social psychological research for the latter part of this century, researchers like A. Bavelas, H.J. Leavitt, H.A. Shepard, M. Horwitz, L. Festinger, H.A. Kelley, K. Bach, M. Deutsch, S. Schacter, among others, spread out at university centers all over the country to set up laboratories for social research. A good many joined Rensis Likert to establish the new Institute for Social Research at the University of Michigan. A few remained at M.I.T., Alex Bavelas and Herb Shepard being the most important for me. With them I managed to create a wild mosaic of a curriculum, with half of my studies at Harvard's Social Relations department, a lot of seminars with Bavelas and Shepard and more courses than I would have liked in economic theory at M.I.T.

My department pre-dated what is now called the Sloan School. It was simply called Course XIV, the Department of Economics and Social Science, numbered that way as are all departments and schools at M.I.T. in a more or less "hierarchical" scientific order, starting with math as Course I, Physics, Course II, etc. The buildings are also "named" thusly as in the famous domed Building 10, the seat of administrative power.

By the time I got there in 1951, under the leadership of Paul Samuelson, Bob Solow and Charles Kindleberger, economic theory was clearly the dominant emphasis and I found myself leaning ever more determinedly away from that and toward the social psychology of human institutions. When I told Paul Samuelson that I had decided not to do my dissertation in economics but in organizational theory, his face was a study of blissful, palpable relief.

*Scene 2 (1956–59) ". . . sperm in the air"*

Cambridge and Boston were alive with talent and ideas. How *incredibly* lucky I thought I was to end up here, not having the slightest idea of what I was getting into and what becoming an academic was all about and feeling culturally inferior to everyone I met. (I realized later that I wasn't alone in feeling that, but we were all too insecure to come clean about it.) The atmosphere was electrifying, intense, competitive, challenging, animating, intimidating, incandescent, almost oppressively "hot." Many years later I wrote a book about Great Groups inspired by that era; and recently my colleagues and friends, Jean Lipman-Blumen and Hal Leavitt wrote an outstanding book with a similar theme, *Hot Groups*. Even today, when I think back to those times, they still, to use the words of the Doors, light my fire.

Perhaps the best way to describe the intellectual excitement in the air is an anecdote about Sigmund Freud. He was one of the last Jews to escape from Vienna in 1938. After a short stay in Paris, he settled in London. One day he accidentally met a fellow Viennese, the novelist, Stefan Zweig. Freud asked Zweig how he liked London and Zweig's scornful response was, "London," he spat out, " London . . . how can you even mention London and Vienna in the same breath! In Vienna, there was sperm in the air." Politically incorrect or not, when I arrived in Cambridge in 1951, there *was* sperm in air.

That's what I meant earlier when I said that history favored my career. Perhaps it's another of those imponderable "eccentric precursors," I don't know, but I can't exaggerate the importance of place and time in one's intellectual development. In 1955 my thesis was completed and I stayed on that academic year as an Assistant Professor at M.I.T. Aside from teaching, I worked very hard publishing pieces of my thesis in sociological and psychological journals.* But what I'm most proud of is an article I co-authored with my mentor, Herb Shepard, published in *Human Relations,* "A Theory of Group Development." It was based primarily on our experiences in leading T-Groups at M.I.T. and at Bethel, Maine. In its neo-Hegelian and perhaps overly formalistic way, Herb and I tried to make sense out of the two basic issues all groups have to confront, the issue of power and authority and the issue of intimacy. How those issues were addressed and resolved pretty much determined, in our view, whether or not groups could accomplish creative and productive work.

Between 1956 and 1959, I was awash with ideas and exciting colleagues, in fact in *way* over my head. With that portentous headiness of youth and promise, reflecting and basking in the *zeitgeist* of that time, we thought our research and writing could change the world. Ken Benne and Bob Chin asked me to join them at Boston University. I held four positions there: teaching six hours of undergraduate social psychology at the school of business, co-teaching the introductory General Psychology course to the Ph.D. students in the Dept. of Psychology with the department chair, Nathan Maccoby, and teaching what was then called the Pro-Seminar with Ken and Bob in the Human Relations Center. My fourth job was directing a research project on the role of the Out-Patient Department nurse in nine major Boston hospitals, a study sponsored by the American Nursing Foundation that was later turned into a small book. That was 12 hours of teaching plus leading

*Actually, the very first academic article I wrote was published in 1953 for the M.I.T. Graduate Magazine, "Antigone, Billy Budd and The Caine Mutiny: The Individual vs. Society."

a research team composed of two doctoral students, both gifted social psychologists, Malcolm Klein, who retired recently as chair of USC's sociology department, and Norm Berkowitz, who migrated over to Boston College in the 70s. We were also helped by the head of nursing at Peter Bent Brigham Hospital, Molly Malone, who provided the knowledge of nursing that we sorely needed.

BU also had an active evening school so to augment my salary, I taught a course there. Not a bad "load," I thought, for my annual salary (including summer teaching) of $6,500.

That was my day job. I also accepted an appointment at Harvard Social Relations department teaching a section of a group course that met three days a week. The other "section men" were Freed Bales, Phil Slater, and Ted Mills. I also spent a lot of time at Harvard with two other researchers whose future paths went in somewhat parallel directions. Will Schutz was working at Harvard on a quantitative study of compatibility in small groups with the instrument that later became known as FIRO-B. The other was Timothy Leary, who was developing an observational scale based on Harry Stack Sullivan's interpersonal theories to elucidate the dynamics of groups. That was in Leary's antediluvian (pre-LSD) days when he could accurately be described as a brass-instrument empiricist. Schutz became a guru and pioneer at Esalen and now leads a management consulting business. About Leary, well, I'm not really sure.

They were all my teachers and a wildly diverse lot. My "boss" at BU's school of business was a proper Bostonian with a name that bespeaks his Brahmin status, Lowell Trowbridge; Ken Benne, a Columbia trained philosopher, one of John Dewey's last students, who could talk and always did so on any topic with cosmic virtuosity; Bob Chin, also a Columbia trained social psychologist who worked with all the Greats there, but especially with Gardner Murphy and Otto Klineberg plus the philosopher, Morris Cohen, then at the City College of New York, where Bob did his undergraduate work. Then there was Nathan Maccoby, the redoubtable and crusty chairman of BU's psychology department. I asked him many years later why he asked me to co-teach that general psychology Ph.D. course with him, as I knew so little at that time. He said, "I know. That's why I asked you. I thought that everyone in the psychology department should know at least a *little* general psychology." There was also Mikki Ritvo, later to become a high-flying management consultant, who deserves more than a sentence and who turned me into a feminist. And the young Ph.D. candidates I mentioned earlier, Klein and Berkowitz, along with the wildly bright and funny Barry Oshry and the deadly serious and saturnine Arthur M. Cohen, provided the acid antidotes to any and all pomposities that were in the air. They never lacked for material.

Those three years swarmed with Great Groups, perhaps the most lasting one being the troika of Benne, Chin and myself. Together we co-authored and edited *The Planning of Change,* my first book, published in 1961, an attempt to encompass in one volume the most seminal and original essays in the yet unborn field of organizational change. The book is still in print after 40 years and was in its way and in its day influential. In that volume, Ken coined the phrase, "change agent" and Bob's essay on system change still sets the standard on that topic. Of course, the very title, *The Planning of Change,* betrays our hubris, I suppose, but says far more about the optimistic climate of the time—that we could actually *plan* change. A humorous sidenote to all of this is that my mother, forever proud and innocent of my work, was convinced that a "change agent" was the person who made change at the turnstiles in New York's subway system.

On the other side of the Charles River, Schutz, Slater, Mills and I did a massive amount of research on group psycho therapy, specifically developing measures of group interaction by observing the groups of a preternaturally gifted and amiably naïve psychoanalyst and Chief of Clinical Psychiatry at Harvard, Elvin Semrad. He wanted us to help him figure out why his clinical interventions seemed to be so effective. So for three years we observed his groups, composed of about 15 first-year psychiatric residents, which met every Saturday morning. The following Wednesday afternoon, we would meet with Semrad and would spend between three to four hours poring over the protocols of the previous Saturday morning's meeting sharing our observations and ideas about groups and leadership. They were often riveting discussions and we learned a lot and every once in awhile, we thought we were on the bleeding edge of discovery. But we never did fathom the mystery of Semrad's magic.

Also, during that time, I spent a fair amount of time with Mills at his small group research lab at Harvard. He was taken with Georg Simmel's work on the effect of numbers on group decision making, especially three-person groups since that number is uniquely vulnerable to isolation and coalition building. Aside from helping him analyze the data, he got me to play the "stooge" in one of his ingenious experiments. Later on I got even with Ted by recruiting him to SUNY-Buffalo (from Yale, where he was the Chair of sociology) something for which he's not completely forgiven me.

*Scene 3: 1959–67, M.I.T.*

It wasn't the salary that brought me back to M.I.T. in 1959. The $9,500 was only $500 more than what I was making at BU and the academic marketplace was booming with opportunities. Leaving BU and its sunny collegiality wasn't easy. From Ken Benne, especially, I learned what it was like to be an intellectual; on my next "co-op job," I learned how to be an academic.

What lured me to M.I.T. was my Antioch role model, Doug McGregor, who returned to establish a new "area" (there were no departments in the Sloan School) focusing on the study of human organizations. He was in the process of assembling a remarkable group of people including Ed Schein, Don Marquis, Dave Berlew, Per Soelberg, Bill Evan and later on with either visiting or adjunct status, Dick Beckhard, Bob Kahn, Harry Levinson, and Bob Greenleaf. Doug, among other things, taught me everything I needed to know about recruiting, which served me well later on during my administrative years. *Any* offer Doug made would be one I couldn't refuse.

As I've noted in the past, those seven years at M.I.T. were perhaps the most extraordinarily intense and *academically* productive of my career. Back in those days for reasons which still remain obscure to me, M.I.T. didn't grant tenure until you were 36. To my knowledge, the only exception to this rule was made for the future Nobelist, Bob Solow. It has often been said that academics should have remained the unmarried clerics they once had been and it was true enough there. Life on the M.I.T. faculty was the academic fast track. The competition was from the start unbearably intense. So what else is an under-36 year old, untenured associate professor to do but publish? I published like a madman, as though there were no tomorrow. Checking over an old vitae, I saw that there that I had written something like eight books, some co-edited or co-authored, 27 academic articles in referreed journals, including my first article on leadership, published in *Administrative Science Quarterly* "Leadership Theory and Administrative Behavior: The Problem of Authority," Dec. 1959; my first major article on organizational change, also in the *ASQ,* "A New Role for the Behavioral Sciences: Effecting Organizational Change," Sept. 1963, and a slew of other articles in journals like *Sociometry, The American Psychologist, American Sociological Review* and others. You could tell I was a real academic. There wasn't an article I wrote which wasn't punctuated with a colon in the title.

But there were a few exceptions because somewhere in my bookbag, I came upon a "prophet's rod" and wrote several articles about the future. The future has fascinated me since my *bar mitzvah,* when I based the traditional, "Today-I-Am—a-Man" speech—something I slaved over for months—on the prophet Jeremiah, an interesting choice for me since few Jeremiads have come to my lips since.

With a passion for the future in my heart, my prophet's rod in hand and Phil Slater's genius at my side, we wrote an article that was published in the March/April, '64 issue of the

*Harvard Business Review* forecasting the demise of the Soviet Union and the triumph of democratic capitalism. We based our 1968 book, *The Temporary Society,* on those ideas, a book which later won *HBR's* McKinsey Award for the best business book for that year. It was, I have to say, a *succes d'estime* with mostly glowing reviews in places like *The New York Times* as well as academic periodicals. It was also a total flop commercially, remaindered scarcely 18 months after publication, never to be heard from again until Jossey-Bass republished it in 1998.

I wrote several "more academic" papers around that time as well. My favorite was actually a keynote speech given at the American Psychological Association meeting in Los Angeles in 1964. I entitled it "Organizational Developments and the Fate of Bureaucracy," at which time I took aim at the Weberian classic work on bureaucracy and predicted its demise. Of course, I always took careful academic refuge behind such terms as "between now and the next 50 years or so," just to be on the safe side. In any case, I re-drafted that speech into a paper which only the IBM house organ, *THINK* (Nov./Dec.'66), thought well enough of to publish. It was entitled, "The Coming Death of Bureaucracy." That was one article they should have taken seriously since they soon became victims of that scourge. As I peruse that same old vitae I see that for reasons still mysterious to me, the *Junior League Magazine* reprinted it in 1968. My readership was becoming strangely eclectic—especially when I removed the colon.

My argument was based on a number of factors which I developed in a reprise of the 1964 APA speech, "A Funny Thing Happened on the Way to the Future," (American Psychologist, July 1970) from which I will now quote:

**1.** The growing influence of intellectual technology, and the growth of research and development.

**2.** The growing confluence between men of knowledge and men of power (or as I wrote about it in 1964, 'a growing affinity between those who make history and those who write it.).

**3.** A fundamental change in the basic philosophy which underlies managerial behavior, reflected most of all in the following three areas: (a) a new concept of man, based on increased knowledge of his complex and shifting needs, which replaces the simplistic, innocent push-button concept of man; (b) a new concept of power, based on collaboration and reason, which replaces a model of power based on coercion and fear; and (c) a new concept of organizational values, based on humanistic-democratic ideals, which replaces the depersonalized mechanistic value system of bureaucracy.

**4.** A turbulent environment which would hold relative uncertainty due to the increase of R & D activities. The environment would become increasingly differentiated, interdependent, and more salient to the organization embedded in it. There would be greater inter-penetration of the legal policy and economic features of an oligopolistic and government-business controlled economy. Three main features of the human organizations would be interdependence rather than competition; turbulence; rather than a steady, predictable state; and large rather than small enterprises.

**5.** A population characterized by a younger, more mobile, and better educated workforce.

"These conditions," I argued, "would lead to significant organizational changes. First of all, the key word would be *temporary: organizations,* adaptive, rapidly changing temporary systems. Second, they would be organized around problems-to-be-resolved. Third, these problems would be solved by people who represent a diverse set of professional skills. Fourth, the groups would be conducted on organic rather than on mechanical lines; they would emerge and adapt to the problems, and leadership and influence would fall to those who seem most able to solve the problems rather to programmed role expectations."

Those words, written close to four decades ago, no longer seem quirky or outrageous. Certainly in the new, wired economy, we'll behave more like a biological community: growing, evolving, merging, developing, adapting organically without the necessity of centralized control.

I've left for last my work with Ed Schein. First of all, we authored a book John Wiley published in 1965, *Personal and Organizational Change Through Group Methods,* wherein we took a hard look at the successful and unsuccessful examples of changing social systems through behavioral science interventions. Many of our colleagues protested because we included some examples of woebegone failures and pointed to some of the adamantine qualities of bureaucratic systems. Before undertaking that, we were the senior partners of a compendium of readings and essays, *Interpersonal Dynamics: Essays and Readings on Human Dynamics* (Irwin-Dorsey,1963).

Working with us as co-editors were Dave Berlew and Fritz Steele, the latter, an M.I.T. Ph.D. and as bright as they come, and Dave Berlew, one of the most elegant minds and writers, who, with Dave McClelland, his Harvard Ph.D. thesis advisor, started the hugely successful firm, McBer. John van Maanen was senior editor of the fifth and final volume of *Interpersonal Dynamics.*

On top of all that publishing, Ed Schein, Dick Beckhard and I were able to interest Addison-Wesley in a series of paperbacks on the nascent and inchoate field of Organizational Development. I dropped out of the editing and left it in the able hands of my two colleagues and, as of now, it's fair to say that the series has proved to be extremely successful with at least 40 titles in print.

Two other events must be mentioned. The first has to do with two international adventures. Serving in Germany in World War II was not exactly an experience that would develop one's understanding of the "global economy." You got dog tags, not passports. So when overseas opportunities presented themselves at M.I.T.—and because of it being M.I.T., there were many such opportunities—I jumped at them. And the encouragement of Dean Howard Johnson, later to become M.I.T.'s President, provided the support I needed to take advantage of overseas activities.

The first was anything but a hardship post. I was invited to spend a year ('61-'62) teaching at IMEDE in Lausanne, Switzerland, now known as IMD, one of Europe's leading business schools. At that time, IMEDE was primarily an executive finishing school for Nestlé's high potentials and primarily supported by that company. There were 50 senior executives in the class, about a third of them from Nestlé, the rest from all over the world. Their modal age was the same as mine, 36. IMEDE then drew its faculty from the Harvard Business School. I was one of the few exceptions. The year was memorable for two quite different things. First, because IMEDE was an HBS satellite where the Case Study method was king, I learned-again, with the faculty tic of disapproval and cynicism—how powerful and subtly nuanced the case method can be. I was a novice at it but my office mate, Ed Learned, one of the founders of the policy area at Harvard, and Frank Aguilar, then a DBA candidate and Baker Scholar, and Dave Leighton were among my many mentors.

Far more cosmic was my introduction to the global economy. The European Economic Community (EEC) was just getting its sea legs and, along with the student mix at IMEDE and global business cases plus writing a case, with my students on a French company in Annecy, my eyebrows were continually raised about both the future of globalism and its discontents.

When the possibility of another global adventure came up, this time as faculty director of the Indian Institute of Management at Calcutta, I went for it. Just as IMEDE was an HBS proxy in its early days, the IIM-Calcutta was initially staffed by Sloan School professors conjointly with an outstanding, primarily Bengali, faculty. When I left IMEDE, I thought I understood, perhaps at most, 40% of what was going on in my students' heads; at IIM-C, max: 10%; but that 10% was far more provocative and interesting than the cultural knowledge I picked up in Europe.

I loved working with the Bengali faculty. Intellectually, they were world-class, argumentative, brilliant, and ferociously articulate on any number of matters. Just to give you a little idea of what I was facing there: recently, a playwright and the Home Minister for the state's Communist government said, "Intellectually, I humbly proclaim we are more advanced than anyone else. We discuss the great questions: What is postmodernism? What does Noam Chomsky have to say about this or that? The Bengali may have no food on the table, but he's off arguing somewhere about the Viet Nam War or the last book he has read or whether it is a good idea to change every signboard in the city from Calcutta to Kolkata."

In addition to co-directing the School, I helped to establish an international organization on OD known as INCOD. My cohorts on that project were my Indian colleagues, Suresh Srivastva, Ishwar Dayal, and Nitish De; a social psychologist from the University of Michigan and the Director of our sister institute at Ahmadabad, IIM-A, Kamala Chowdhury; Allen Cohen, on leave from HBS and that year at IIM-A, John Thomas, from M.I.T., Barry Richman, from UCLA and Howard Baumgartel from the University of Kansas were all U.S. representatives. Two others joyfully contributed in translating our dreams into reality, one an Indian, Udai Pareek, and his U.S. counterpart, Rolf Lynton. These stalwarts, working at the very soul of social change, ridiculously ahead-of-its-time, established the Aloka Institute to train Indian change agents.

The other event is a sad one for me to recall now, let alone write about. Doug McGregor suffered a massive heart attack and died at the tragically early age of 58. He was the emotional and intellectual center of our group. I was—we all were—very dependent on him: his brio, his informed optimism and most of all, his unbridled capacity for joy. No one could light up a room the way Doug could after two martinis, smoking his pipe and telling an off-color joke. He was a thoroughly engaged man and totally supportive. Doug was, in the finest sense of that phrase, a "change agent," able to change an entire concept of the hollow, Organizational Man and replace it with a theory that stressed our human potential, our capacity for growth, and a theory that elevated man's role in an industrial society. The truth is that a large segment of our professional lives now operate in an environment which he created.

He was also a close personal friend. I remember the time in 1960 when I wanted to buy a small town-house in a mews on Beacon Hill and asked him whether he thought it was a sound investment for someone (without tenure). In a heartbeat, he said, "I'll lend you the money for the down payment. And don't worry about tenure." His word was always good. I still worried.

I was his reluctant successor at M.I.T. and in a way I don't think it's too fanciful to think that my next career move was a way to incarnate his dreams along with my own.

## Act II: Just Do It, 1967–78

*This act takes place at two universities, SUNY-Buffalo and the University of Cincinnati. Our protagonist served as provost at the former for four years and president of the latter for seven.*

University campuses, throughout the world but especially in the U.S., were roiling with conflict and riots, and to someone whose own education (at least that part of it that led to degrees), was completed when campus was synonymous with a certain degree of detachment, even civility, the late 60s and early 70s were a nightmare. It was first of all baffling and unreal. One could not believe that a campus could be dangerous, that a student could fire-bomb an office or a policeman beat up a faculty member. But all those things were happening on campuses in those days. Sometimes the mist in the early evenings was smog and sometime it was tear gas. Fear and violence, emotions we had only recently come to identify with the American urban experience, became part of the university climate as well.

The moments of horror were captured in gut-rending photographs, rows of police and guardsmen behind masks, a shattered science building in Wisconsin, the Bank of America in flames in Santa Barbara, a dying student sprawled in the grass at Kent State. Universities had moments of horror during that period and it also had periods of almost frantic joy. The atmosphere was that of wartime. Between the terrible reality of the battles were the stretches characterized by boredom, sometimes by enormous freedom as if one were relieved by the special circumstances of all normal duties and responsibilities. When the students weren't denouncing their ideological enemies or confronting (and often being beaten by) the police, they seemed to be having a wonderful time. In this ambivalent emotional climate, the mundane business of going to class, teaching and learning, often went on uninterrupted.

It was the worst of times . . . and it was the worst of times. "So why," an M.I.T. colleague asked, "did you choose the period of greatest campus upheaval in history and leave a full professorship, with a corner office overlooking the Charles River, and go to Buffalo as provost?" He spat out *Buffalo* with the same sort of contempt that Stefan Zweig spoke of London. I suspect that he gave up on me completely when I accepted the presidency of the University of Cincinnati in 1971, because I've not heard from him since.

Having written a great deal about this period elsewhere in this book and in *The Leaning Ivory Tower and Why Leaders Can't Lead,* I won't elaborate further here. While these years were a detour from my role as a pure scholar, Chapter One helps spell out the important ways in which being a practitioner shaped my later writings for an era in which management books had grown into a national obsession.

## Act III: A Return to the Scholarly Life
## (USC 1979-Today)

In 1978 I resigned from UC and received a Twentieth Century Fund grant to write a book on leadership. Shortly after, in April of 1979 I found myself in a London hospital recovering from what my British doctors called a "moderately roughish" heart attack. I had been attending a conference at St. George's House in Windsor Castle. It so happened that my long-time friend from M.I.T. days, Charles Handy, was provost of St. George's House, the newly established center for continuing education center for the Church of England. Charles was also chairing the conference I was attending during which I collapsed. I was recuperating in improbable quarters, the flat of Elizabeth and Charles Handy, compressed into the ancient wall of Henry the Third's wing of Windsor Castle. The Handys graciously and generously looked over me for three long months as I wobbled back to health.

It was during that time that I was recruited by Jim O'Toole to join the University of Southern California's business school faculty. I thought, "Oh yes, oh yes, here is a chance to really make a dent in the universe and make some useful mischief."

I felt like Rip van Winkle when I joined USC, or to be more current, like Austin Powers. It wasn't 20 or 30 years, only 11 since I left the world of scholarship, but the field I left in 1967 was unrecognizable. It hadn't just blossomed, it had become a heavy industry. I felt that the tiny municipality I had known was now Brobdingnag. Virtually every business school and other professional schools as well had their own version of an Organization Behavior department often parading under a variety of names such as Management and Organization (our version at USC) or just management sometimes co-mingled with strategy and other combinations. There were, to my astonishment, a number of hugely successful, best-selling business books—mega-hits such as Peters and Waterman's *In Search of Excellence,* Naisbitt's *Megatrends,* Blanchard and Johnson's *The One-Minute Manager,* Covey's *The Seven Habits* and anything Drucker wrote.

To put this in perspective, Doug McGregor's book on management, *The Human Side of Enterprise,* sold in its peak year, 1965, 30,000 copies and Abe Maslow's book on management—admittedly, it had a weird title, *Eupsychian Management*—sold only 3,000 copies when it was published. In 1998, when it was republished by Wiley, it sold 3,000 copies in its first week on the market.

I suspect that one of two factors, or probably both, may have caused this explosive interest: one was the unexpected and reluctantly accepted notion that maybe the attitudes, perceptions and feelings of the work force and the social architecture they worked under could have something to do with productivity. The other factor may have been the unprecedented competition that American industry was facing from Japan and Germany, which was occurring most dramatically in the late 70s and 80s. In many industrial sectors, like automobiles and consumer electronics they were, to put it politely, eating our lunch. Tom Peters credits the multi-million book sales of his best seller primarily to the latter. Whatever explanation you prefer, one thing was clear: the U.S. was no longer Numero Uno and enlightened business leaders were no longer as supremely confident as they had been for the four decades following World War II. They opened their minds to our ideas.

It's also been one long boom for business schools. The last statistic I saw showed that 85,000 MBAs graduated in 1998. A concomitant of that is the widespread growth of Ph.D. programs. In 1959 I chaired the Sloan School's committee to design its first Ph.D. program. Up to that point, most business schools did not offer Ph.D.s. In fact, business schools were not thought to be an integral part of the intellectual life of the modern university. Most professors of business did not have doctorates. Those who did were either DBAs or had came out of industrial engineering or held an advance degree in accounting.

What drastically changed the intellectual landscape of business education was the influence of two major foundation reports, both published in 1959. The Gordon/Howell report, sponsored by the Ford Foundation, and the Pierson study funded by the Carnegie Foundation supported were enormously influential and had a formidable impact on how business education was done. And the reason these two reports were so successful—no surprise here: each put their money where their mouth was. They gave vast amounts of dollars to a new breed of business professors and to a new type of business school. So we observed the New Schools such as Carnegie-Mellon's Graduate School of Industrial Administration, the already-mentioned Sloan School, the Stanford School of Management and too many others to mention here, carving out new curricula, new research agendas and, in the process, escaping their Rodney Dangerfield "no respect" syndrome.

If I could put the important findings of these two foundation reports into one pithy statement (doing a grave injustice to both), it would be this: business schools had to get away from their almost exclusive reliance on "clinical experience" and develop a more rigorous and scientifically based canon. The tension between empirical experience and codified, systematic knowledge is still a live-wire issue, regularly contested in all professional schools. The extent to which schools of management learn how to make this a creative, rather than a divisive, tension will determine whether or not they can accomplish their academic purposes successfully.

USC, for me, emerging after 11 years of fairly grueling administrative duties, was like joining an intellectual spa, an "intellectual fitness center."* This was *home,* writing and teaching again; finding my own voice. To paraphrase Jerry Garcia, the only one doing what I can do.

These past 20 years may not have been as intense as those Cambridge/Boston ones, but I've never been happier or enjoyed so many significant intellectual partnerships. Working with Ian Mitroff and Dick Mason, we inaugurated a series of management books under the Jossey-Bass label. I've co-authored a number of books with colleagues: with Burt Nanus, *Leaders;* with Ian Mitroff, *The Unreality Industry;* with Pat Biederman, *Organizing Genius;* and with Dave Heenan, *Co-Leaders.*

---

*I stole this phrase from Mort Meyerson. When he was CEO of Perot Systems, he would, on occasion, take a group of diverse and different executives from brain storming sessions. He called these "Intellectual Fitness Centers."

The most intense and exciting collaboration going on at the present time is co-teaching an undergraduate course on leadership with USC's president, Steve Sample. We recruit 50 of USC's best and brightest students and introduce these sharp 20-year olds to leadership through the Great Books, novels, movies, Socratic-like discussions, weekly essays and a wide selection of guest speakers, from Michael Dukakis to former California Governor Pete Wilson, from the Reverend Cecil Murray to Los Angeles Mayor Richard Riordan.

Great cities and great institutions have the Spirit of Place. Certainly, the Boston area had it when I was there earlier in the century. I would argue that now Southern California and the university which is most emblematic of this region, USC, has that spirit.

We do know that cities which have remained great and glorious over long periods of time are those with a rich variety of population, economic enterprise, and social functions. Diversity endows them with resilience and for maintaining identity in the midst of endless changes. Perhaps this is all an elegant justification for why these past 20 years have been, for me, so alive, so absorbing, and so invigorating—who knows.

Thus, it isn't merely history that favored my career, it is also geography, the spirit of the *place.* Perhaps, then, Tolstoy was right. We are slaves to history and to forces we can't control, but we can be rightly grateful for the extraordinary creative possibilities presented by them.

# 18

# *The Wallenda Factor*

*"The Wallenda Factor" is as much about life as about management. In this short essay, based on a study of 90 leaders, I tried to home in on the characteristic that allows a few people to do extraordinary things. I found that those who successfully walked the high wire in whatever field they chose had much in common. They took risks without dwelling too much on the downside. They saw error, not in terms of failure, but in terms of growth. I'm convinced that the late Karl Wallenda found in the tight-rope the answer to a question all of us should ask ourselves: "When do I feel most alive?"*

One of the most impressive and memorable qualities of the leaders I studied was the way they responded to failure. Like Karl Wallenda, the great tight-rope aerialist, who once said, "The only time I feel truly alive is when I walk the tight-rope," these leaders put all their energies into their task. They simply don't think about failure, don't even use the word, relying on such synonyms as *mistake* or *glitch* or *bungle* or countless others, such as *false start, mess, hash, bollix,* or *error.* Never *failure.* One of them said during the course of an interview that "a mistake is just another way of doing things." Another said, "I try to make as many mistakes as quickly as I can in order to learn."

Shortly after Wallenda fell to his death in 1978 (traversing a 75-foot-high tight-rope in downtown San Juan, Puerto Rico), his wife, also an aerialist, discussed that fateful San Juan walk, "perhaps his most dangerous." She recalled, "All Karl thought about for three straight months prior to it was *falling.* It was the first time he'd *ever* thought about that, and it seemed to me that he put all his energy into *not falling,* not into walking the tight-rope."

Mrs. Wallenda went on to say that her husband even went so far as to personally supervise the installation of the tight-rope, making certain that the guy-wires were secure, "something he had never even thought of before." From what I learned from my interviews with successful leaders, I can say that when Karl Wallenda poured his energies into *not falling* rather than walking the tight-rope, he was virtually destined to fail. Indeed, I call that peculiar combination of vision, persistence, consistency, and self-confidence necessary for successful tight-rope walking—the combination I found in so many leaders—the Wallenda Factor.

An example of the Wallenda Factor comes in an interview with Fletcher Byrom, who retired recently from the presidency of the Koppers Company, a diversified engineering, construction, and chemicals company. When asked about the "hardest decision he ever had to make," he said, "I don't know what a hard decision is. I may be a strange animal, but I don't worry. Whenever I make a decision, I start out recognizing there's a strong likelihood I'm going to be wrong. All I can do is the best I can. To worry puts obstacles in the way of clear thinking."

Or consider Ray Meyer—perhaps the winningest coach in college basketball—who led DePaul University to 40 straight years of winning seasons. When his team dropped its first home game after 29 straight home-court victories, I asked him how he felt about it. His response was vintage Wallenda: "Great! Now we can start concentrating on winning, *not* on not losing." And then there is Harold Prince, the Broadway producer. He regularly calls a press conference the morning after one of his Broadway plays opens—before reading any reviews—in order to announce plans for his *next* play.

Effective leaders overlook error and constantly embrace positive goals. They pour their energies into the task, not into looking behind and dredging up excuses for past events. For a lot of people, the word "failure" carries with it a finality, the absence of movement characteristic of a dead thing, to which the automatic human reaction is helpless discouragement.

But, for the successful leader, failure is a beginning, the springboard of hope.

One CEO I interviewed, James Rouse, the famed city planner and developer, said that when he was dissatisfied with the looks of some housing in his Columbia, Maryland, project, he tried to influence the next design by nagging and correcting his team of architects. He got nowhere. Then he decided to stop correcting them and tried to influence them by demonstrating what he wanted, *what he was for.* Inspired by Rouse's vision, the architects went on to create some of the most eye-catching and functional housing in the country. What this illustrates is that the self-confidence of leaders is *contagious.* Two more examples: In the early days of Polaroid, Edwin Land continually inspired his team to "achieve the impossible." Land's compelling self-confidence convinced his managers and researchers that they couldn't fail. When William Hewitt took over Deere and Company in the mid-1950s, he turned a sleepy, old-line farm implements firm into a leader among modern multinational corporations. His secret? Commitment. Confidence. Vision. And always asking, "Can't we do this a little better?" And the employees rose to the occasion. As one long-time Deere employee put it: "Hewitt made us learn how good we were." Because they know where they are going, great leaders inspire the people who work for them so that they, too, can walk the tight-rope. That is one of the reasons why organizations run by great leaders often appear so productive.

Although leading is a "job" for which leaders are handsomely paid, where their rewards come from—and what they truly value—is a sense of adventure and play. In my interviews, they describe work in ways that scientists and other creative types use: "exploring a new space," "solving a problem," "designing or discovering something new." Like explorers, scientists, and artists, they seem to focus their attention on a limited field—their task—forget personal problems, lose their sense of time, feel competent and in control. When these elements are present, leaders truly enjoy what they're doing and stop worrying about whether the activity will be productive or not, whether their activities will be rewarded or not, whether what they are doing will work or not. They are walking the tight-rope.

I've wondered, from time to time, if this fusion of work and play, where, quoting from a Robert Frost poem, "love and need are one," is a positive addiction. My guess is that it is a healthy addiction, not only for individual leaders but for society. Great leaders are like the Zen archer who develops his skills to the point where the desire to hit the target becomes extinguished, and man, arrow, and target become indivisible components of the same process. That's good for the leaders. And when this style of influence works to attract and empower people to join them on the tight-rope, that's good for organizations and for society. Hail the Wallenda Factor!

# 19

## *When to Resign*

*Many of today's leaders, especially within the realm of high technology, are under the age of 35. As such, they may not be terribly familiar with the lives and predicaments of Daniel Ellsberg, Ed Muskie and Robert McNamara, persons whose names are prominent in this essay. Yet even though this piece is close to three decades old, I remain extremely fond of it due to the manner in which it explores when a leader has to draw the line.*

*Friends from the South talk about having to make "hurting decisions," those choices which tear at the soul but which still must be made. None is more painful than deciding you must leave a once beloved institution, whether it's a marriage or a job. This article, written with Patricia Ward Biederman, weighs both the high cost of quitting and the higher cost of staying on in a role in which you are no longer effective.*

No matter how often Daniel Ellsberg reminds the public that not he but a seemingly endless war in Indochina is at issue, I find that it is Ellsberg the man who touches the imagination. One can't help speculating on his personal odyssey from loyal insider to defiant outsider, from organization man to prison-risking dissident. It is the process of that change of heart that fascinates me. What interaction of man and organization produces a commitment like the younger Ellsberg's and then leads only a few years later to equally passionate rejection? How much, I wonder, of the Ellsberg affair is idiosyncratic and how much reflects general principles of organizational life? After all, Ellsberg is not the first government adviser to become suspicious of the work in which he has engaged. What is singular about Ellsberg is that he has found a dramatic way to make his dissent articulate. The organizational ethic is typically so strong that even the individual who dissents and opts for the outside by resigning or otherwise dissociating himself does so with organization-serving discretion. Ellsberg may not have broken the law, but he surely did something more daring. He broke the code. He has not only spoken out, he has produced documentation of his disillusionment.

The stakes are rarely as great, but many people who work in large, bureaucratic organizations find themselves in a position similar to Ellsberg's. They oppose some policy, and they quickly learn that bureaucracies do not tolerate dissent. What then? They have several options. They can capitulate. Or they can remain within the group and try to win the majority over to their own position, enduring the frustration and ambiguity that goes with this option. Or they can resign. Remaining can be an excruciating experience of public loyalty and private doubt. But what of resigning? Superficially resignation seems an easy out, but it also has its dark and conflictful side. As the Stevenson character in *MacBird!* says:

> In speaking out one loses influence.
> The chance for change by pleas and prayer is gone.
> The chance to modify the devil's deeds
> As critic from within is still my hope.
> To quit the club! Be outside looking in!
> This outsideness, this unfamiliar land,
> From which few travelers ever get back in. . .
> I fear to break; I'll work within for change.

If resignation is the choice, the problem of how to leave, silently or openly voicing one's position, still remains.

These options are a universal feature of organizational life and yet virtually nothing has been written on the dynamics of dissent in organizations, although a recent book by Harvard political economist Albert O. Hirschman almost single-handedly makes up for past deficiencies. Oddly enough, the book still remains "underground," largely unread by the wide audience touched by the processes Hirschman describes. I first began seriously considering the question of resignation and other expressions of dissent as organizational phenomena in the Spring of 1970. At that time I had just resigned as Acting Executive Vice-President of State University of New York at Buffalo. As so often happens, my interest in the phenomenon grew out of unpleasant personal experience. I had resigned in protest against what I considered undue use of force on the part of the University's Acting President in dealing with a series of student strikes on our campus that spring. In my case, resigning turned out to be a remarkably ineffective form of protest.[1] When I tried to analyze why, I found that my experience was hardly unique, that most large organizations, including government agencies and universities, have well-oiled adaptive mechanisms for neutralizing dissent. The individual who can force the organization into a public confrontation, as Ellsberg did, is rare indeed.

The garden-variety resignation is an innocuous act, no matter how righteously indignant the individual who tenders it. The act is made innocuous by a set of organization-serving conventions that few resignees are able (or even willing, for a variety of personal reasons) to break. When the properly socialized dissenter resigns, he tiptoes out. A news release is sent to the media on the letterhead of the departing one's superior. "I today accepted with regret the resignation of Mister/Doctor Y," it reads. The *pro forma* statement rings pure tin in the discerning ear, but this is the accepted ritual nonetheless. One retreats under a canopy of smiles, with verbal bouquets and exchanges, however insincere, of mutual respect. The last official duty of the departing one is to keep his mouth shut. The rules of play require that the last word goes to those who remain inside. The purpose served by this convention is a purely institutional one. Announcement of a resignation is usually a sign of disharmony and possibly real trouble within an organization. But without candid follow-up by the individual making the sign, it is an empty gesture. The organization reasons, usually correctly, that the muffled troublemaker will soon be forgotten. With the irritant gone, the organization pursues its chosen course, subject only to the casual and untrained scrutiny of the general public.

The striving of organizations for harmony is less a conscious program than a consequence of the structure of large organizations. Cohesiveness in such organizations results from a commonly held set of values, beliefs, norms, and attitudes. In other words, an organization is also an appreciative system in which those who do not share the common set, the common point of view, are by definition deviant, marginal, outsiders.

Ironically, this pervasive emphasis on harmony does not serve organizations particularly well. Unanimity leads rather quickly to stagnation which, in turn, invites change by nonevolutionary means. The fact that the organizational deviant, the individual who "sees" things differently, may be the institution's vital and only link with, for lack of a better term, some new, more apt paradigm does not make the organization value him any more. Most organizations would rather risk obsolescence than make room for the nonconformists in their midst. This is most true when such intolerance is most suicidal, that is, when the issues involved are of major importance (or when important people have taken a very strong or a personal position). On matters such as whether to name a new product "Corvair" or "Edsel," or whether to establish a franchise in Peoria or Oshkosh, dissent is reasonably well tolerated, even welcomed, as a way of insuring that the best of all possible alternatives is finally implemented. But when it comes to war or peace, life or death, growth or organizational stagnation, fighting or withdrawing, reform or status quo—desperately important matters—dissent is typically seen as fearful. Exactly at that point in time when it is most necessary to consider the possible consequences of a wide range of alternatives, public show of consensus becomes an absolute value to be defended no matter what the human cost.

Unanimity, or at least its public show, is so valued within the organizational context that it often carries more weight with an individual than his own conscience. Thus, we see in the March 31, 1971, issue of The New York *Times* that "Muskie regrets silence on war" and wishes that he had made public as far back as 1965 his "real doubts about involvement in the Vietnam war." Instead, he said, "he voiced his concerns privately to President Johnson." "There are two ways," he said, "and they're both legitimate ways of trying to influence public policy. And I can guess the tendency is, when the President is a member of your own party and you're a Senator, to try to express your doubts directly to him, in order to give him a chance to get the benefit of your views." Senator Muskie said he often had done that, "but wished that I'd expressed my doubts publicly at that time." The article goes on to say that Muskie "was far less hesitant to criticize President Nixon's conduct of the war." In an adjoining article about Humphrey, The *Times* reports him as describing to a student audience "publicly for the first time the pressure he had been under from President Johnson not to speak out on the Vietnam issue. Many times during the first month of the 1968 campaign, he recalled, he had wanted to speak out more forcefully on the Vietnam issue only to be dissuaded by the President. This, he said, posed a personal dilemma. On the one side, he said, he saw his chances for winning the Presidency slipping away. But if he sought headlines on the Vietnam issue by taking a more critical stance, he said, he was being warned by the President that he would jeopardize the delicate negotiations then under way to bring South Vietnam and the Vietcong to the Paris negotiating table."

"That's the God's truth. . . . How would you like to be in that jam?" Humphrey asked a student.

Actually, Humphrey's "jam" is a classic one. A member in good standing of an organization, in this case the Johnson Administration, suddenly finds himself opposed to his superior and his colleagues in regard to some policy. If the policy is relatively unimportant or not yet firm, the objection may be absorbed by bargaining or compromise. If the issue at stake is actually trivial, it may simply be avoided. But if the issue is important and the dissenter adamant, the gulf begins to widen. At first, the dissenter tries to exert all possible influence over the others, tries to bring the others around. In Albert Hirschman's compact terminology, this is the option of *voice*. Short of calling a press conference, this option can be exercised in several ways from simply grumbling to threatening to resign. But usually the individual gives voice to his dissatisfaction in a series of private confrontations like those of Muskie and Humphrey with Johnson. When these fail, as they usually do, he must face the possibility of resigning (or, as Hirschman calls it, exercising the option to *exit*). Resigning becomes a reasonable alternative as soon as voice begins to fail. The individual realizes that hours of sincere, patient argument have come to nothing. He realizes that his influence within the organization is waning, and so probably is his loyalty. If he stays on, he risks becoming an organizational eunuch, an individual of no influence publicly supporting a policy against his will, judgment, personal value system, at times even his professional code.

As bleak as this prospect is, exit on matters of principle is still a distinctly uncommon response to basic institutional conflict. This is particularly true of American politics. In many nations with parliamentary systems, principled resignation from high office is common. But in the United States the concept of exit as a political act has never taken hold. The Walter Hickels are the exception. The last time a cabinet official left in protest and said why was when Labor Secretary Martin Durkin resigned because President Eisenhower refused to support his proposed amendments to the Taft-Hartley Act. As James Reston wrote recently in a postmortem on the Johnson Administration:

"One thing that is fairly clear from the record is that the art of resigning on principle from positions close to the top of American government has almost disappeared. Nobody quits now, as Anthony Eden and Duff Cooper left Neville

Chamberlain's cabinet, with a clear and detailed explanation of why they couldn't be identified with the policy any longer.... Most [of those who stayed on] at the critical period of escalation gave to the President the loyalty they owed to the country. Some . . . are now wondering in private life whether this was in the national interest."

What accounts for our national reluctance to resign and our willingness, when forced to take the step, to settle for a "soft exit," without clamor, without a public statement of principle, and ideally without publicity? Tremendous institutional pressures and personal rationalizations work together to dissuade the dissident from exit in favor of voice. Most of us would much rather convince the boss or top group to see "reason" rather than quit. Resignation is defiant, an uncomfortable posture for most organization men (including politicians and academics). Worse, it smacks of failure, the worst of social diseases among the achievement-oriented. So instead of resigning, we reason to ourselves that the organization could go from bad to worse if we resigned. This may be the most seductive rationalization of all. Meanwhile, we have become more deeply implicated in the policy that we silently oppose, making extrication progressively more difficult. If resignation cannot be avoided, there are selfish reasons for doing it quietly. Most resignees would like to work again. Only Nader's Raiders love a blabbermouth. Speaking out is not likely to enhance one's marketability. A negative aura haunts the visibly angry resignee, while the individual who leaves a position ostensibly to return to business, family, teaching or research reenters the job market without any such cloud. Many resignees prefer a low profile simply because they are aware that issues change. Why undermine one's future effectiveness by making a noisy but ineffectual stand? However selfish the reasons, the organization reaps the major benefits when an individual chooses to resign quietly. A decorous exit conceals the underlying dissension that prompted the resignation in the first place. And the issue at contest is almost sure to be obscured by the speechmaking.

Like the Zen tea ceremony, resigning is a ritual, and woe to the man who fails to do it according to the rules. For example, when Fred Friendly resigned as President of CBS News in 1966 over the airing of Vietnam hearings, he sinned by releasing a news story *before* the Chairman of the Board, William S. Paley, could distribute his own release. Friendly writes in his memoir of this episode:

> Around two o'clock a colleague suggested that I should have called Paley, who was in Nassau, and personally read my letter [of resignation] to him over the phone. When I called Stanton to ask him if he had read my letter to the chairman, he said that he had just done so, and that Paley wanted me to call him. When I did, Paley wanted to know only if I had released my letter; when I told him that I had, all useful communication ceased. "You volunteered to me last week that you would not make a public announcement," he said. . . . The last thing the chairman said to me was: "Well, if you hadn't put out that letter, maybe we could still have done something." I answered that my letter was "after the fact, long after."

Paley's response is explicable only if we remember that the *fact* of resignation and the *reasons* behind it are subordinated in the organizational scheme to the issue of institutional face-saving. A frank resignation is regarded by the organization as an act of betrayal. (To some degree, this is, of course, an issue of personal face-saving. Those in power may wish for institutional harmony in part as a protection against personal criticism.)

Because a discreet resignation amounts to no protest at all, a soft exit lifts the opprobrium of organizational deviation from the resignee. When Dean Acheson bowed out as Under Secretary of the Treasury in 1933 after a dispute with F.D.R. over fiscal policy, his discretion was boundless and F.D.R. was duly appreciative. Some years later, when another official left with less politesse, sending the White House a sharp criticism of the President's policies, Roosevelt returned the letter with the tart suggestion that the man ought to "ask Dean Acheson how a gentleman resigns."

But "hard" or "soft," exit remains the option of last resort in organizational life. Remarkably, the individual who is deeply opposed to some policy often opts for public acquiescence and private frustration. He may continue to voice his opposition to his colleagues but they are able to neutralize his protest in various ways. Thus we see George Ball becoming the official devil's advocate of the Johnson Administration. As George E. Reedy writes:

> During President Johnson's Administration I watched George Ball play the role of devil's advocate with respect to foreign policy. The cabinet would meet and there would be an overwhelming report from Robert McNamara, another overwhelming report from Dean Rusk, another overwhelming report from McGeorge Bundy. Then five minutes would be set aside for George Ball to deliver his dissent, and because they expected him to dissent, they automatically discounted whatever he said. This strengthened them in their own convictions because the cabinet members could quite honestly say: "We heard both sides of this issue discussed." Well, they heard it with wax in their ears. I think that the moment you appoint an official devil's advocate you solidify the position he is arguing against.

One can hardly imagine a predicament more excruciating than Ball's. Often an individual in such conflict with the rest of his organization simply removes himself, if not physically then by shifting his concern from the issues to practical problems of management and implementation. He distracts himself. Townsend Hoopes suggests that this was the case with Robert McNamara. According to Hoopes, who was Under Secretary of the Air Force, there was growing evidence in the Autumn of 1967 that the President and McNamara were growing further and further apart in their attitudes toward escalating the Vietnam war. Hoopes saw in McNamara the fatigue and loneliness of a man "in deep doubt" as to the course the war was taking. But, writes Hoopes:

> *Owing to his own strict conception of loyalty to the President, McNamara found it officially necessary to deny all doubt and, by his silence,*

*to discourage doubt in his professional associates and subordinates.* . . . The result of McNamara's ambivalence, however, was to create a situation of dreamlike unreality for those around him. *His staff meetings during this period were entirely barren affairs: a technical briefing, for example, on the growing strength of air defenses around Hanoi, but no debate on what this implied for the U.S. bombing effort, and never the slightest disclosure of what the President or the Secretary of State might consider the broad domestic and international implications to be.* It was an atmosphere that worked to neutralize those who were the natural supporters of his concerns about the war. (Italics are for emphasis.)

What Hoopes describes is ethical short-circuiting. Conflict-torn McNamara busies himself with the minutiae of war planning because lists of numbers and cost estimates have a distracting, if illusory, moral neutrality. According to Hoopes, toward the end of McNamara's tenure, the despairing Secretary stopped questioning the military and political significance of sending 206,000 more troops into Indochina and concentrated in the short time he had on the logistical problems of getting them to the port of debarkation safely and efficiently.

One sees a remarkably similar displacement of energy from moral or political concerns to managerial or technological ones in the career of Albert Speer. I do not mean to label McNamara a Fascist by literary association. But the pages of *Inside the Third Reich* reveal that Speer dealt with ambivalence brought on by intense organizational stress in a remarkably similar way. Speer did not allow his growing personal reservations about Hitler to interfere with his meticulous carrying out of administrative duties. Speer kept the Nazi war machine running in high gear and increasingly productive until 1945. As Eugene Davidson writes: "A man like Speer, working with blueprints, ordering vast projects, is likely to exhaust himself in manipulation, in transforming the outer world, in carrying out production goals with all the means at hand."

Whether such activity exhausts an individual to the point of moral numbness is questionable, but certainly the nature of the large organization makes it possible for a McNamara or an Albert Speer or an Ellsberg (while at Rand), for that matter, to work toward an ultimately immoral end without an immediate sense of personal responsibility or guilt. Organizations are by definition systems of increased differentiation and specialization, and, thus, the morality of the organization is the morality of segmented acts. As Charles Reich wrote in *The New Yorker,* "A scientist who is doing his specialized duty to further research and knowledge develops a substance called napalm. Another specialist makes policy in the field of our nation's foreign affairs. A third is concerned with the most modern weaponry. A fourth manufactures what the defense authorities require. A fifth drops napalm from an airplane where he is told to do so." In this segmented environment, any one individual can easily develop tunnel vision, concentrating on the task at hand, completing his task with a sense of accomplishment, however sinister the collective result of all these individual jobs well done. This segmented structure characteristic of all large organizations encourages indifference and evasion of responsibility. A benefit of membership in such an organization is insurance against the smell of burning flesh. Speer, for example, still does not seem particularly troubled by the horrors of slave labor in his wartime munitions plants even when making his unique public confession.

Speer reports that it never occurred to him to resign even though he was aware of what his loss would do to hasten the end of Hitler's regime. Faced with a much more subtle and complex situation, McNamara seriously considered resigning, according to Hoopes. But that he did not do so in 1967 when his doubts were so oppressive is remarkable. Hoopes provides a fascinating clue to McNamara's reluctance to resign or even to voice his uneasiness in any except the most private audiences with the President. In the following short portrait by Hoopes in his book *The Limits of Intervention,* we see McNamara wrestling with an ingrained organizational ethic stronger than his own intelligence and instinct:

> Accurately regarded by the press as the one moderate member of the inner circle, he continued to give full public support to the Administration's policy, including specific endorsement of successive manpower infusions and progressively wider and heavier bombing efforts. Inside the Pentagon he seemed to discourage dissent among his staff associates by the simple tactic of being unreceptive to it; he observed, moreover, so strict a sense of privacy in his relationship with the President that he found it virtually impossible to report even to key subordinates what he was telling the President or what the President was saying and thinking. . . . All of this seemed to reflect a well-developed philosophy of executive management relationships, derived from his years in industry; its essence was the belief that a busy, overworked chairman of the board should be spared the burden of public differences among his senior vice-presidents. Within such a framework, he could argue the case for moderation with the President—privately, selectively, and intermittently. But the unspoken corollary seemed to be that, whether or not his counsel of moderation were followed, there could arise no issue or difference with President Johnson sufficient to require his resignation—whether to enlighten public opinion or avoid personal stultification. It was this corollary that seemed of doubtful applicability to the problems and obligations of public office. *McNamara gave evidence that he had ruled out resignation because he believed that the situation would grow worse if he left the field to Rusk, Rostow, and the Joint Chiefs. But also because the idea ran so strongly against the grain of his temperament and his considered philosophy of organizational effectiveness.*

Does this mean that McNamara would not resign because quitting violated some personal notion of honor? Or does it mean that he believed that dissent and "organizational effectiveness" are negatively correlated? I suspect that the latter is closer to the truth. Like any other corporation president, McNamara was raised on organizational folklore. One of the central myths is that the show of unanimity is always desirable.

That this belief is false and even dangerous does not limit its currency. Yes, there are times when discretion is required. Clearly organizations should not fight constantly in public. But what is the gain of forbidding at all costs and at all times any emotional give-and-take between colleagues? A man has an honest difference of opinion with the organizational powers. Why must he be silenced or domesticated or driven out so that the public can continue to believe—falsely—that organizational life is without strife? And yet organizations continue to assume the most contrived postures in order to maintain the illusion of harmony. Postures like lying to the public.

Our inability to transcend the dangerous notion that we don't wash our dirty linen in public verges on the schizophrenic. It implies that dissent is not only bad but that our public institutions such as government are made up not of men but saints who never engage in such vulgar and offensive activities. Thus, government strives to be regarded as a hallowed shrine where, as George Reedy reports from his experience as White House press secretary under President Johnson, "the meanest lust for power can be sanctified and the dullest wit greeted with reverential awe." In fact, organizations, including governments, are vulgar, sweaty, plebeian; if they are to be viable, they must create an institutional environment where a fool can be called a fool and all actions and motivations are duly and closely scrutinized for the inevitable human flaws and failures. In a democracy, meanness, dullness, and corruption are always amply represented. They are not entitled to protection from the same rude challenges that such qualities must face in the "real" world. When banal politeness is assigned a higher value than accountability or truthfulness, the result is an Orwellian world where the symbols of speech are manipulated to create false realities.

"Loyalty" is often given as a reason or pretext for muffling dissent. A variation on this is the claim that candor "gives comfort to the enemy." Ellsberg's national loyalty was repeatedly questioned in connection with his release of the so-called Pentagon Papers. In the first three installments of the document as run in The *Times*, practically nothing that wasn't well known was revealed. A few details, an interesting admission or two, but basically nothing that had not come to light earlier in other less controversial articles and books on the Indochina war. But government officials trying to suppress the publication of the classified material chose to make much of the "foreign consequences" of its release. "You may rest assured," a government official was quoted as saying by the Buffalo *Evening News*, "that no one is reading this series any more closely than the Soviet Embassy."

All of the foregoing pressures against registering dissent can be subsumed under the clumsy label of "loyalty." In fact, they represent much more subtle personal and organizational factors including: deep-rooted psychological dependence, authority problems, simple ambition, co-optive mechanisms (the "devil's advocacy" technique), pressure to be a member of the club and fear of being outside looking in, adherence to the myth that gentlemen settle their differences amicably and privately, fear of disloyalty in the form of giving comfort to "the enemy," and, very often, that powerful Prospero-aspiration: the conviction that one's own "reasonable" efforts will keep things from going from bad to worse.

There is a further broad cultural factor that must be considered before the other defenses against exit can be understood. It simply doesn't make sense for a man as intelligent and analytically sophisticated as our nation's Number One Problem Solver, Robert McNamara, to delude himself that he couldn't quit because "duty called." Duty to whom? Not to his own principles? Nor, as he saw it, to the nation's welfare. McNamara's real loyalty was to the code of the "organizational society" in which most of us live out our entire active careers. Ninety percent of the employed population of this country works in formal organizations. Status, position, a sense of competence and accomplishment are all achieved in our culture through belonging to these institutions. What you *do* determines, to a large extent, what you *are*. "My son, the doctor" is not only the punch line of a thousand Jewish jokes. It is a neat formulation of a significant fact about our culture. Identification with a profession or other organization is a real-life passport to identity, to selfhood, to self-esteem. You are what you do, and work in our society (as in all other industrialized societies) is done in large, complex, bureaucratic structures. If one leaves the organization, particularly with protest, one is nowhere, like a character in a Beckett play, without role, without the props of office, without ambience or setting.

In fact, a few more resignations would be good for individual consciences and good for the country. Looking back, veteran diplomat Robert Murphy could recall only one occasion when he thought he should have resigned. The single instance was the Berlin Blockade of 1948–49, which he thought the U.S. should have challenged more vigorously. "My resignation almost certainly would not have affected events," he wrote in regret, "but if I had resigned, I would feel better today about my own part in that episode." *Time* magazine, from which Murphy's quotation was taken, goes on to say in its essay:

> In the long run, the country would probably feel better, too, if a few more people were ready to quit for their convictions. It might be a little unsettling. But it could have a tonic effect on American politics, for it would give people the assurance that men who stay truly believe in what they are doing.

My own resignation was a turning point. The decision represented the first time in many years of organizational life that I had been able to say, No, I cannot allow myself to be identified with that particular policy, the first time I had risked being an outsider rather than trying to work patiently within the system for change. Many factors entered into the decision but in the last analysis my reason for resigning was an intensely personal one. I did not want to say, a month or two months after the police came onto campus, "Well, I was against that move at the time." I think it is important for everyone in decision-making positions in our institutions to speak out. And if we find it impossible to continue on as administrators because we are at total and continuous odds with institutional policy, then I think we must quit and go out shouting. The alternative is petit-Eichmannism, and that is too high a price.

### Note

1. For many reasons, notably my decision to retain another administrative position while resigning the acting post. The distinction between the positions was clear only to other members of the administration, and the public generally interpreted my equivocal exit as a halfhearted protest.

# 20
# Followership

*Like "When to Resign," this short piece is about doing the right thing. Subordinates sometimes pay the ultimate institutional price for candor, but that doesn't relieve them of the obligation to tell their leaders what they may not want to hear. This piece is also a reminder that morality is not solely an executive function.*

It is probably inevitable that a society as star-struck as ours should focus on leaders in analyzing why organizations succeed or fail. As a long-time student and teacher of management, I, too, have tended to look to the men and women at the top for clues on how organizations achieve and maintain institutional health. But the longer I study effective leaders, the more I am convinced of the under-appreciated importance of effective followers.

What makes a good follower? The single most important characteristic may well be a willingness to tell the truth. In a world of growing complexity, leaders are increasingly dependent on their subordinates for good information, whether the leaders want to hear it or not. Followers who tell the truth, and leaders who listen to it, are an unbeatable combination.

Movie mogul Samuel Goldwyn seems to have had a gut-level awareness of the importance of what I call "effective backtalk" from subordinates. After a string of box-office flops, Mr. Goldwyn called his staff together and told them: "I want you to tell me exactly what's wrong with me and M.G.M., even if it means losing your job."

Although Mr. Goldwyn wasn't personally ready to give up the ego-massaging presence of "yes men," in his own gloriously garbled way he acknowledged the company's greater need for a staff that speaks the truth.

Like portfolios, organizations benefit from diversity. Effective leaders resist the urge to people their staffs only with others who look or sound or think just like themselves, what I call the doppelgänger, or ghostly-double, effect. They look for good people from many molds, and then they encourage them to speak out, even to disagree. Aware of the pitfalls of institutional unanimity, some leaders wisely build dissent into the decision-making process.

Organizations that encourage thoughtful dissent gain much more than a heightened air of collegiality. They make better decisions. In a recent study, Rebecca A. Henry, a psychology professor at Purdue University, found that groups were generally more effective than individuals in making forecasts of sales and other financial data. And the greater the initial disagreement among group members, the more accurate the results. "With more disagreement, people are forced to look at a wider range of possibilities," Ms. Henry said.

Like good leaders, good followers understand the importance of speaking out. More important, they do it. Almost 30 years ago, when Nikita Khruschev came to America, he met with reporters at the Washington Press Club. The first written question he received was: "Today you talked about the hideous rule of your predecessor, Stalin. You were one of his closest aides and colleagues during those years. What were you doing all that time?" Khruschev's face grew red. "Who asked that?" he roared. No one answered. "Who asked that?" he insisted. Again, silence. "That's what I was doing," Mr. Khruschev said.

Even in democracies, where the only gulag is the threat of a pink slip, it is hard to disagree with the person in charge. Several years ago TV's John Chancellor asked former Presidential aides how they behaved on those occasions when the most powerful person in the world came up with a damned fool idea. Several of the aides admitted doing nothing. Ted Sorenson revealed that John F. Kennedy could usually be brought to his senses by being told, "That sounds like the kind of idea Nixon would have."

Quietism, as a more pious age called the sin of silence, often costs organizations—and their leaders—dearly. Former President Ronald Reagan suffered far more at the hands of so-called friends who refused to tell him unattractive truths than from his ostensible enemies.

Nancy Reagan, in her recent memoir, "My Turn," recalls chiding then–Vice President George Bush when he approached her, not the President, with grave reservations about White House chief of staff Donald Regan.

"I wish you'd tell my husband," the First Lady said. "I can't be the only one who's saying this to him." According to Mrs. Reagan, Mr. Bush responded, "Nancy, that's not my role."

"That's exactly your role," she snapped.

Nancy Reagan was right. It is the good follower's obligation to share his or her best counsel with the person in charge. And silence—not dissent—is the one answer that leaders should refuse to accept. History contains dozens of cautionary tales on the subject, none more vivid than the account of the murder of Thomas à Becket. "Will no one rid me of this meddlesome priest?" Henry II is said to have muttered, after a contest of wills with his former friend.

The four barons who then murdered Becket in his cathedral were the antithesis of the good followers they thought themselves to be. At the risk of being irreverent, the right answer to Henry's question—the one that would have served his administration best—was "No," or at least, "Let's talk about it."

Like modern-day subordinates who testify under oath that they were only doing what they thought their leader wanted them to do, the barons were guilty of remarkable chutzpah. Henry failed by not making his position clear and by creating an atmosphere in which his followers would rather kill than disagree with him. The barons failed by not making the proper case against the king's decision.

Effective leaders reward dissent, as well as encourage it. They understand that whatever momentary discomfort they experience as a result of being told from time to time that they are wrong is more than offset by the fact that reflective backtalk increases a leader's ability to make good decisions.

Executive compensation should go far toward salving the pricked ego of the leader whose followers speak their minds. But what's in it for the follower? The good follower may indeed have to put his or her job on the line in the course of speaking up. But consider the price he or she pays for silence. What job is worth the enormous psychic cost of following a leader who values loyalty in the narrowest sense?

Perhaps the ultimate irony is that the follower who is willing to speak out shows precisely the kind of initiative that leadership is made of.

# 21

## *The Leader as Storyteller*

Leading Minds: An Anatomy of Leadership
*by Howard Gardner, with the collaboration of Emma Laskin*
*New York: BasicBooks, 1995*

*One of the best books on leadership in recent years,
Howard Gardner's* Leading Minds, *was unusual in
the way it focused on public leadership without
addressing corporate leadership. Its lessons are
nonetheless powerful for everyone. The following
review, published in the* Harvard Business Review *in
1996, examined Gardner's intriguing notion that the
most effective leaders—the evil ones as well as the
noble ones—are good storytellers, persons who can
both relate and embody a powerful narrative in a way
that draws others alongside them.*

Writing on leadership has become a growth industry in
recent years, with writers churning out thousands of articles
and hundreds of books on the subject over the last two
decades. Of the handful that seem likely to endure, two that
immediately come to mind are James MacGregor Burns's
still resonant *Leadership* (Harper & Row, 1978) and James
O'Toole's *Leading Change: Overcoming the Ideology of Comfort and the Tyranny of Custom* (Jossey-Bass, 1995). These
two have now been joined by a third, Howard Gardner's
superb new book, *Leading Minds.*

Subtitled *An Anatomy of Leadership,* Gardner's book is
extraordinarily ambitious. It attempts to do nothing less
than create a cognitive framework for all that has been
learned about leadership. Like Gardner's earlier *Frames of
Mind* (BasicBooks, 1983), *The Mind's New Science* (Basic-

Books, 1986), and *Creating Minds* (BasicBooks, 1993), his new book is the product of his research into creativity and influence, undertaken at Harvard University's Graduate School of Education.

Because Gardner is a good teacher, who knows that the most effective lessons are often couched in good stories, he does not just present his theory of leadership in a text full of the italicized terms and simplistic charts that have become as obligatory as page numbers in recent leadership books. Instead, he fleshes out his theoretical notions in lively mini-biographies of 11 twentieth-century leaders, beginning with Margaret Mead and ending with Mahatma Gandhi. In the context Gardner creates, these condensed lives have the force of letters from some of the great leaders of the recent past-letters that tell us, if only in a fragmentary way, what these men and women learned about the conduct of public life during their remarkable careers. The brief biographies are a delight and an education, full of useful hints and signposts, if not answers.

Before analyzing Gardner's achievement in some detail, let me say why his book is so important. Around the globe, humanity currently faces three extraordinary threats: the threat of annihilation as a result of nuclear accident or war, the threat of a worldwide plague or ecological catastrophe, and a deepening leadership crisis in most of our institutions. Unlike the possibility of plague or nuclear holocaust, the leadership crisis will probably not become the basis for a best-seller or a blockbuster movie, but in many ways it is the most urgent and dangerous of the threats we face today, if only because it is insufficiently recognized and little understood.

The signs of a leadership crisis are alarming and pervasive. Witness the change in leadership at some of our most respected corporations—General Motors, IBM, and American Express. Gardner acknowledges the deterioration of leadership in our corporations when he compares the leadership capabilities of two of GM's former leaders, Alfred P. Sloan, Jr., and Roger Smith.

In politics, it is the same. No head of a developed, democratic nation has more than a tentative hold on his or her constituency. President Bill Clinton has an approval rating that threatens to dip below 40% and faces opposition from Congress unmatched in recent history. In Great Britain, John Major's Conservative government teeters. Italy and Japan must manage with interregnum governments. A recent survey taken in Canada shows that its Progressive Conservative Party, in office for a decade, has the support of only 3% of the population. The same poll indicates that twice as many respondents–6%–believe Elvis is still alive.

The leadership crisis appears to be spreading. In the United States, senators are resigning, some without encouragement of scandal. The mood of the populace is unsettled, angry, sometimes foul, and, in a few horrifying recent cases, even murderous. And those who ostensibly lead agree only that things are terrible and getting worse. Among the general population, cynicism is rampant. I don't recall such a widespread loss of faith in our major institutions even during the tumultuous 1960s. Indeed, I can't remember a time when so many of our leaders themselves were so vocally disenchanted with government, including their own political parties, as they are today. Vice President Al Gore recently told an apocryphal story that perfectly captures the tenor of the times. A government pollster, clipboard in hand, asks people whether they are more satisfied with government today. Five percent say they are more satisfied, 10% say less, and 85% refuse to answer because they think the question is part of a government plot.

It was with this crisis very much in mind, with "Where Have All the Leaders Gone?" playing in my head, that I read Gardner's book. And although *Leading Minds* offers no magic formula, no quick cure, it does provide a framework for thinking about leadership in clear, unemotional terms that is the necessary first step toward resolving the leadership crisis that faces us.

One of Gardner's central ideas is that effective leaders—the Hitlers as well as the Roosevelts—tell or embody stories that speak to other people. By leaders, Gardner does not mean only CEOs or heads of state. In his view, leaders are all those "persons who, by word and/or personal example, markedly influence the behaviors, thoughts, and/or feelings of a significant number of their fellow human beings." (Gardner prefers the term *audience* to *followers* for those who are influenced.) He describes a continuum of leadership that starts with indirect leadership, exerted through scholarly work or other symbolic communication, and progresses to direct leadership of the sort exercised by world leaders through speeches and other means.

Gardner also charts leadership in terms of its widening impact: from influence exercised within relatively narrow domains, such as academic specialties, to influence exercised over larger communities, such as the influence Pope John XXIII exerted over the Roman Catholic Church. In addition, he describes a hierarchy of leadership based on creativity, with smaller-scale leaders such as educator Robert Maynard Hutchins at the bottom and visionaries such as Gandhi at the top.

The four factors Gardner lists as essential for effective leadership are a tie to a community or audience, a rhythm of life that includes isolation and immersion, a relationship between the stories leaders tell and the traits they embody, and arrival at power through the choice of the people rather than through brute force. Readers may or may not agree with the theoretical framework that Gardner modestly describes as not a model of leadership but merely the ingredients for a model. Whether they agree or not, however, they will find his stories of actual leaders full of insights into the myriad ways leadership expresses itself. Gardner is never so committed to his cognitive theory that he limits his observations to what fits neatly within his paradigm. With remarkable economy, he gives us more, not less; he provides not only the abstract and theoretical but also the concrete and historical.

Gardner's attempt to analyze leadership systematically is courageous, given the vulnerability of any overarching explanation to critical assault. But the magic of the book is this jux-taposition of the theoretical with the telling particulars. It is useful to learn that J. Robert Oppenheimer, head of the Manhattan Project and later a controversial spokesman for the responsible use of nuclear energy, began as an indirect leader within the relatively limited universe of theoretical physics. More interesting, however, is the idiosyncratic nature of Oppenheimer's leadership, vividly revealed in Gardner's account of Oppenheimer's career.

Gardner knows that the right anecdote can be worth a thousand theories, and he is best when he shows instead of tells. For example, rather than write at length on how Oppenheimer's leadership sometimes failed because of his arrogance, Gardner gives a single indelible example: Oppenheimer's icy dismissal of publisher Philip Graham for having failed to read some text in the original Sanskrit. In the same chapter, Gardner provides a glimpse of moral leadership when he recounts how President Lyndon Johnson (not one of Gardner's 11) ended Oppenheimer's unofficial banishment from public life by presenting him with the Enrico Fermi Award. Oppenheimer showed his profound understanding of the significance of Johnson's action when he said, "I think it is just possible, Mr. President, that it has taken some charity and some courage for you to make this award today. That would seem to me a good augury for all of our futures."

Again and again, Gardner gives us opportunities to think deeply about leadership by defining terms in which to do so and by describing and ordering the many forms that leadership takes. If this schematic approach sometimes gets a bit tedious, we know that in a page or two we will come to another illuminating moment, another small take-home lesson. This is the primary return on our investment of time. A secondary pleasure of the book is that it has us jotting notes to ourselves to find out more about leaders whom we might otherwise have overlooked, such as Angelo Giuseppe Roncalli, the future Pope John XXIII, who paused on his journey to the papacy to save Jews in the Balkans during World War II. Gardner's creativity, recognized with a MacArthur "genius" award, transforms what could have been a tedious slog through weighty subject matter into an intellectual thrill ride.

One of the great strengths of Gardner's book is that it avoids the false dichotomies that mar so much of the contemporary literature about leadership. However well intentioned, those who write about leadership have tended to become embroiled in one or more of the now familiar controversies on the subject. Three debates in particular have preoccupied those concerned with leaders and leadership.

The first of these debates is whether leaders are larger-than-life figures—heroes who can change the weather, as Winston Churchill said his ancestor John Churchill could—or whether they are simply vivid embodiments of forces greater than themselves. I think of this as a debate between Tolstoy and Carlyle. In Tolstoy's *War and Peace,* Napoleon and his Russian counterparts have very little to do with the ultimate outcome of the great battles with which they are identified. To use a metaphor that might have left Tolstoy tugging his beard in confusion, the leader in Tolstoy's view is just another surfer riding the waves of the zeitgeist, albeit the surfer with the biggest board. Carlyle, on the other hand, argues that every institution is the lengthened shadow of a great man. Had he been a Southern Californian, he might have written that great leaders don't just ride waves, they make them.

Instead of embracing either of these polarized views of leadership, Gardner is able to transcend them, even to reconcile them. Gardner never succumbs to the either/or thinking that is the province of what he describes as the five-year-old mind—five being the age Gardner chooses as representing the unschooled mind of the general public. In writing about General George C. Marshall, for instance, Gardner describes both the behavior of a hero—Marshall as a young officer who dares to confront General Pershing at their first meeting—and the career trajectory of a leader who sought to repair the economies of former enemies. If Gardner occasionally tips the scale in favor of Carlyle's view of leadership, who can blame him? After all, this is a book that recognizes the importance of stories in human affairs, and what stories are more compelling than those about heroes?

Gardner also rises above the persistent controversy over whether leaders are born or made. This debate is sufficiently widespread to have inspired a cartoon in which a nervous teenager presents a report card blackened with Fs to his CEO father and asks, "What do you think, Pop, genes or the environment?" Gardner acknowledges the controversy, which has occasioned raised voices in a thousand faculty clubs, but instead of choosing sides, he presents useful data from both as part of the matrix of what we know about leaders. He reports that leaders do seem to have certain experiences in common. A remarkable number of the prominent figures of our time, including President Clinton, suffered the early loss of a father. And leaders seem to have certain traits in common as well. As my own study of dozens of contemporary leaders has revealed, whether in the arts, the political arena, or the corporation, leaders are almost always risk takers. (They also tend to be curious, energetic, and gifted with an acute sense of humor.)

Gardner not only can examine the controversy over nature versus nurture equitably, he also can consider it without obsessing about it. His ability to juggle contradictory notions is a sign of his maturity. To argue over whether leaders are born or made is an indulgent diversion from the urgent matter of how best to develop the leadership ability that so many have and that we so desperately need. A Nobel Prize awaits the person who resolves the question of whether leaders are born or made. But until some unanticipated breakthrough occurs or compelling new data emerge, the argument leads nowhere. The need for leadership in every arena of public life has become so acute that we don't have the luxury of dwelling on the unresolvable.

The third of the false dichotomies that Gardner so artfully avoids is the perceived conflict between expedient and idealistic leadership. The literature on leadership uses several different terms to describe those leaders who seize the moment without regard for the impact of their actions on the quality of other people's lives. *Machiavellian* is the harshest of these terms. The gentler ones typically crop up in discussions of contingency theory and "situationalism." But Gardner wisely avoids labels, choosing instead to show us that leaders are often both pragmatists and idealists. He correctly characterizes Hutchins, for example, as a "pragmatically tinged idealist," and talks of Sloan's desire to serve the nation while making money for General Motors.

In four decades of studying leaders, I have repeatedly found them to be what I call pragmatic dreamers—men and women whose ability to get things done is often grounded in a vision that includes altruism. Thus when Steve Jobs was recruiting John Sculley, then head of PepsiCo, for Apple Computer, Jobs knew to appeal not just to Sculley's ambition but also to his desire to leave a legacy that would go beyond boosting profit margins. Jobs is said to have asked the man who was to become Apple's next president and CEO how many more years of his life he wanted to spend making flavored water.

Scholars tackle two kinds of subjects. Some, like dry-fly fishing and the iconography of sixteenth-century French poetry, can be plumbed to their depths. Others, like leadership, are so vast and complex that they can only be explored. The latter subjects are inevitably the more important ones. You may question a few of Gardner's specific choices. For example, you may wonder if his work would have been more applicable to corporate life if he had chosen to focus almost exclusively on public leadership and its large-scale issues. But any such quibbles are only that, given the remarkable achievement of the book.

In the patterns of leadership that Gardner traces, several elements recur that have not been emphasized enough in earlier work on the subject. Travel, for instance, was even more important than formal education in shaping many of Gardner's leaders, including Roncalli and Gandhi. Gardner points out that nonauthoritarian leaders are more likely than authoritarian leaders to have traveled extensively abroad. Many leaders went on almost mythic interior journeys involving testing and rebirth. Gardner shows how Eleanor Roosevelt, who had to deal with both her husband's polio and his love for another woman, responded by reinventing herself as an increasingly independent advocate for the causes that were most important to her, notably women's rights and civil rights.

It is important, though, that we do not become too Carlylean in our view of leadership. Leadership is never exerted in a vacuum. It is always a transaction between the leader, his or her followers, and the goal or dream. A resonance exists between leaders and followers that makes them allies in support of a common cause. The leader's role in this process has been much analyzed. My studies show, for instance, that leaders are highly focused, that they are able to inspire trust, and that they are purveyors of hope. But followers are more essential to leadership than any of those individual attributes. As Garry Wills writes in *Certain Trumpets: The Call of Leaders* (Simon & Schuster, 1994), "The leader most needs followers. When those are lacking, the best ideas, the strongest will, the most wonderful smile have no effect."

Leaders are capable of deep listening: Gandhi demonstrated that when he traveled throughout India learning the heart of his people. But what distinguishes leaders from, say, psychotherapists or counselors is that they find a voice that allows them to articulate the common dream. Uncommon eloquence marks virtually every one of Gardner's leaders, but I have yet to see public speaking listed on a résumé. We seem to regard the ability to galvanize an audience as something almost tawdry, even dangerous. Yet it was the eloquence of Martin Luther King, Jr., grounded in the cadences of thousands of his father's sermons, that gave him the voice of a national, even international leader. That fact should be kept in mind by anyone trying to draw up a curriculum for future leaders.

Effective leaders put words to the formless longings and deeply felt needs of others. They create communities out of words. In *Leading Minds,* Gardner shows that he himself is just such a leader, able to articulate and clarify what many of us have been thinking on the subject for a long time.

# 22
## *Operating on Instinct*

*Two things seemed pretty apparent to me. One was, that in order to be a [Mississippi River] pilot a man had got to learn more than any one man ought to be allowed to know; and the other was, that he must learn it all over again in a different way every 24 hours.*

Mark Twain
Life on the Mississippi

*A recurring theme in this collection of essays is the challenge of finding what Oliver Wendell Holmes called "the simplicity that lies at the end of complexity." The following essay, which originally appeared in* On Becoming a Leader, *describes how a number of significant leaders in a range of fields have been able to do just that, by trusting what Emerson called "the blessed impulse" that arises quietly within ourselves. Yielding to that impulse, I believe, is a principal function of a leader.*

Life has never been simple and is growing more complex all the time, yet we persist in attempting to reduce it to bumper-sticker dimensions. The advocates of simplicity see reality as mechanical, static, segmented, and rational, when it is, in fact, organic, dynamic, whole, and ambiguous. They see relationships as linear, sequential and serial, discrete, singular and independent, when they are, in fact, parallel and simultaneous, connected, murky, multiple and interdependent. They are determinists, believers in cause-and-effect, when, in fact, probability is the rule and the inevitable hardly ever happens. They wear square hats, when they should try sombreros.

Lest anyone feel overwhelmed by complexity, however, I'd like to offer this thought from Carl Sagan's *The Dragons of Eden:*

> *We can imagine a universe in which the laws of nature are immensely more complex. But we do not live in such a universe. Why not! I think it may be because all those organisms who perceived their universe as very complex are dead. Those of our arboreal ancestors who had difficulty computing their trajectories as they brachiated from tree to tree did not leave many offspring.*

The universe may not be *very* complex, but it is, nevertheless, complex. And as I mentioned earlier, the social laws are more complex and less certain than the natural ones. But despite the complexity, we cannot stand still. We must continue to swing from tree to tree, although the trees may be ideas, and we may be using axons instead of arms to make the connections. We might want to take Alfred North Whitehead's advice here: "Seek simplicity, then distrust it."

It was the mechanistic view that produced the organization man, and it was the organization man, as I have noted, who ironically enough has caused many of the problems in our organizations. It is the individual, operating at the peak of his creative and moral powers, who will revive our organizations, by reinventing himself and them.

American organizational life is a left-brain culture, meaning logical, analytical, technical, controlled, conservative, and administrative. We, to the extent we are its products, are dominated and shaped by those same characteristics. Our culture needs more right-brain qualities, needs to be more intuitive, conceptual, synthesizing, and artistic. And so, of course, do we. As I talked with the people I interviewed for this book, I was struck again and again by the fact that, whatever their occupations, they relied as much on their intuitive and conceptual skills as on their logical and analytical talents. These are whole-brained people, capable of using both sides of their brain.

In any corporation, managers serve as the left brain and the research and development staff serves as the right brain, but the CEO must combine both, must have both administrative and imaginative gifts. One of the reasons that so few corporate executives have successfully made the leap from capable manager to successful leader is that the corporate culture, along with society as a whole, recognizes and rewards left-brain accomplishments and tends to discount right-brain achievements. Bottom-line thinking is a manifestation of left-brain dominance. Habits are born in the left brain and unmade in the right.

AAUW executive director Anne Bryant uses something she calls "the hot air balloon exercise" to encourage her staff to think imaginatively. "You take people up in an imaginary balloon and from up there you can see the entire entity. Then you examine what you see, who you see, what they're doing, and what other things they might be doing. You imagine, for instance, what might happen if you put $500,000 toward child development research or what might be done about teen pregnancy."

Acknowledging the constant dilemma of organizations, and the pull between left-brain habits and right-brain visions, Richard Schubert, CEO of the American Red Cross, told me, "I'm constantly torn between the obvious need to support the existing structure and the equally obvious need to change it."

Frances Hesselbein, executive director of the Girl Scouts of the USA, sees social changes and envisions how her organization will be prepared for them: "By the year 2000, one-third of this country will be minority. So girls' needs are changing, and we're exploring different ways to meet those needs and deliver our services. I'm establishing a center for innovation. It isn't a place. It's people and a concept. The team . . . will work directly with Girl Scout Councils in developing models through which we can reach highly diverse communities and locate and train indigenous leadership, which will be increasingly important."

Bryant, Schubert, and Hesselbein each take a whole-brain approach in leading their nonprofit organizations out of traditional patterns and into innovative modes. Not coincidentally, all three of them had been previously successful in the private sector and made major career changes in midlife. And all three say they've never done anything that they enjoy as much as their current assignments. Schubert says succinctly, "This is the most exciting, challenging thing I've ever done."

Scientist Mathilde Krim, who also moved recently from the private to the public sector, said, "Growth requires curiosity to experience both the difference and the synchrony, to explore and immerse yourself in new surroundings, to be able to contemplate your experiences and get something out of them."

A part of whole-brain thinking includes learning to trust what Emerson called the "blessed impulse," the hunch, the vision that shows you in a flash the absolutely right thing to do. Everyone has these visions, leaders learn to trust them.

I want to remind you here of something Norman Lear said regarding the profound influence that Emerson's "Self Reliance" had on his growth as a leader: "Emerson talks about listening to that inner voice and going with it, all voices to the contrary. I don't know when I started to understand that there was something divine about that inner voice—I certainly didn't in high school, college, or even in young manhood—but somewhere along the line, I appreciated that, too. How is it possible that as a writer I can go to bed a thousand times with a second act problem and wake up with the answer? Some inner voice. To go with that—which I confess I don't do all of the time—is the purest, truest thing we have. And when we forgo our own thoughts and opinions, they end up coming back to us from the mouths of others. They come back with an alien majesty. . . . So the lesson is, you believe it. *When I've been most effective, I've followed that inner voice.*"

Following the "blessed impulse" is, I think, basic to leadership. This is how guiding visions are made real. But the need for other right-brain qualities came up again and again in my conversations.

Author and feminist leader Gloria Steinem said of being an entrepreneur, "It helps if you're a nonlinear thinker. And it takes a certain amount of persuasion, which means empathy. . . . Entrepreneurs always seemed to me like the artists of the business world, because we put together things that haven't gone together in the past." She used similar words when she talked about success: "To me, the model of progress is not linear. Success is completing the full circle of yourself."

Herb Alpert described how he works this way: "I'm a right-brain animal. I'm not a businessman in the traditional sense. And I do a lot of buckshotting and I rely on my gut reaction. When my shoulders feel tight, I know something's off. I use my body as a barometer. . . . I try to listen like a piece of Silly Putty when someone plays me a song. I try to let my biases just blow in the breeze. For the most part, I'm listening for the feeling."

That reliance on instinct has made Alpert a successful recording star and an equally successful businessman. His partner Gil Friesen said of Alpert, "Instinctively he knows what's right and what should be done. And he has the ability to detach himself from time to time and look and see and ask questions. He's running his own career within the framework of the company, which is an ideal scenario. As he makes decisions, he reinvents his career."

Alpert believes that you need a vision of the future at the same time that you're dealing with the present. And Alpert believes in trust. In speaking of Friesen and the third partner, Jerry Moss, Alpert said, "The real motor of this company is the basic trust that Jerry, Gil, and I have for each other, and the trust that artists have for us. They say they're more comfortable and more inspired because our people care about what they're doing. Also, we're a privately owned and independent label, so we're able to move quickly."

Friesen continued, "I can't tell you how important that word *independent* is, how important it is to our staff and to the artists. It has a kind of magic about it." Then he added with a smile, "And we never refer to our recordings or our artists as 'product,' because we think it's demeaning."

Apple CEO John Sculley encourages diversity of opinion around him, and goes with vision over market research. "One of the biggest mistakes a person can make is to put together a team that reflects only him. I find it's better to put teams together of people who have different skills and then make all those disparate skills function together. The real role of the leader is to figure out how you make diverse people and elements work together.

"Often people don't know what they want and can't describe it until they see it. If we'd done market research on the Macintosh prior to its introduction, and asked people to describe the ideal personal computer, they would have come up with something entirely different. But when we show people the Macintosh and say, 'Is this what you want?' they say, 'Yes.' You have to be able to make the abstract recognizable, because only then can people accept or reject it."

Alfred Gottschalk looks for right-brain characteristics when he hires. "I first look for character, whether the individual can inspire trust. Then I look for imagination and perseverance, steadfastness of purpose. If, for example, I am engaging somebody who is going to be the chief controller of the institution, and I see that as an undergraduate he had difficulty with intermediate algebra or calculus, and he nevertheless manages to go into accounting, I wonder what kind of a financial imagination he has. I try to find out as much as I can about the individual, and then a largely intuitive decision is made. I have to feel right about the person."

Right-brain characteristics come in handy even when you're dealing with things, not people. Mathilde Krim talked about the importance of instinct in her early work: "I always had a good instinct for biological problems. I don't remember ever having worked at something that fizzled into nothing. . . . I could recognize a chromosome. One time a colleague said that he had isolated a new cell line from a dog. And I looked at it and saw immediately that it wasn't a dog cell. I could tell that it was a rat cell just by looking at the chromosomes, and I was right, because we did cellulogical tests afterwards. In the case of prenatal diagnosis, it was obvious to me from the beginning, the first time I looked at the lymphatic cells, that there was a difference between male and female cells, so then we studied it systematically. At the time it made quite a splash in the press, but it was a very simple kind of work to do."

For Krim, who had the vision and trusted her instincts, it was a very simple kind of work to do. But it had never been done before.

The leaders I spoke with believed also in the importance of luck, but they put a particular spin on it, one reminiscent of Vince Lombardi's dictum that luck is a combination of preparation and opportunity. Jim Burke, who described himself as an "intuitive, instinctive person" with an overlay of logic, said of leadership positions, "A lot of luck occurs to get people to these places. A lot of what happened in my life was an accident. You wouldn't be here talking to me if it hadn't been for Tylenol. I happened to be exquisitely prepared for that problem—by accident, though."

Boston prosecutor Jamie Raskin also spoke of luck and preparation. "The general advice I would have for people about leadership is to find out what's truest in yourself and stick to it. But I really believe in the role of luck in human affairs. Machiavelli said that fortune favors the bold. I think the prepared mind is basically the same thing as the bold, but fortune is in there. Napoleon said that of all the qualities his lieutenants had, the one he most favored was luck. Luck continues to intervene at every point in your life."

Sydney Pollack described right-brain leadership best, when he said that it comes out of "a certain kind of controlled free association. All art comes out of that. We say daydreams, we say inspiration, but scientifically what it is, is free association. It's the ability to be in touch with that. That's where you get the ideas. And then it's the ability to trust the ideas once you have them, even though they may break certain rules.

And then it's the confidence and courage to carry out the ideas once you've found them and once you've trusted them. Then you can't be afraid to fail. Otherwise it's just imitative. Otherwise you go to leadership school, and try to pitch your voice the same way that the boss did there, and have your office decorated the same way his is, and that's not real leadership. Real leadership probably has more to do with recognizing your own uniqueness than it does with identifying your similarities."

Pollack told me a story that illustrates marvelously the "blessed impulse" of leadership. "Years ago, I did a film with Barbra Streisand and Robert Redford called *The Way We Were*. Streisand played a character who wanted desperately to be a writer, who worked very, very hard at it, but nothing came easily to her. Redford played a character where everything came easy. He was a kind of a prince. He had no particular aspirations to be a writer, but he happened to be good and talented. She had worked and struggled and worked and struggled in her writing class to do a very serious paper, a little short story. And the professor chose that day to read Redford's story. It just devastated her. She ran out of the classroom, and the scene called for her to run to a trash basket, rip up her story, throw it in the trash basket, and just sob.

"I had set up the shot so that the camera was at the trash basket pointing toward a tree behind which she was standing, so that when I would call, 'Action,' she would emerge running from behind this tree, run toward the camera, straight at us, throw the story in the trash basket, and I would move into her face when she leaned against the trash basket and cried. The first assistant director on the picture, Howard Koch, Jr., had been the first A.D. on her previous picture, *Up the Sandbox*. Howard came to me while we were working on the scene and said, 'You know, she's very nervous.' I asked why. He said, 'She's very upright because she thinks she can't cry. She had some terrible problems crying in *Up the Sandbox*, and in her head she equates that with being a bad actress, so she's very nervous.'

"We have a device in the picture business, little ammonia crystals that go into a little test tube with holes in the bottom like a salt shaker and gauze over the front end. The makeup man blows in it, and the ammonia aroma comes out and gets in your eyes and makes tears. It makes your eyes bloody and it stinks, but it works for film. Barbra had the makeup man behind the tree. I said to Howard, 'I don't believe she can't cry. Anybody who sings the way she sings can cry. You stay here. I will go behind the tree. When I wave my hands, you roll the camera.'

"I went back to the tree, and I found Barbra pacing. The makeup man was there with his test tube, and I sent him away. She got alarmed and said, 'Where are you going? Wait, wait, what are you doing?' I said, 'Just relax. Just relax.' I went over and I put my arms around her, and the minute I put my arms around her, she just started to sob. And I waved my hand, and he rolled the camera, and around the tree she went.

"Now, I didn't say anything to her. I didn't think up some wonderful piece of direction to give her. But I knew that there was juice going on in her, and she was just too tense to let it come out. She had built it all up in her mind, and something touched her when I put my arms around her. Something just made her let loose. And she cried all the way through the picture. You can say, 'How did you think of it? What made you know what would work?' To tell you the truth, I didn't have the faintest idea what I was going to do when I sent away the makeup man. I just was so convinced that she could cry, because I had seen so much emotion in her work, and I knew her to be a very emotional woman, and I had no idea what to do—and then the impulse. I don't know where the impulse to hug her came from.

"Now where did the impulse happen? Did it happen on the walk to the tree? I don't think so. I don't think the impulse happened until I saw her. What does it represent in terms of problem solving? It represented a very efficient and quick solution at the time, probably better than a lot of talk, or a lot of saying, 'Well, think about the time something bad happened to you.' If I had come near her and said, 'Look, I know you can do this, I believe in you,' she would have said, 'Get out of here!' That would have just put more pressure on her. I think what happened was—and I'm guessing—that she felt a sense of real support, and that touched her. I think that moment was a simple, emotional thing, that somebody was really on her side, and it touched her, and that's all."

These leaders have proved not only the necessity but the efficacy of self-confidence, vision, virtue, plain guts, and reliance on the blessed impulse. They have learned from everything, but they have learned more from experience, and even more from adversity and mistakes. And they have learned to lead by leading.

Grace under pressure might be this group's motto. None began life with an edge. Some began with genuine handicaps. All have risen to the top because leaders are made, and made by themselves. To quote Wallace Stevens, they have lived "in the world, but outside of existing conceptions of it." And they have made new worlds, because they themselves are, each and every one, originals. They have worn sombreros.

They would say themselves that they can teach you nothing, but they have shown you the ways to learn everything you need to know.

No leader sets out to be a leader. People set out to live their lives, expressing themselves fully. When that expression is of value, they become leaders.

So the point is not to become a leader. The point is to become yourself, to use yourself completely—all your skills, gifts, and energies—in order to make your vision manifest. You must withhold nothing. You must, in sum, become the person you started out to be, and to enjoy the process of becoming.

Henry James, midway through a life filled with writing marvelous novels, wrote in his *Notebooks:*

*I have only to let myself go! So I have said to myself all my life—so I said to myself in the far-off days of my fermenting and passionate youth. Yet I have never fully done it. The sense of it—of the need of it—rolls over me at times with commanding force: it seems the formula of my salvation, of what remains to me of a future. I am in full possession of accumulated resources—I have only to use them, to insist, to persist, to do something more—to do much more than I have done. The way to do it to affirm one's self sur la fin—is to strike as many notes, deep, full and rapid, as one can. All life is—at my age, with all one's artistic soul the record of it—in one's pocket, as it were. Go on, my boy, and strike hard. . . . Try everything, do everything, render everything—be an artist, be distinguished to the last.*

James's major novels were written after this self-exhortation. So strike hard, try everything, do everything, render everything, and become the person you are capable of being.

# 23
## Postscript:
## The Future Has No Shelf Life

*"In my room, the world is*
*beyond my understanding;*
*But when I walk I see that it*
*Consists of three or four hills,*
*and a cloud."*
—Wallace Stevens

In his *Report to Greco,* Nikos Kazantzakis tells us of an ancient Chinese imprecation, "I curse you; may you live in an important age." So we are all damned, encumbered and burdened as well as charmed, exhilarated and fascinated by this curse. What a time! Tom Friedman, in his recent book, *The Lexus and the Olive Tree,* tells us that the world is only ten years old; what he means by this is that the Berlin Wall fell roughly ten years ago, in November of 1989, marking the end of the Cold War. The symbol of the Cold War, he wrote, was The Wall; the symbol of our "important age" is the Web; the former, an armed fortress, the latter, a boundariless world. In the Cold War world, we feared destruction at the hands of an enemy we knew all too well; in our new age, we fear economic and technological forces we can't see, touch or feel—forces which can change our lives at any moment.

The world is ten years old when you consider that all of the old foundations of success are gone; e.g. controlling natural resources, land, gold and oil. Now it's information and, as Bill Gates recently said, "The only factory asset we have is human imagination." I think he can say that without being accused of hyperbole. (At last count, Microsoft's market capitalization is $470 billion; I suspect that the factory assets don't add up to more than 1 or 2% of that.) And just consider:

- Ten years ago there were maybe 400 people who understood the power of the Web and today there are countless millions.
- Ten years ago there was virtually no E-Commerce and in '98, there was $43 billion in sales and according to Forrester Research there will be $1.3 trillion in 2003. I think it's going to be closer to $2 trillion.
- Ten years ago Japan was riding high and we were entering a recession.
- Ten years ago AT&T was a moribund giant and now it's an agile giant betting its future on cable TV as much as fiber optics.
- Ten years ago the top 10 growth stocks would have been a combination of energy, banking and manufacturing companies and today the top ten are all informational technology firms: Dell Computer, Cisco Systems, Sun Microsystems, Qualcomm, EMC and down to #10, Intel.
- Ten years ago C. Everett Koop was a kindly, avuncular Surgeon General of the U.S. and now he's Dr.Koop.com, dispensing medical advice on the Web with an $84 million IPO.
- Ten years ago Amazon was a river in Brazil...and today it's a verb, as in, we've been "amazoned."
- And ten years ago, you could never have seen this cartoon (page 297) in the pages of the *New Yorker*.

And what CEOs are worrying about today and what keeps them awake after midnight are such non-trivial issues as keeping their best talent, disruptive technologies, new channels of distribution, being dis-intermediated out of business, over capacity and hyper-competition, phantom competitors (dramatized by two boys in a garage coming up with a new Great App), internal communication (not a new issue but more problematical now), growing or being taken prisoner, having to cannibilize one's best-selling product. And finally, ten years ago most senior executives were reading *In Search of Excellence* and now they're reading *Only the Paranoid Survive* or *The Innovator's Dilemma: When New Technologies Cause Great Firms to Fail.*

"*Big Tony's Web site—get rid of it.*"

So the world we occupy today is a vastly different world than the world of just ten years ago vastly different than the world of 50 years ago when I started work for my Ph.D. or 40 years ago when Benne, Chin and I ingenuously put together *The Planning of Change.* Of course, we Americans have always lived on the fast track but today's hyper-turbulent, spastic, volatile, uncertain, vertiginous—I promise you I won't run out of descriptors—is qualitatively different, more chasmatic, to coin a word, more consequential, affecting more of our life-space than other tectonic changes we've experienced, even electricity or the turbine engine.

I can only assert that, of course, not prove it. But it seems entirely plausible to me because my old prophet's rod has failed me and when I wander from my room, I seem unable to see over the three or four hills and the cloud Wallace Stevens saw when he wandered from his room. No, the future has no shelf life these days, but it certainly poses a number of questions that leaders of human organizations, as well as scholars and students, should be thinking about. In conclusion, I'd like to raise a few of these difficult questions both because of their pressing urgency and because they are questions that will help light our path.

**1.** Playing with the idea that the world is only 10 years old, what will the world of organizations look like on their 20th anniversary, in 2010? Will they resemble the huge mega-mergers of GE, AOL-Time Warner, PB-Amoco-Arco, Viacom and Intel? Or will they look like a smallish, ramshackle Hollywood model, where groups from diverse disciplines gather together for short periods of time, develop or finish a product and then after a spell, regroup? Or will there be some kind of combination, a hybrid of "Great Groups" working rather independently under some large, decentralized behemoth?

**2.** And what about the new leaders? When the world is 20, will they look like C. Michael Armstrong of AT&T, Andy Grove of Intel, or Jack Welch of GE? Or will they resemble the younger Carly Fiorina of Hewlett Packard, Jim Clark of Netscape, Scott McNealy of Sun, Tim Koogle of Yahoo, Mark Andreesssen (formerly) of Netscape and AOL, John Chambers of Cisco and Jeff Bezos of Amazon.com? Will the "new leaders" have the same competencies as the over-60 crowd?

**3.** What about the future of "high-involvement" organizations?" American democracy, as Tocqueville told us long ago, is not always and in all ways the very best kind of thing. It often goes too far, he thought, and when it does it has a tendency to pervert the very values it tries to foster. How does this relate to contemporary organizations, to so-called "empowered organizations," where workers are demanding and getting more autonomy, more say in decision-making, and where self-managed teams are becoming less exceptional?

Will modern organizations turn into parliamentary democracies where leaders are chosen by the led, where employee-owned management companies, like United Airlines, will have board members who are employees calling the shots?

**4.** Another dilemma of democracy and one we tend to evade (including me) is, what are we to do with disparities in talent? Not to sound Nietzschean, but what do we do with— or do we even admit to—superior and inferior talent? Is it Hitler's Ghost, the fear of the *uber-mensch,* that blocks the view to that question? The future is here, but as someone said, it's distributed unequally. So is talent. This raises at least two pertinent questions for us: As far as organizations go, can everyone be a leader? Should everyone want to be a leader? Burt Nanus and I argued strongly for "yes" to the first question and ducked the second. Don't people vary a great deal with respect to intelligence, whether it's emotional or cognitive? Don't certain neurosurgeons, cello players, tennis players, and yes, leaders, have the "touch"? How many Agassi's and Yo-Yo Ma's or Welch's do we have in any given population sample?

The second question is more complex, but must be asked by leaders and scholars alike. The increasing chasm of income between the top quintile and the bottom quintile along with the obscene differential between the average worker and the average CEO (419 dollars to 1 dollar at last count) is a serious issue. It's important to note that nearly 90% of stocks are owned by only 10% of the population with the top 1% owning 51.4%. Add to that the disparities in education and family background. Should we not be worrying about the "Brazilification" of our society? Do we have any responsibility for that or ways of doing something about those achingly stubborn inequalities?

**5.** What about important demographic changes that are now upon us? I'm thinking specifically about agism, both young and old agism. It came to mind recently when I was invited to speak at a conference called TED (Technology, Entertainment and Design). Richard Wurman, the founder of this highly successful conflab, told me that in the Y2K conference, the invited speakers would either be in their 30s and under or 70s and older. Interesting, I thought; but illustrated more sharply in a *New York Times* article with the headline, "Andreessen Steps Down from AOL." The story went on to say that Andreessen's successor, a 53-year-old former professor, may be more suited to the ways of America On Line, where executives tend to be in their late 30s and 40s than the 28-year-old co-founder of Netscape. I recalled that Andreessen was only 23 when he helped found the Internet browser.

Now put that together with the other side of the equation, the 60-and-older crowd who are not only living longer and living healthier but, according to all reports, want to work way beyond 60 or 65. In fact a recent study by Civic Ventures reports that 50% of older Americans (however that's defined) are working for pay in their "retirement" and another 40% do volunteer work. The golden years are dead, the report claims.

Think of this: As recently as 1960, according to a recent *Economist,* "men could expect to spend 50 of their 68 years of life in paid work. Today, they are likely to work for only 38 of their 76 years." So what do we do with these old duffers who have their energy and health and hopefully their marbles? What should organizations do to retain the wisdom without forestalling the futures of the coming generations? And what about the bored, twentysomething millionaires: will they have to suffer a long life starting up startups as Mr. Andreessen wants to do? Or will they become philanthropizers?

The policy issues these demographics raise have serious implications. Just to take one: If workers continue to take early retirements, and the average age of retirement seems to be declining to the early 60s in the U.S., much lower in all the European countries, and with the boomers in massive numbers hitting retirement in the near future, there won't be enough wage earners to support the retirement of the boomer spike.

**6.** What about the Social Contract between employers and employees, that hallowed implicit contract which usually offered some form of loyalty and responsibility to both parties? Roughly 25% of the US workforce has been dumped since 1985 and even at present, when the unemployment rate is 4.2%, the lowest in over 30 years, you can figure on a half to three-fourths of a million employees in flux every year. What's interesting is that in 1998, about 750,000 workers were laid off or quit or retired, and of those, 92% found jobs that paid either more or were equal to what they were getting. A recent survey reported in *The Wall Street Journal* revealed that four out of ten employees were less than three years in their job, only one-third of the workforce works in an "old fashioned" 9-5 job and the quit rate this year is 14.5%. It was about 3% ten years ago. I figure that the *churn* of the workforce at any given time is between 20 to 25%; that is, the number of workers who are temporarily out of work or looking for new opportunities is roughly that figure.

I'd like to put a more "human face" on those numbers. I was fascinated to read in Peter Capelli's new book the *explicit* social contract at Apple:

> Here's the deal *Apple* will give you. Here's what we want from you. We're going to give you a really neat trip while you're here. We're going to teach you stuff you couldn't learn anywhere else. In return . . . we expect you to work like hell, buy the vision as long as you're here. . . .We're not interested in employing you for a lifetime, but that's not the way we are thinking about this. It's a good opportunity for both of us that is probably finite.
>
> P. Capelli, *The New Deal at Work* '99

Along these lines, John Sculley told me that one of the reasons he found the culture of Apple difficult (after Pepsi) was what he considered a total lack of loyalty when he was there. Groups of people would abruptly leave, empty their desks in the middle of the night and set up a new and competing business before the next work day was over. And not long ago, I was having dinner with a faculty colleague and his parents. His father was in his late 80s and had been an extremely successful banker. In passing he told me that when he was running his business, he would never—"I mean NEVER"—he proclaimed, hire anyone who held more than three jobs. "Because I have to assume they're either disloyal or incompetent." Considering today's serial monogamy of the workforce where the average worker may have five to eight jobs in a lifetime, I thought his statement was rather quaint.

So what about the Social Contract in our Temporary Society, in our Free Agency Society, where the new contract seems to resemble Apple's: "We're not interested in employing you for a lifetime . . . that's not the way we're thinking about this. It's a good opportunity for the both of us that is probably finite." Is it all going to be one neat, finite trip?

7. Do we have or even need *a* current theory of organizational change? There has been so much good work on leading change, on major interventions of change management, from a variety of researchers and consultants, but is there any consensus around the major strategic variables which can lead to sustainable change or a paradigmatic model of organizational change? Are complex human institutions too diverse in history, product, demography, and markets to have one monolithic model?

When I think of the prevalent business models today, it appears as if two extremes paradoxically co-exist. On one hand, in this Internet Era, we have the Silicon Valley model: three people under 25 with a hot idea. Small is beautiful. Sound familiar? At the same time, we can cite another bromide: Size matters. In 1998, there were $1.6 trillion in worldwide mergers and in 1999 the figure rose to $3 trillion! Given those extremes, is it quixotic to think we can come up with *the* theory of organizational change?

And by the way, regarding these mega-mergers—let's call them by their real name: take-overs—do they perform well and are they good or bad for the consumer? I have my doubts, especially with the recent creation of the media monolith Viacom being the most recent example. The potential for the bureaucratization of imagination, to say nothing of the conflict issues (e.g., CBS reviewing a Paramount film or a Simon & Schuster book and pretending it's objective reporting) should concern all of us.

**8.** Since writing *Organizing Genius,* a book about "Great Groups," I've been concerned about a puzzling moral and ethical issue that has no name and that continues to haunt me—an issue that was left unexamined in the book itself. I can illustrate my question with examples more easily than I can describe it, let alone understand it. The paradigmatic Great Group in the book was the Manhattan Project under the leadership of the distinguished physicist, J. Robert Oppenheimer. Beginning in January of 1943, that small group of scientists and engineers designed a nuclear device that brought an end to World War II. Exactly a year earlier, some 5,000 miles away, another group met, this time in Wannsee, a suburb of Berlin and, ironically, a district where before the War, many wealthy Jews lived. That group, under the leadership of the Chief of Nazi Security, Reinhard Heydrich, assisted by Adolf Eichmann, his secretary, were brought together to design the Final Solution, a plan to exterminate all of Europe's remaining Jews. Another Great Group which formed itself during the last quarter of the 18th Century was made up of six men, under the leadership of George Washington, and designed and implemented a plan to establish a new republic.

In a way, all of these groups were "great" using the criteria ordinarily used in the literature to describe "high performing systems." They all had exemplary leadership, a high degree of commitment, alignment and trust; they all developed innovative solutions and carried them out successfully. What's wrong with that picture? Are there any important differences between groups and organizations that on one hand leave a scar on history and on the other hand, create one of the most significant social inventions of all time, the first modern, democratic nation? Should we consult for HMOs that are not doing right by the patients or a tobacco company that sells a product that kills? Is there any difference between a movie company that produces "snuff" films, a type of porn film where real people are strangled and mutilated, and the studio that produced *Forest Gump?* I could go on and on, but I'm not quite sure how to pose the question any more than I can get my nervous conceptual arms around it.

**9.** One of the most Frequently Asked Questions I get on the lecture circuit is about "balance." By balance, the questioner usually means: Can I make it at work and at home? Can I have fun and a marvelous home life *and* get a terrific bonus? My first impulse is to respond, "You're asking the wrong guy." I resist that. My second impulse, is "Brother, can you spare a nano-second?" I resist that, too.

First of all I should make clear that balance is a mechanical term implying an equilibrium; the first definition of balance in my *OED* is a "weighing instrument." Somehow I believe that the search for balance, though deeply felt and not to be dismissed, is chimerical. We just don't do one thing at a time anymore. We multi-task in the car, with a latte, with a phone, a fax machine . . . we floss. It's interesting to note a new fraction has worked its way into our vocabulary, 24/7 as an abbreviation for everything running all the time, like our computers, 24 hours, 7 days a week. *The New Random House Historical Dictionary of Slang* is working on a definition of 24/7 which, according to the editor, will probably be "constantly." James Gleick's new book, *Faster: The Acceleration of Everything,* sums it up. Dear Ann Landers, do you know anyone who is taking a nano-second to smell the roses?

I do have a few friends who tell me they've done this; you know, a second home in Aspen, no phone calls on Sunday, four weeks with the kids on a bike trip in the Appenines. Funny, their cell phone line is always busy and when I do manage to get through, I hear their fax machine chirping away in the background. And it was Sunday! I wonder if any 30- or 40-something who is trying to make it at their E company with two children plus another one on the way or a 30-

year-old assistant professor with a working spouse and a child or two and going for tenure can have balance in this rat-a-tat world where the only thing we have time for is a three-minute egg. This sounds more like an editorial than a question, but, tell me: do you know anyone who has reached that state of nirvana called "balance"?

Before letting go of this question, I do think that Charles Handy is right and that we are all "hungry spirits" and that work should contain more meaning than stock options. Recently, I spoke before an audience of software executives, average age 29; average compensation, $2.5 million. They were not especially happy campers; all seemed to have a certain malaise about, yes, meaning—a kind of "is-this-all-there-is" type of question. A bad case of "affluenza,"* I called it. Maybe balance *qua* meaning can be found at work because I don't think the world is slowing down. As the historian Stephen Kern remarked, "Human beings have never opted for slower."

**10.** What do we make of "CEO churning"? There's been a lot of interest recently on the revolving doors for CEOs. A recent Harvard Business School study shows that Boards are 30% more likely to oust a CEO than they were 10 years ago. Doubtless, a number of complex factors are involved in the diminishing half-life of executive tenure: hyper-competition, internet volatility, turbo-globalism, trillion dollars of mergers . . . you can round up the usual suspects. Reflecting this interest, *Fortune* ran a cover story in mid-1999 on 10 notable CEOs who had been axed by their Boards, including the likes of Robert Allen at AT&T, Eckert Pfeiffer at the Pfeiffer Co., John Sculley at Apple in their Hall of Failures. Since that article, we could add M. Douglas Ivester at Coca-Cola and others to the list of casualties.

Both Morgan McCall and Dan Goleman have written seminal books on the social and emotional dramas that often lead

---

*Don't think for a minute that this is only an American disease. A recent report done in the UK, "The Paradox of Prosperity," found that the professional classes who have a 90% rise in disposable income will be too busy working to enjoy it.

to executive de-railing. Jim O'Toole and I have written an article based on our belief that Boards of Directors have an enormous and not fully understood impact on executive failure. I've been intensely curious about how leaders sustain creativity, keep their juices flowing and I think a lot of Gary Hamel's powerful question: "Are we learning as fast as the world is changing?"

How do we keep our eyes and ears open to nascent and potentially disruptive inflection points? Is the speed of the Internet Era to blame as Ben Rosen, non-executive chairman of Compaq, believed when he "resigned" Mr. Pfeiffer? How much does sheer luck play or are executives just not up to the warp speed nature of change, and if so, why? Or why is it that we're witnessing this *tsunami* of senior executive churning?

**11.** What is the role of business education for the next generation? Do we continue to do what we have been doing, just a little fine-tuning and tweaking? We *are* doing fairly well as it is, or so it seems; certainly in terms of prestige and importance and yes, endowments. I would wager that over the last decade more business schools have been *named* and given major bucks than the combined decades preceding the 90s. So why fix what ain't broke?

But what inflection points are we ignoring or not paying attention to? Are we providing an education that will provide the cognitive, emotional, interpersonal, and leadership competencies that will be required for sustained success in the New Economy? Is there space in our clogged curriculum for the philosophy, the metaphysics, the critical thinking of the enterprise? Are we giving our students a passion for continual learning, a refined, discerning ear for the moral and ethical consequences of their actions, and for an understanding of the purposes of work and human organizations? My greatest wish is that our students and alumni don't end up like some of those 29-year-old software millionaires, with their cell phones buzzing in their second homes in Aspen, suffering from a new kind of bug that causes affluenza and who wonder, when they retire, "Is this all there is?"

**12.** About 20 years ago I wrote an article with the poignance of a flower child entitled, "Where Have all the Leaders Gone?"; what I wonder about today is, where will the leaders come from? Not too long ago, I did some *pro bono* consulting for an outstanding research center with a small research faculty with a gazillion Nobel Laureates on staff. Over the last few years, they've had a lot of difficulty with their leadership. The problem was simple and also seemed intractable. Anybody who was good enough to pass the rigorous scientific criteria of the search committee didn't want the job. They wanted to do science. Having served on dozens of search committees for academic deans and presidents, the same problem presents itself. There is a genuine dearth of people who are accomplished in their disciplines and want to do leadership and are competent at it. So every other year, the aforementioned research institute, after a long, drawn out process hires some reluctant soul who, after a year or so, finds out he really wants to go back to his lab and the search starts again. *Ad infinitum.*

More recently, a large financial house in New York asked if I would partner with them in developing a leadership development program. After interviewing a few of their senior partners, I decided against it because most of them were more interested in trading or doing investment banking than they were managing and leading. By the way, they didn't seem to have the foggiest notion of what leadership is, nor did they care. On top of that, many of the partners felt that doing management was somewhat beneath them, if not demeaning, certainly not worth their time. In a way, I can't fault them. They loved what they were doing, trading millions of dollars a day seemed to have more of an edge to it than worrying about the supply chain or whatever. The problem is how do they get someone to "manage Asia"? Beats me. But perhaps that's why I should have accepted their invitation.

Now what's interesting about all this is that more and more of our workers are, to use Peter Drucker's 25-year-old phrase, "knowledge workers." And today, I should add that more and more of the workforce are "investor workers," bringing their own profitable ideas into the company. Most organizations will soon resemble that research institute and the modern research university and that NY financial house. And then what: where will the leaders come from to run this new economy?

These are questions that should exhilarate and hopefully energize us. The years ahead of us promise to be uniquely exciting ones, times that seem to mock any effort to define or shape them. But just as the Biblical hero Joseph was able to interpret the dreams of the Pharoah, charting a course for the future that rescued a nation, so must we be intepreters of our complex times and the dreams that arise within them. Could there be a more thrilling time to be a leader?

# Index

314 | MANAGING THE DREAM